822.914 WES 8/40163 ⁷⁰⁶

of Literature Series

...e Wesker Trilogy

D0307405

The Heritage of Literature Series

Founder General Editor: E. W. Parker, M. C.

The titles in this series include modern classics, and a wide range of novels, short stories and drama

A selection from the series includes

THE WESKER TRILOGY   *Arnold Wesker*
ROOTS   *Arnold Wesker*
SUNSET SONG   *Lewis Grassic Gibbon*
CRY THE BELOVED COUNTRY   *Alan Paton*
THE LONELINESS OF THE LONG-DISTANCE RUNNER   *Alan Sillitoe*
   BILLY LIAR   *Keith Waterhouse*   (in one volume)
THE WORLD OF THE SHORT STORY   An anthology chosen by
   A. H. M. Best and M. J. Cohen
FARMER'S BOY   *John R. Allan*

A complete list of the series is available on request

The Wesker Trilogy

Chicken Soup with Barley

Roots

I'm Talking About Jerusalem

ARNOLD WESKER

With Introduction and Notes by

A. H. M. BEST, M.A.

and

MARK COHEN, B.A.

SALISBURY
COLLEGE OF
TECHNOLOGY
LIBRARY

LONGMAN

LONGMAN GROUP LIMITED
*Longman House, Burnt Mill,
Harlow, Essex CM20 2JE, England
and Associated Companies throughout the World.*

The Wesker Trilogy First published by Jonathan Cape 1960
Chicken Soup with Barley © 1959 Arnold Wesker
Roots © 1959 Arnold Wesker
I'm Talking About Jerusalem © 1960 Arnold Wesker
Introduction and Notes © Longman Group Ltd
(formerly Longmans, Green & Co., Ltd.) 1965

All rights reserved. No part of this publication may be
reproduced, stored in a retrieval system, or trans-
mitted in any form or by any means, electronic,
mechanical, photocopying, recording, or otherwise,
without the prior permission of the Copyright owner.

*First published in this edition 1965
Tenth impression 1984*

ISBN 0 582 34884 6

8/40163   *Printed in Hong Kong by
Wilture Printing Co., Ltd.*

822.91 WES Jun '90

All performing rights of these plays are fully protected, and
permission to perform must be obtained in advance: for pro-
fessional performances from Theatrework (London) Limited,
12 Abingdon Road, London, W.8; for amateur performances,
from Evans Brothers Limited (Evans Plays Department),
Montague House, Russell Square, London, W.C.1. These
are the original versions of the plays and they do not
quite conform with the Lord Chamberlain's requirements.

ACKNOWLEDGEMENTS

We are grateful to the following for permission to include copyright
material in this edition:

To Faber and Faber Ltd for material from *Autumn Journal* by Louis
MacNeice; to Lawrence and Wishart Ltd for the melody of the first verse of
'The Coal Owner and the Pitman's Wife' from *Come All Ye Bold Miners* by
A. L. Lloyd; to Keith Prowse Music Publishing Co Ltd (Reynolds Music)
for the melody of the latter part of the chorus of 'My Old Dutch' (music
by Charles Ingle). The cover photograph is reproduced by permission of
the Observer.

CONTENTS

First presentation of the complete WESKER TRILOGY was at the Royal Court Theatre, London, in the summer of 1960. First performances of the individual plays, in this initial presentation of the complete trilogy, were as follows:

Chicken Soup with Barley	7th June 1960
Roots	28th June 1960
I'm Talking About Jerusalem	27th July 1960

Directed by John Dexter
Designed by Jocelyn Herbert

A play is ultimately a co-operative effort, and I would like to acknowledge my indebtedness to all the actors and actresses who eventually brought my plays alive on the stage. And in particular I cannot offer enough thanks for the understanding brought to the production by John Dexter, the director, many of whose ideas are contained in the versions as published.

NOTE TO ACTORS AND PRODUCERS

My people are not caricatures. They are real (though fiction), and if they are portrayed as caricatures the point of all these plays will be lost. The picture I have drawn is a harsh one, yet my tone is not one of disgust – nor should it be in the presentation of the plays. I am at one with these people: it is only that I am annoyed, with them and myself.

FAMILY TREES

KAHNS

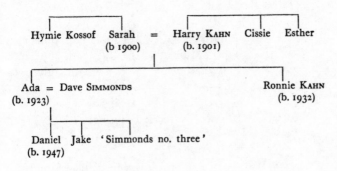

BRYANTS

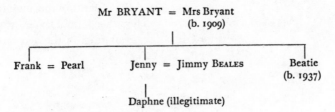

Chicken Soup with Barley

For

Leah and Joe

*

Characters of the Play

SARAH KAHN
HARRY KAHN, *her husband*
MONTY BLATT
DAVE SIMMONDS
PRINCE SILVER
HYMIE KOSSOF, *Sarah's brother*
CISSIE KAHN, *Harry's sister, a trade-union organizer*
ADA KAHN, *daughter of Sarah and Harry*
RONNIE, *son of Sarah and Harry*
BESSIE BLATT, *wife of Monty*

Act I

SCENE 1: October 4th 1936
SCENE 2: The same evening

Act II

SCENE 1: June 1946
SCENE 2: Autumn 1947

Act III

SCENE 1: November 1955
SCENE 2: December 1956

*First presented at the Belgrade Theatre, Coventry,
on 7th July 1958*

Act One

October 4th, 1936.

The basement of the Kahns' house in the East End of London. The room is warm and lived in. A fire is burning. One door, at the back and left of the room, leads to a bedroom. A window, left, looks up to the street. To the right is another door which leads to a kitchen, which is seen. At rear of stage are the stairs leading up into the street.

SARAH KAHN is in the kitchen washing up, humming to herself. She is a small, fiery woman, aged thirty-seven, Jewish and of European origin. Her movements indicate great energy and vitality. She is a very warm person. HARRY KAHN, her husband, comes down the stairs, walks past her and into the front room. He is thirty-five and also a European Jew. He is dark, slight, rather pleasant looking, and the antithesis of Sarah. He is amiable but weak. From outside we hear a band playing a revolutionary song.

SARAH (*from the kitchen*). You took the children to Lottie's?
HARRY (*taking up book to read*). I took them.
SARAH. They didn't mind?
HARRY. No, they didn't mind.
SARAH. Is Hymie coming?
HARRY. I don't know.
SARAH (*to herself*). Nothing he knows! You didn't ask him? He didn't say? He knows about the demonstration, doesn't he?
HARRY. I don't know whether he knows or he doesn't know. I didn't discuss it with him – I took the kids, that's all. Hey, Sarah – you should read Upton Sinclair's book about the meat-canning industry – it's an eye-opener . . .
SARAH. Books! Nothing else interests him, only books. Did you see anything outside? What's happening?

3

HARRY. The streets are packed with people, I never seen so many people. They've got barricades at Gardiner's Corner.

SARAH. There'll be such trouble.

HARRY. Sure there'll be trouble. You ever known a demonstration where there wasn't trouble?

SARAH. And the police?

HARRY. There'll be more police than blackshirts.

SARAH. What time they marching?

HARRY. I don't know.

SARAH. Harry, you know where your cigarettes are, don't you? (*This is her well-meaning but maddening attempt to point out to a weak man his weakness.*)

HARRY. I know where they are.

SARAH. And you know what's on at the cinema?

HARRY. So?

SARAH. And also you know what time it opens? (*He grins.*) So why don't you know what time they plan to march? (*Touché!*)

HARRY. Leave me alone, Sarah, will you? Two o'clock they plan to march – nah!

SARAH. So you do know. Why didn't you tell me straight away? Shouldn't you tell me something when I ask you?

HARRY. I didn't know what time they marched, so what do you want of me?

SARAH. But you did know when I nagged you.

HARRY. So I suddenly remembered. Is there anything terrible in that?

> She shakes a disbelieving fist at him and goes out to see where the loudspeaker cries are coming from. The slogan 'Madrid today – London tomorrow' is being repeated. As she is out HARRY looks for her handbag, and on finding it proceeds to take some money from it.

SARAH (*she is hot*). Air! I must have air – this basement

4

will kill me. God knows what I'll do without air when I'm dead. Who else was at Lottie's?

HARRY (*still preoccupied*). All of them.

SARAH. Who's all of them?

HARRY. All of them! You know. Lottie and Hymie and the boys, Solly and Martin.

He finds a ten-shilling note, pockets it and resumes his seat by the fire, taking up a book to read. SARAH *returns to front room with some cups and saucers.*

SARAH. Here, lay these out, the boys will be coming soon.

HARRY. Good woman! I could just do with a cup of tea.

SARAH. What's the matter, you didn't have any tea by Lottie's?

HARRY. No.

SARAH. Liar!

HARRY. I didn't have any tea by Lottie's, I tell you. (*Injured tone*) Good God, woman, why don't you believe me when I tell you things?

SARAH. *You* tell *me* why. Why don't I believe him when he tells me things! As if he's such an angel and never tells lies. What's the matter, you never told lies before I don't think?

HARRY. All right, so I had tea at Lottie's. There, you satisfied now?

SARAH. (*preparing things as she talks*). Well, of course you had tea at Lottie's. Don't I know you had tea at Lottie's? You think I'm going to think that Lottie wouldn't make you a cup of tea?

HARRY. Oh, leave off, Sarah.

SARAH. No! This time I won't leave off. (*Her logic again.*) I want to know why you told me you didn't have tea at Lottie's when you know perfectly well you did. I want to know.

HARRY *raises his hands in despair.*

I know you had tea there and *you* know you had tea there

– so what harm is it if you tell me? You think I care whether you had a cup of tea there or not? You can drink tea there till it comes out of your eyes and I wouldn't care only as long as you tell me.

HARRY. Sarah, will you please stop nagging me, will you? What difference if I had tea there or I didn't have tea there?

SARAH. That's just what I'm saying. All I want to know is whether you're all of a liar or half a liar!

HARRY (*together with her.*) . . . all of a liar or half a liar!

> *A young man,* MONTY BLATT, *comes down the stairs. He is about nineteen, Jewish, working-class, and cockney. His voice is heard before he is seen, shouting: 'Mrs Kahn! Sarah! Mrs Kahn!' He has interrupted the row as he dashes into the room without knocking.*

MONTY. Ah, good! You're here! (*Moves to window and, looking out, shouts up.*) It's O.K. They're here. Here! (*Offering parcel*) Mother sent you over some of her strudel. C'mon down. (*To* HARRY) Hello, Harry boy, how you going? All fighting fit for the demo?

HARRY. I'm fit, like a Trojan I'm fit!

SARAH. You won't see him at any demo. In the pictures you'll find him. (*Goes to landing to make tea.*)

MONTY. The pictures? Don't be bloody mad. You won't hear a thing! You seen the streets today? Sarah, you seen the streets yet? Mobbed! Mo-obbed! The lads have been there since seven this morning.

> *Two other young men in their early twenties come down the stairs,* DAVE SIMMONDS *and* PRINCE SILVER. *They are heatedly discussing something.*)

PRINCE. But Dave, there's so much work here to do. Hello, Sarah!

DAVE. I know all about the work here, but there are plenty

of party members to do it. Hello Sarah. Spain is the battle-front. Spain is a real issue at last.

SARAH. Spain? Spain, Dave?

HARRY. Spain?

PRINCE. Dave is joining the International Brigade. He's leaving for Spain tomorrow morning. (*To* DAVE) But Spain is only one issue brought to a head. You're too young to ...

HARRY. Dave, don't go mad all of a sudden. It's not all glory, you know.

DAVE. Harry, you look as though you didn't sleep last night.

MONTY. He didn't – the old cossack. (*To the tune of 'All the nice girls love a sailor'*) For you know what cossacks are ... Am I right, Harry?

PRINCE. I saw your sister Cissie at Aldgate, Harry. She was waving your mother's walking-stick in the air.

HARRY. She's mad.

MONTY (*loudly calling*). Where's this cup of tea, Sarah?

SARAH (*bringing in tea*). Do your fly-buttons up, Monty, you tramp you. Now then, Dave, tell me what's happening and what the plans are.

Everyone draws up a chair by the table.

DAVE. It's like this. The Party loudspeaker vans have been out all morning – you heard them? The Fascists are gathering at Royal Mint Street near the bridge. They plan to march up to Aldgate, down Commercial Road to Salmon Lane in Limehouse – you know Salmon Lane? – where they think they're going to hold a meeting. Then they plan to go on to Victoria Park and hold another meeting.

SARAH. *Two* meetings? What do they want to hold two meetings for?

HARRY. Why shouldn't they hold two meetings?

SARAH. What, *you* think they should hold two meetings?

HARRY. It's not what I think – she's such a funny woman – it's not what I think, but they want to hold two meetings – so what's so strange about that?

SARAH. But it costs so much money.

HARRY. Perhaps you want we should have a collection for them?

DAVE. Now. They could go along the Highway by the docks and then up Cable Street, but Mosley won't take the Highway because that's the back way, though the police will suggest he does.

SARAH. I bet the police cause trouble.

PRINCE. They've had to call in forces from outside London.

SARAH. You won't make it a real fight, boys, will you? I mean you won't get hurt.

MONTY. Sarah, you remember they threw a seven-year-old girl through a glass window? So don't fight the bastards?

PRINCE. Now Monty, there's to be discipline, remember. There's to be no attack or bottle-throwing. It's a test, you know that, don't you, it's a test for us. We're to stop them passing, that's all.

MONTY. Sure we'll stop them passing. If I see a blackshirt come by I'll tap his shoulder and I'll say: 'Excuse me, but you can't come this way today, we're digging up the road.' And he'll look at my hammer and sickle and he'll doff his cap and he'll say: 'I beg your pardon, comrade, I'll take the Underground.'

DAVE. Comrades! You want to know what the plans are or **you** don't want to know? Again. As we don't know what's going to happen we've done this: some of the workers are rallying at Royal Mint Street – so if the Fascists want to go through the Highway they'll have to fight for it. But we guess they'll want to stick to the main route so as not to lose face – you follow? We've therefore called the main rally at Gardiner's Corner. If, on the other hand, they do attempt to pass up Cable Street—

SARAH. Everything happens in Cable Street.

HARRY. What else happened in Cable Street?

SARAH. Peter the Painter had a fight with Churchill there, didn't he?

MONTY. You're thinking of Sidney Street, sweetheart.

HARRY. You know, she gets everything mixed up.

SARAH. You're very wonderful I suppose, yes? You're the clever one!

HARRY. I don't get my facts mixed up, anyway.

SARAH. Per, per, per, per, per! Listen to him! My politician!

MONTY. Sarah, do me a favour, leave the fists till later.

DAVE. If, on the other hand, they do try to come up Cable Street then they'll meet some dockers and more barricades. And if any get through that lot then they still can't hold their meetings either in Salmon Lane or Victoria Park Square.

SARAH. Why not?

PRINCE. Because since seven this morning there's been some of our comrades standing there with our platforms.

MONTY. Bloody wonderful, isn't it? Makes you feel proud, eh Sarah? Every section of this working-class area that we've approached has responded. The dockers at Limehouse have come out to the man. The lot!

PRINCE. The unions, the Co-ops, Labour Party members and the Jewish People's Council—

SARAH. The Board of Deputies?

HARRY. There she goes again. Not the Jewish Board of Deputies – *they* asked the Jewish population to keep away. No. the Jewish People's Council – the one that organized that mass demo against Hitler some years back.

    SARAH *pulls face at him.*

MONTY. There's been nothing like it since the General Strike.

HARRY. Christ! The General Strike! That was a time, Sarah, eh?

SARAH. What you asking me for? You want I should re-

9

member that you were missing for six days when Ada
was ill?

HARRY. Yes, I was missing, I'm sure.

SARAH. Well, sure you were missing.

HARRY. Where was I missing?

SARAH. How should I know where you were missing. If
I'd have known where you were missing you wouldn't have
been missing.

*There is heard from outside a sound of running feet
and voices shouting. Everyone except* HARRY *moves
to the window.*

FIRST VOICE. They're assembling! They're assembling!
Out to the barricades – the Fascists are assembling!

SECOND VOICE. Hey, Stan! Where's the best place?

FIRST VOICE. Take your boys to Cable Street. The Fascists
are assembling! Come out of your houses! Come out of
your houses!

MONTY. What about us, Dave?

SARAH. You haven't suggested to Harry and me where to go
yet.

DAVE. There's plenty of time. They won't try to march till
two, and it's only twelve thirty.

SARAH. You eaten? You boys had lunch?

PRINCE. We all had lunch at my place, Sarah; sit down, stop
moving a few seconds.

DAVE. Take your pick, Sarah. If you fancy yourself as a nurse
then go to Aldgate, we've got a first-aid post there, near
Whitechapel Library.

SARAH. Such organization! And you lot?

DAVE. Monty is taking some of the lads to the left flank of
Cable Street, Prince is organizing a team of cyclist messen-
gers between the main points and headquarters, I'm going
round the streets at the last minute to call everyone out
and – and that's the lot.

MONTY (*rubbing his hands*). All we have to do is wait.

DAVE. Where is Ada?

SARAH. Ada and Ronnie are at Hymie's place. I thought it best they get right out of the way.

DAVE (*guiltily*). You think she'll stay away? Your precocious daughter is a born fighter, Sarah.

MONTY. 'Course she is! She'll be round the streets organizing the pioneers – you see.

SARAH. Never! I told her to stay there and she'll stay there.

HARRY. I'm sure!

SARAH. God forbid she should be like you and run wild.

HARRY. All right, so she should be like you then!

SARAH. I'm jolly sure she should be like me! Ronnie isn't enough for him yet. A boy of five running about at nights and swearing at his aunts. (*Smiles at thought.*) Bless him! (*To the others*) He didn't half upset them: they wouldn't let him mess around with the radio so he started effing and blinding and threw their books on the floor. (*Turning again to* HARRY) Like you he throws things.

HARRY. Have you ever come across a woman like her before?

MONTY. I'd love another cup of tea.

HARRY (*jumps up and goes to kitchen*). I'll make it. I'll make it.

SARAH. He's so sweet when anybody else is around. I'll make some sandwiches.

PRINCE. But we've eaten, Sarah.

SARAH. Eat. Always eat. You don't know what time you'll be back.

> SARAH *goes to cupboard and cuts up bread ready for cheese sandwiches. A very distant sound of people chanting is heard:* 'They shall not pass, they shall not pass, they shall not pass.'

MONTY. The boys! Listen. Hear them? You know, Sarah, that's the same cry the people of Madrid were shouting.

PRINCE. And they didn't get past either. Imagine it! All

those women and children coming out into the streets and making barricades with their beds and their chairs.

DAVE (*sadly*). It was a slaughter.

PRINCE. And then came the first International Brigade.

DAVE. The Edgar André from Germany, Commune de Paris from France, and the Dombrovsky from Poland.

MONTY. Wait till our Dave gets over there. You'll give 'em brass balls for breakfast, Dave, eh?

SARAH. You really going, Dave? Does Ada know?

DAVE. Don't tell her, Sarah. You know how dramatic calf-love is.

PRINCE. Calf-love? If you get back alive from Spain she'll marry you at the landing stage – mark me.

SARAH. How are you going?

DAVE. They tell me it's a week-end trip to Paris and then a midnight ramble over the Pyrenees. The back way!

SARAH. It's terrible out there, they say. They say we've lost a lot of good comrades already.

PRINCE. We've lost too many comrades out there – you hear me, Dave?

MONTY. Sammy Avner and Lorimer Birch at Boadilla, Felicia Brown and Ernst Julius at Aragon.

SARAH. Julius? The tailor who used to work with us at Cantor's? But he was only a young boy.

PRINCE. And Felicia an artist and Lorimer an Oxford undergraduate.

MONTY. And Cornford was killed at Cordova.

PRINCE. And Ronnie Symes at Madrid.

MONTY. And Stevie Yates at Casa del Campo.

SARAH. Casa del Campo! Madrid! Such beautiful names and all that killing.

Pause.

MONTY. Hey! You know who organized the first British group? Nat Cohen! I used to go to school with him. Him and Sam Masters were on a cycling holiday in France. As

12

soon as they heard of the revolt they cycled over to Barcelona and started the Tom Mann Centuria.

HARRY (*coming to the door*). He's a real madman, Nat
Cohen, He chalks slogans right outside the police station. I
used to work with him.

SARAH. God knows if they'll come back alive.

DAVE. When three Fascist deserters were asked how they
reached our lines they said they came through the hills of
the widows, orphans and sweethearts; they'd lost so many
men attacking those hills.

MONTY. And may they lose many more!

DAVE (*angrily*). The war in Spain is not a game of cards,
Monty. You don't pay in pennies when you lose. May they
lose many more! What kind of talk is that? Sometimes,
Monty, I think you only enjoy the battle, and that one day
you'll forget the ideal. You hate too much. You can't have
brotherhood when you hate. There's only one difference
between them and us—we know what we're fighting for.
It's almost an unfair battle.

HARRY *now returns to kitchen to pour out tea.*

MONTY. Unfair, he says! When Germany and Italy are
supplying them with guns and tanks and aeroplanes and
our boys have only got rifles and mortars – is that unfair?
You call that unfair, I don't think?

DAVE. When you fight men who are blind it's always unfair.
You think I'm going to enjoy shooting a man because he
calls himself a Fascist? I feel so sick at the thought of firing
a rifle that I think I'll board that boat with a blindfold
over my eyes. Sometimes I think that's the only way to
do things. I'm not even sure that I want to go, only I know
if I don't then – then – well, what sense can a man make
of his life?

SARAH. You're really a pacifist, aren't you, Dave?

DAVE. I'm a terribly sad pacifist, Sarah.

HARRY. I understand you, Dave – I know what you mean,

boy. What do you want we should say? You go – we're
proud of you. You stay behind – we love you. Sometimes
you live in a way you don't know why – you just do a thing.
So you don't have to shout – you're shouting at yourself!
But a pacifist, Dave? There's going to be a big war soon,
a Fascist war: you think it's time for pacifism?

SARAH. He's right, Dave.

DAVE. I know it's not time yet. I know that. I know there is
still some fighting to be done. But it'll come. It will come,
you know – when there'll be a sort of long pause, and people
will just be frightened of each other and still think they
have to fight. That'll be the time – But now – well, I feel
like an old gardener who knows he won't live through to
the spring to plant his seeds.

> HARRY *comes in with the teas and at the same
> time a voice from the streets is heard frantically
> shouting:* 'Man your posts! Men and women of the
> East End, come out of your houses! The blackshirts
> are marching! Come out! Come out!' *There is a
> hurried movement from the people in the room.*
> DAVE *and* MONTY *rush to the window.* PRINCE
> *rushes upstairs knocking a cup of tea out of*
> HARRY'S *hand.*

MONTY. Christ! They've started before time.

DAVE. It might be a false alarm.

PRINCE (*from the stairs.*) We can't take the risk. Let's get
going.

> MONTY *moves off quickly, taking a poker from the
> fireplace on his way out and concealing it in his
> clothes.*

MONTY. I'll clean it and bring it back later.

HARRY. But I've made your tea.

DAVE. Stick it back in the pot. We'll drink it later. Now you
two, you know where the posts are – Cable street, Royal
Mint Street and Gardiner's Corner.

HARRY (*at the window*). The street is mobbed. Jesus! Look at them, everybody is coming out, everybody.

SARAH (*putting on her coat in general rush*). Where's the first-aid post?

DAVE (*having helped* SARAH *with coat, moves off*). White-chapel Library. Harry, you coming?

HARRY (*still at window*). I'm coming, I'm coming. You go on. Good God, there's Alf Bosky and his wife. She's got the baby with her. (*Shouts up.*) Hey Alf – good luck, comrade – we're coming. Sarah, there's Alf Bosky and his wife.

SARAH (*looking for something in kitchen*). I heard, I heard! (*She finds a rolling pin and, waving it in the air, dashes into the front room.*) Are you coming now, Harry? I'm going to Gardiner's Corner – come on, we'll be late.

HARRY (*backing away from rolling pin*). Don't hit anybody with that thing, Sarah, it hurts.

SARAH. Fool!

SARAH *dashes to the stairs but stops and, remembering something, returns to front room. From a corner of the room she finds a red flag with a hammer and sickle on it and thrusts it in* HARRY'S *hand.*

SARAH. Here, wave this! Do something useful!
Exits upstairs.

HARRY (*grabbing his coat*). Hey, Sarah, wait for me – Sarah! Hey, wait for me!
He follows her, banner streaming. The voices outside grow to a crescendo: 'They shall not pass, they shall not pass, *they shall not pass!*'

CURTAIN

Act One

*Same room, later that evening. There is commotion and
some singing from the streets outside.* MONTY *and* PRINCE
are coming down the stairs leading HYMIE KOSSOF. *He
has blood all over his face. He is a short, rotund man with
a homely appearance.*

MONTY (*leaving* PRINCE *and* HYMIE *to go into the room*).
I'll get some water on the stove. Sit him in a chair. (*Shouts
upstairs.*) Cissie! Don't come down yet, go and get some
first-aid kit from somewhere. (*Fills kettle.*)

PRINCE. Now don't talk too much and don't move, Hymie.
Jesus! What a state you're in. Sarah'll go mad.

HYMIE. Well, clean me up quickly then.

MONTY (*rushing from kitchen to window*). Cissie! *Cissie!*
Try that sweet shop near Toynbee Hall. I saw a first-aid
group there. They might still be there. (*Comes away, but,
remembering something else, sticks his head out again.*)
Aspros! Try and get hold of some Aspros.

SARAH (*from the top of the stairs – off*). Monty! Is Hymie
down there?

HYMIE. Oh, my goodness, she's here. If there is one thing
Sarah loves it's someone who's ill to fuss over. Why didn't
I go home?

MONTY. Because you know Lottie would say serves you
right!
(SARAH *appears;* MONTY *rushes to her.*) Now don't panic,
Sarah, he's all right, he's all right.

SARAH (*entering*). Hymie!

HYMIE. Sarah Nightingale!

MONTY. Now don't frighten him, I tell you.

SARAH (*taking over towel and wiping him*). Fool you! They
told me you were hurt – I nearly died.

HYMIE. So did I!

16

SARAH. Fool! *you* had to go straight into it.

HYMIE. I was only hit by a truncheon. Now do me a favour, Sarah, and just make some tea, there's a good girl.

SARAH. Nobody else got hurt. Only him. The brave one!

MONTY (*significantly handling the poker*). Plenty got hurt! Oh, he's all right. Aren't you all right, Hymie?

HYMIE. I'm here, aren't I?

SARAH (*taking off her coat*). Well, why hasn't anybody done something?

PRINCE. Cissie has gone to get some first aid.

SARAH. Cissie? Harry's sister?

PRINCE. Yes. Where is Harry, by the way. Anybody seen him?

SARAH (*ominously*). Wait till I see him. I'll give him. You expected him to stay there?

MONTY. I saw him at Cable Street; he was waving the old red flag, but he didn't stay long. He took one look at the artillery and guns and said he was going to find us some sandwiches.

SARAH. They had guns at Cable Street? Did they use them?

MONTY. Nah! it was only brought out to frighten us. *Frighten* us, mark. If they'd have dropped a bomb today we wouldn't have been frightened. Christ! What a day!

HYMIE. I mean, did you ever see anything like it? We threw stones and bottles at them, Sarah. They were on horseback with batons and they kept charging us, so we threw stones. And you should have seen Monty when one policeman surrendered. Surrendered! A policeman! It's never happened before. He didn't know what to do, Monty didn't. None of us knew. I mean, who's ever heard of policemen surrendering? And after the first came others – half a dozen of them. My goodness, we made such a fuss of them. Gave them cigarettes and mugs of tea and called them comrade policemen.

PRINCE. There's no turning back now – nothing can stop the workers now.

MONTY. I bet we have a revolution soon. Hitler won't stop at Spain, you know. You watch him go and you watch the British Government lick his arse until he spits in their eye. Then *we'll* move in.

HYMIE. I'm not so sure, Monty. We won today but the same taste doesn't stay long. Mosley was turned back at Aldgate pump and everyone shouted hurrah. But I wonder how many of the people at Gardiner's Corner were just sightseers. You know, in every political movement there are just sightseers.

MONTY. Ten thousand bloody sightseers? Do me a favour, it wasn't a bank holiday.

> SARAH *goes to the kitchen to pour the water into the bowl.* CISSIE *appears.*

HYMIE. Any big excitement can be a bank holiday for a worker, believe me.

> Enter CISSIE. *Woman of about thirty-three. She is a trade-union organizer – precise in her manner, dry sense of humour.*

CISSIE. Ointment, lint, bandage and plaster. Let's have a look at him.

SARAH (*entering with bowl of water*). I'm coming, it's all right, I can manage.

> CISSIE *makes way and* SARAH *begins to sponge her brother's face and then puts bandage round his head.*

PRINCE. Where were *you*, Cis?

CISSIE. Gardiner's Corner holding a banner. The union banner. And you?

MONTY. Digging up the paving stones in Cable Street.

CISSIE. Paving stones? (*She hoists the back of her skirt to warm her behind in front of the fire.*)

MONTY. We pulled out the railings from a near-by church

and the stones from the gutter. I'll get some more coal for
the fire. (*Goes to kitchen, pinching* CISSIE'S *behind on
the way*.) We turned over a lorry.

SARAH. A lorry?

HYMIE. But it was the wrong one. The lorry we'd laid on was
in a near-by yard and when the call went up to bring the
lorry the boys, if you don't mind, grabbed one at the top
of the street. I ask you!

SARAH. Keep still. There, you look more respectable now.
  MONTY *re-enters with coal and on his way to fire
  takes a feather from a hat near by and plants it
  among* HYMIE'S *bandages*.

HYMIE. Anyone get hurt your way, Cissie?

CISSIE. Some of the boys from my union got arrested.

SARAH. I'll go and make some tea now.

CISSIE. Mick and Sammy and Dave Goldman – and that
bloody fool, if you'll excuse the expression, Sonny Becks.
Everybody is standing behind the barricades waiting for
the blackshirts to appear. The place is swarming with
policemen waiting, just waiting, for an opportunity to lay
their hands on some of us. So look what he does: not content with just standing there – and Sonny knew perfectly
well that the orders were for the strictest discipline – not
content with just standing he chose that moment to get up
on Mrs O'Laoghaire's vegetable barrow and make a political speech. 'Let us now remember the lessons of the Russian
revolution,' he starts like he was quoting Genesis, the nitwit. And then he finds that the barrow isn't safe so he steps
over to an iron bedstead and put his foot through the
springs just as he was quoting Lenin's letter to the toiling
masses!

MONTY. You can never stop Sonny making a speech.

CISSIE. But not in bed! Anyway, you know Sonny – a
mouth like a cesspool and no shame – so he lets out a
torrent of abuse at the capitalist bed-makers and the police

just make a dive at him. Mick and Sammy tried to argue with the police so they were hauled off and then Dave Goldman tried to explain – that was when he was hauled off, poor bastard, if you'll excuse the expression!

HYMIE. What'll happen?

CISSIE. The union'll have to find the lawyers and probably pay their fine – what else? Which reminds me – Monty and Prince. Get all the boys and girls you can find and bring them to that social next Saturday, the one for Sally Oaks.

HYMIE. Wasn't it her husband caught his bicycle in a tram-line and was killed?

CISSIE. That's right. She's a Catholic. The local priest is trying to raise some money to keep her going for a bit and we promised we'd support it. Well, I'm going.

SARAH (*entering with tea*). Cissie, have you seen Harry?

CISSIE. Harry? No!

SARAH. He's not at your place, I suppose?

CISSIE. How should I know? I haven't been there all day.

SARAH. He always is at your place.

CISSIE. Sarah, I'm not responsible for my brother's actions. None of us have ever been able to control him, the eldest brother! We warned you what you were taking on – you wanted to change him! She wanted to change him.

SARAH. It's your mother who spoils him, you know that?

CISSIE. Spoils him! Do me a favour – the woman's been bed-ridden for the last ten years. Spoils him!

SARAH. He knows he can go to her – she'll feed him.

CISSIE. He's her son, for God's sake.

SARAH. Don't I know it. He's her son all right – and he wants to be looked after like everyone looks after her. Only it's such a pity – he can walk!

CISSIE. Yes, yes – so I know all this already. Good night, everyone.

CISSIE *exits amid varied goodbyes and* 'I'll be seeing you'.

SARAH. I hate her!

HYMIE. Don't be a silly girl. Cissie is a good trade-union
organizer.

SARAH. She's a cow! Not a bit of warmth, not a bit! What's
the good of being a socialist if you're not warm.

HYMIE. But Cissie has *never* liked Harry.

SARAH. Not a bit of warmth. Everything cold and calcula-
ted. People like that can't teach love and brotherhood.

PRINCE. Love comes later, Sarah.

SARAH. Love comes now. You have to start with love. How
can you talk about socialism otherwise?

MONTY. Hear, hear, Comrade Kahn. Come on now, what is
this? We've just won one of the biggest fights in working-
class history and all we do is quarrel.

> MONTY *settles down and all is quiet. Suddenly,*
> *softly, he starts to sing.*
>
> England arise, the long long night is over.
>
> *Others join in.*
>
> Faint in the East behold the dawn appears.
> Out of your evil sleep of toil and sorrow,
> England arise, the long long day is here.
> England arise . . .

SARAH (*suddenly*). Hymie! The children! God in heaven,
I've forgotten the children.

HYMIE. They're at my place. What's the matter with you?

SARAH (*putting on her coat*). But I can't leave them there.
How could I forget them like that; what am I thinking of?
Won't be long.

> *Exits.*

HYMIE (*calling up to her*). But Ronnie'll be asleep. Don't tell
Lottie I got hit. Tell her I'm coming home soon. (*Returning to front room*) Impetuous woman!

They all settle themselves comfortably round the fire. SARAH *is heard calling from the street.*

SARAH (*off*). Make yourself some food! And there's tea in the pot.

HYMIE (*coming away from window*). Make yourself some food! With her it's food all the time. Food and tea. No sooner you finished one cup than you got another.

MONTY. She's a sweetheart.

HYMIE. God forbid you should ever say you're not hungry. She starts singing that song: As man is only human he must eat before he can think.

MONTY (*picking up the song and singing it*).

As man is only human
He must eat before he can think,
Fine words are only empty air
But not his meat or his drink.

Others join in chorus.

Then left right left, then left right left,
There's a place, comrade, for you.
March with us in the ranks of the working class
For you are a worker too.

Harry enters. As they finish the song he stands in the doorway and, waving the banner, cries

HARRY. We won! Boys, we won the day!

MONTY. Harry! Welcome home the hero! Where are those bloody sandwiches?

HYMIE. Your wife's looking for you.

HARRY. What, she's gone *out* for me? (*Places banner in corner and looks concerned.*)

MONTY. Yes! Just this minute.

HARRY. Did she have a rolling pin in her hand?

HYMIE. No, no. She's gone to my place to collect the children.

HARRY. Blimey, Hymie! What happened to you? You all right, Hymie?

22

HYMIE. Now don't you fuss, Harry; drink your tea.

MONTY. That's it, Harry, swill up, mate.

HARRY. Sure, sure. (*Goes to kitchen.*) The children, you say?
But I saw Ada in the streets.

PRINCE (*looking to* MONTY). She was helping me, Harry,
but don't tell Sarah. She was taking messages from Cable
Street to headquarters. I knew she wouldn't stay in on such
a day. Marched with us on the victory march, then went to
look for Dave.

MONTY. She'll break her little heart when she hears he's
going to Spain.

ADA *comes tearing down the stairs at this point –
she is the Kahns' daughter, aged* 14.

ADA. Mother! Mother! Hello everyone – Dad, where's
Mother? (*She snatches a slice of bread and butter from
table.*)

HARRY. Hello, Ada – you haven't seen her yet? You'll cop it.
She's gone to look for Ronnie.

ADA. (*going off again*). Be back in quarter of an hour – excuse
me.

HARRY. Where you going now?

ADA. Must check up on the last few posts, see that all the
other pioneers are safe. (*She calls back through the window.*) Christ, what a day, comrades! (*Exits.*)

HARRY. Comrades! And *we* didn't force her to be in the
pioneers. Wasn't necessary. I tell you, show a young person
what socialism means and he recognizes life! A future! But
it won't be pure in our lifetime, you know that, don't you,
boys? Not even in hers, maybe – but in her children's lifetime – *then* they'll begin to feel it, all the benefits, despite
our mistakes. Now boys, tell me everything that happened.

PRINCE. Don't you know? Sir Philip Game, the police commissioner, got the wind up and banned the march. He told
Mosley to fight it out with the Home Secretary. He wasn't
going to have any trouble. And what happened to you?

HARRY (*proudly*). I was nearly arrested.

MONTY. You?

HARRY. I was running through the streets waving a red banner Sarah gave me and a policeman told me to drop it.

PRINCE. So?

HARRY. I dropped it! And then I turned into Flower and Dean Street and raised it again. He must have guessed what I was going to do. Christ! I never saw so many policemen appear so quickly. They seemed to pour out of all the windows when they heard that penny-farthing whistle. I only just had time to hop into my mother's place.

MONTY. And you stayed there?

HARRY. I had a cup of tea and at about four o'clock I came out. I got to Gardiner's Corner and police were charging the barricades. I didn't see no Fascists. Any get there?

PRINCE. They stayed in the back streets. The police did all the attacking. So?

HARRY. So I saw the police were picking our boys off like flies and then I saw my policeman – his hat was missing by this time. Oooh! There was a vicious look came into his eye when he saw me. I didn't stop to ask him where he'd lost it. I just ran back to my mother's and read a book.

HYMIE (*ominously*). So you *were* at your mother's. (*To the others*) I think we'd better go before Sarah comes back. Harry, we're going.

HARRY. You're not staying for something to eat?

HYMIE. Lottie's waiting for me, Harry. Come on, you two.

HARRY. Hey, Hymie. You won't tell her I was at my mother's all the time, will you? No?

The boys assure him with pats and shakes of the head. HARRY *pours himself out a cup of tea and, taking it into the front room, he settles down to a book by the fire. After some seconds* SARAH *comes down the stairs with* RONNIE, *a boy of about five.*

24

He is asleep in her arms. She takes him straight into the bedroom. HARRY *tries to appear very absorbed.* SARAH *comes out of the room, takes off her coat and hangs it up. She is eyeing* HARRY *most of the time with a gaze to kill while he does his best to avoid it. She clears a few things from the table, then goes out to get herself a cup of tea. As she watches* HARRY *she seats herself at the table and slowly stirs her drink. He shrinks under her gaze as her head begins to nod. It is an 'I-know-you-don't-I' nod.*

SARAH. You think I'm a fool, don't you?

HARRY *shifts uncomfortably, doesn't answer.* SARAH *watches him.*

Think I can't see, that I don't know what's going on. (*Pause.*) Look at him! The man of the house! Nothing matters to him! (*Pause.*) Well, Harry, why don't you look at me? Why don't you talk to me? I'm your wife, aren't I? A man is supposed to discuss things with his wife.

HARRY (*at last*). What do you want me to say?

SARAH. Must I tell you what to say? Don't you know? Don't you *just* know! (*Pause.*) Artful! Oh, you're so artful!

HARRY. Yes, yes. I'm artful.

SARAH. Aren't you artful, then? You think because you sit there pretending to read that I won't say anything? That's what you'd like – that I should just come in and carry on and not say anything. You'd like that, wouldn't you? That you should carry on your life just the same as always and no one should say anything.

HARRY. Oh, leave me alone, Sarah.

SARAH. Oh, leave me alone, Sarah! I'll leave you alone all right. There'll be blue murder, Harry, you hear me? There'll be blue murder if it carries on like this. All our life is it going to be like this? I can't leave a handbag in the room. You remember what happened last time? You left me! Remember?

HARRY *tries to turn away out of it all and* SARAH
shakes him back again.

Remember? And you wanted to come back? And you
came back – full of promises. What's happened to them
now?

HARRY. Nothing's happened! Now stop nagging! Good
God, you don't let a man live in peace.

SARAH. You can still pretend? After you took ten shillings
from my bag and you know that I know you took it and
you can still be righteous? Say you don't know anything
about it, go on. Say you don't know what I'm talking about.

HARRY. No. I *don't* know what you're talking about.

SARAH (*finally unable to control herself, cursing him*). Fire
on your head! May you live so sure if you don't know what
I'm talking about. The money fell out of my purse, I suppose. I dropped it in the street. (*Screaming at him*) Fire on
your head!

HARRY (*rising and facing her in a rage*). I'll throw this book
at you – so help me I'll throw this book at you.

At this point ADA *rushes in.*

ADA. Harry, stop it. (*She cries.*) Oh, stop it!

HARRY (*shouting*). Tell your mother to stop it, she's the
cause, it's her row. Don't you know your mother by now?
He has moved away to the door.

SARAH. I'm the cause? Me? You hear him, Ada, you hear
him? I'm the cause! (*Throws a saucer at him.*) Swine, you!

HARRY (*in speechless rage, throws his book to the ground*).
She's mad, your mother, she's stark raving mad!

HARRY *rushes out of the room up the stairs.* SARAH
*follows him to bottom of stairs and, picking up a
basin in her hands, brandishes it.* ADA *goes to look
out of the window.*

SARAH. That's it, run away. Go to your mother! She'll give
you peace! She'll do everything for you! Weakling, you!
Weakling!

ADA (*crying*). Everybody's outside, Mummy. Everybody is looking down at us.

SARAH (*turning to comfort her*). There, there, Boobola. There, there, meine kindt. Shuh! Shuh! I'm sorry. (*Bends over her and strokes her.*) Shuh! Shuh! It's finished, I'm sorry, it's over.

HARRY (*from the street*). She's mad, she's gone mad, she has.

SARAH. Shuh! shuh! Ada, don't listen. It'll pass. Shuh – shuh! (*Cooing*) loolinka, Ada, Ada, Ada.

> As she comforts ADA, RONNIE *comes out and stands watching them – listening and bewildered* . . .

CURTAIN

Act Two

June 1946 – the war has come and gone.

The scene is now changed. The Kahns have moved to an L.C.C. block of flats in Hackney – the 1930 kind, with railings. The working class is a little more respectable now, they have not long since voted in a Labour Government. The part of the flat we can see is: the front room, from which lead off three rooms; the passage to the front door – and a door lead-

ing from the passage to the kitchen (off); and part of the balcony with its iron railings.

It is late on a Friday afternoon. HARRY *is lying down on the sofa.* SARAH *walks along the balcony, puts her hand through the letter box, withdraws the key, and enters the front room – energetic as ever.*

SARAH. What! you here already? (*Accepting the fact*) You haven't been working!

HARRY. The place closed down.

SARAH (*takes off coat and unpacks shopping bag*). The place closed down! But you only started there on Monday.

HARRY. Well! So the place closed down! Is it my fault?

SARAH. It always happens where *he* works. You can't bring luck anywhere, can you! When it's a slump you always manage to be the first one sacked and when the season starts again you're the last one to find work. Ah, Harry, you couldn't even make money during the war. The war! When *everybody* made money.

HARRY (*laying pay packet on table*). Nah!

SARAH (*reading it*). What's this? Seven pounds thirteen? Why only seven pounds thirteen?

HARRY. Four days' work.

SARAH. You haven't worked *all* day today? So what you been doing?

28

HARRY. I felt tired.

SARAH. Sleep! That's all he can do. You didn't peel potatoes or anything? (*No answer.*) Oh, what am I standing here talking to you for? Don't I know you by now?

HARRY. I got a headache.

SARAH (*going to kitchen and talking from there*). Yes, yes – headache! Ronnie not home yet?

HARRY. He's distributing leaflets.

SARAH. What leaflets?

HARRY. I don't know what leaflets. What leaflets! Leaflets!

SARAH. Come and make some tea. Ada will be here soon.

HARRY. Leave me alone, Sarah.

SARAH (*from the kitchen*). Make some tea when I ask you!
> HARRY *rises, and* ADA *is seen coming along the balcony. She enters through the front door in the same manner as Sarah. She is 25 years of age, well-spoken, a beautiful Jewess and weary of spirit.*

HARRY (*kissing her*). Hello, Ada.

SARAH. Ada? Ada? You here? Go inside, Daddy'll make some tea. Supper will soon be ready. (*Appears cheerfully from kitchen with all the signs of a cook about her. Kisses* ADA.) Got a nice supper.

ADA. What nice supper?

SARAH. Barley soup. I left it on a small light all day while I was at work. (*Returns to kitchen.*)

ADA. Do you know if Ronnie has gone to my place to see if there is mail from Dave?

SARAH. Suppose so. He usually does when he knows you're coming here straight from work.
> RONNIE *appears on the balcony and lets himself in. Aged 15, enthusiastic, lively, well-spoken like his sister.*

(*Hearing the noise at the door*) Ronnie?

RONNIE. I'm here.

SARAH. He's here.

29

RONNIE (*to* ADA *as he enters*). Two hundred and fifty leaflets in an hour and a half!

ADA. Very good. What for?

RONNIE. The May Day demo. Are you coming?

ADA. I doubt it.

RONNIE (*mocking her*). I doubt it! Don't you find the march exciting any longer?

ADA. I do *not* find the march exciting any longer.

RONNIE. Can't understand it. You and Dave were such pioneers in the early days. I get all my ideas from you two – and now—

ADA. And now the letters, please.

RONNIE. Letters? Letters? What letters?

ADA. Oh, come on, Ronnie – Dave's letters.

RONNIE (*innocently*). But I've been distributing leaflets!

ADA. You didn't go to my home to find . . . ?

RONNIE Miles away – other direction.

ADA (*sourly*). Thank you.

> While ADA *sits down to read a newspaper* RONNIE *withdraws three letters from his pocket and reads some initials on the back.*

RONNIE. I.L.T. Now what could that mean – I love thee?

ADA. Give me those letters, please.

RONNIE (*teasing*). Oh, I love thee, sister.

ADA. You've been reading them.

RONNIE (*reading front of envelope*). Letter number 218 – Christ! he's prolific. And here's number 215 – lousy service, isn't it? And number 219. This one says I.L.T.T., I love thee terribly, I suppose. And if I loved you I'd also love you terribly. (*Bends over and kisses her.*)

ADA. Idiot! (*Reads.*)

RONNIE. Isn't it time that husband of yours was demobbed? The war's been over a year already. Imagine! I was only nine when he left. I've still kept all his letters, Ada, all of them. (*Ambles round the room to wall and tears off a little piece of wallpaper which he hurriedly crumples and stuffs into his pocket, making sure no one has seen him.*) We've been living here for five years – he hasn't even seen this place, God help him! (*Shouting to kitchen*) Harry! Harry! Where's Harry?

> *Harry comes in with some tea and* RONNIE *goes to take a cup.*

Good old Pops. Dad, I saw Monty Blatt. He says you must attend the meeting tonight.

HARRY. Ach! Do me a favour!

RONNIE. Listen to him! Party member! Won't attend branch meetings! How can you know what's going *on* in the world? That's where Ada gets her apathy from. She's you! And you're a lazy old sod – whoopee!

> RONNIE *hoists* HARRY *over his shoulder, fireman fashion, and dances round the room.*

RONNIE. Are you going to the meeting?

HARRY. Let me down, you fool! Let me down!

RONNIE. The meeting?

HARRY. Stop it, you idiot – I've got a headache.

ADA. Do be quiet, you two.

RONNIE (*lowering his father*). I'll fight you. Come on, fists up, show your mettle; I just feel in the mood. (*Assumes quixotic boxing stance.*)

HARRY (*grinning*). Bloody fool! Leave off!

RONNIE. Windy! (*Playfully jabs* HARRY.)

HARRY (*raising his fists*). I'll knock your block off.

> *They follow each other round – fists raised. First* RONNIE *moves forward, then he backs away and* HARRY *moves forward. Thus they move – to and fro, without touching each other, until* SARAH *comes in with some soup in plates.*

SARAH. The table! the table! Lay the table someone.

RONNIE. The table, the table – oh, oh, the table!

> *Everyone moves to lay the table;* RONNIE *in haste,*

ADA *while reading, and* HARRY *clumsily. Then they all sit down.*

ADA. Lovely soup, Mummy.

RONNIE. Magnificent!

SARAH. You like it?

HARRY. They just said they did.

SARAH. I wasn't talking to you.

RONNIE. She wasn't talking to you.

HARRY. Your mother never talks *to* me.

RONNIE. You're so ugly, that's why. I wouldn't talk to you either only you wouldn't give me any spending money.

SARAH. He won't give you any spending money this week anyway.

RONNIE. Don't tell me. He's out of work.

HARRY (*pathetically*). The shop closed down.

ADA. Oh, Daddy, why does it always happen to you?

HARRY. It doesn't always happen to me.

ADA. Always! All my life that's all I can remember, just one succession of jobs which have fallen through.

HARRY. Is it my fault if the garment industry is so unstable?

ADA. It's not the industry – it's you.

HARRY. Yes, me.

ADA. Well, isn't it you?

HARRY. Oh, Ada, leave off. I have enough with your mother. I've got a headache.

ADA. I don't wonder you have a headache, you spend most of your time sleeping.

HARRY. Yes, sleeping.

ADA. What are you going to do now?

HARRY. I'll look for another job on Monday.

ADA. What's wrong with Sunday – on the Whitechapel Road? There's always governors looking for machinists.

HARRY. Those people aren't there for work. They go to gossip. Gossip, that's all! Monday I'll find a job and start straight away. It's busy now, you know.

SARAH (*collecting the soup dishes and taking them out*). Morgen morgen nor nischt heite, sagen alle faule leite.

ADA. Daddy – you are the world's biggest procrastinator.

RONNIE. Give the boy a break, Addy, that's a big word.

ADA. He ought to be ashamed of himself. The industry's booming with work and he's out of a job. You probably got the sack, didn't you?

HARRY (*offended*). I did not get the sack.

ADA. All her life Mummy's had to put up with this. I shall be glad to get away.

> SARAH, *entering with the next course, hears this remark and glares bitterly at* HARRY.

RONNIE. Get away where?

ADA. Anywhere. When Dave comes back we shall leave London and live in the country. That'll be our socialism. Remember this, Ronnie: the family should be a unit, and your work and your life should be part of one existence, not something hacked about by a bus queue and office hours. A man should see, know, and love his job. Don't you want to feel your life? Savour it gently? In the country we shall be somewhere where the air doesn't smell of bricks and the kids can grow up without seeing grandparents who are continually shouting at each other.

SARAH. Ada, Ada.

RONNIE. And no more political activity?

ADA. No more political activity.

RONNIE. I bet Dave won't agree to that. Dave fought in Spain. He won't desert humanity like that.

ADA. Humanity! Ach!

RONNIE. Listen to her! With a Labour majority in the House? And two of our own Party members? It's only just beginning.

ADA. It's always only just beginning for the Party. Every defeat is victory and every victory is the beginning.

RONNIE. But it is, it is the beginning. Plans for town and

country planning. New cities and schools and hospitals. (*Jumping up on chair to* HARRY'*s facetious applause.*) Nationalization! National health! Think of it, the whole country is going to be organized to co-operate instead of tear at each other's throat. That's what I said to them in a public speech at school and all the boys cheered and whistled and stamped their feet – and blew raspberries.

ADA. I do not believe in the right to organize people. And anyway I'm not so sure that I love them enough to *want* to organize them.

SARAH (*sadly*). This – from you, Ada? You used to be such an organizer.

ADA. I'm tired, Mother. I spent eighteen months waiting for Dave to return from Spain and now I've waited six years for him to come home from a war against Fascism and I'm tired. Six years in and out of offices, auditing books and working with young girls who are morons – lipsticked, giggling morons. And Dave's experience is the same – fighting with men who he says did not know what the war was about. Away from their wives they behaved like animals. In fact they wanted to get away from their wives in order to behave like animals. Give them another war and they'd run back again. Oh yes! the service killed any illusions Dave may have once had about the splendid and heroic working class.

HARRY (*pedantically*). This is the talk of an intellectual, Ada.

ADA. God in heaven save me from the claptrap of a three-penny pamphlet. How many friends has the Party lost because of lousy, meaningless titles they gave to people. *He* was a bourgeois intellectual, *he* was a Trotskyist, *he* was a reactionary Social Democrat. Whisht! Gone!

HARRY. But wasn't it true? Didn't these people help to bolster a rotten society?

ADA. The only rotten society is an industrial society. It

34

makes a man stand on his head and then convinces him he is good-looking. I'll tell you something. It wasn't the Trotskyist or the Social Democrat who did the damage. It was progress! There! Progress! And nobody dared fight progress.

SARAH. But that's no reason to run away. Life still carries on. A man gets married, doesn't he? He still has children, he laughs, he finds things to make him laugh. A man can always laugh, can't he?

ADA. As if that meant he lived? Even a flower can grow in the jungle, can't it? Because there is always some earth and water and sun. But there's still the jungle, struggling for its own existence, and the sick screeching of animals terrified of each other. As if laughter were proof!

HARRY. And we and the Party don't want to do away with the jungle, I suppose?

ADA. No, you do not want to do away with the jungle, I suppose. You have *never* cried against the jungle of an industrial society. You've never wanted to destroy its *values* – simply to own them yourselves. It only seemed a crime to you that a man spent all his working hours in front of a machine because he did not own that machine. Heavens! the glory of owning a machine!

SARAH. So what, we shouldn't care any more? We must all run away?

ADA. Care! Care! What right have we to care? How can we care for a world outside ourselves when the world inside is in disorder? Care! Haven't you ever stopped, Mother – I mean stopped – and seen yourself standing with your arms open, and suddenly paused? Come to my bosom. Everyone come to my bosom. How can you possibly imagine that your arms are long enough, for God's sake? What audacity tells you you can harbour a billion people in a theory? What great, big, stupendous, egotistical audacity, tell me?

RONNIE. Whoa, whoa!

HARRY. But it *is* an industrial age, you silly girl. Let's face facts—

ADA (*mocking*). Don't let us kid ourselves.

HARRY (*with her*). Don't let us kid ourselves – it's a challenge of our time.

ADA. Balls!

HARRY. You can't run away from it.

ADA. Stop me!

HARRY. Then you're a coward – that's all I can say – you're a coward.

SARAH (*sadly*). She had a fine example from her father, didn't she?

HARRY (*to this stab in the back*). What do you mean – a fine example from her father?

SARAH. You don't understand what I'm saying, I suppose?

HARRY (*he is hurt and throws a hand at her in disgust*). Ach! you make me sick.

SARAH (*mocking*). Ach, you make me sick. *I* make *him* sick. Him, my fine man! You're the reason why she thinks like this, you know that?

HARRY. Yes, me.

SARAH. Well, of course you. Who else?

RONNIE (*collecting dishes and escaping to the kitchen*). I'll wash up.

HARRY. I didn't bring her up – she's all your work.

SARAH. That's just it! You didn't bring her up. You weren't concerned, were you? You left it all to me while you went to your mother's or to the pictures or out with your friends.

HARRY. Yes. I went out with my friends. Sure!

SARAH. Well, didn't you? May I have so many pennies for the times you went up West to pictures.

HARRY. Oh, leave off, Sarah.

SARAH. Leave off! That's all he can say – leave off, leave

me alone. That was it. I did leave you alone. That's why I had all the trouble.

ADA. I'm going home, Mummy.

SARAH (*caressingly and apologetically*). Oh no, Ada, stay, it's early yet. Stay. We'll play solo.

ADA. I'm feeling tired and I must write to Dave.

SARAH. Well, stay here and write to Dave. We'll all be quiet. Ronnie's going out. Daddy'll go to bed and I've got some washing to do. Stay, Ada, stay. What do you want to rush home for? A cold, miserable, two-roomed flat, all on your own. Stay. We're a family, aren't we?

ADA (*putting on her coat*). I've also got washing to do, I must go—

SARAH. I'll do it for you. What's a mother for? Straight from work I'll go to your place and bring it back with me. Stay. You've got company here – perhaps Uncle Hymie and Auntie Lottie'll come up. What do you want to be on your own for, tell me?

ADA. I'm not *afraid* of being on my own – I must go.

SARAH (*wearily*). Go then! Will we see you tomorrow?

ADA. Yes, I'll come for supper tomorrow night. Good night. (*Calling*) Good night, Ronnie.

RONNIE (*appearing from kitchen*). 'Night, Addy.

SARAH. You washing up, Ronnie?

RONNIE. I'm washing up.

SARAH. You I don't have to worry about – but your sister runs away. At the first sight of a little bother she runs away. Why does she run away, Ronnie? Before she used to sit and discuss things, now she runs to her home – such a home to run to – two rooms and a shadow!

RONNIE. But, Ma, she's a married woman herself. You think she hasn't her own worries wondering what it'll be like to see Dave after all these years?

SARAH. But you never run away from a discussion. At least I've got you around to help me solve problems.

RONNIE. Mother, my one virtue – if I got any at all – is that I always imagine you can solve things by talking about them – ask my form master! (*Returns to kitchen.*)

SARAH (*wearily to* HARRY). You see what you do? That's your daughter. Not a word from her father to ask her to stay. The family doesn't matter to you. All your life you've let the family fall around you, but it doesn't matter to you.

HARRY. I didn't drive her away.

SARAH (*bitterly*). No – you didn't drive her away. How could you? You were the good, considerate father.

> HARRY *turns away and hunches himself up miserably.*

Look at you! Did you shave this morning? Look at the cigarette ash on the floor. Your shirt! When did you last change your shirt? He sits. Nothing moves him, nothing worries him. He sits! A father! A husband!

HARRY (*taking out a cigarette to light*). Leave me alone, please leave me alone, Sarah. You started the row, not me, you!

SARAH (*taking cigarette from his hand*). Why must you always smoke? – talk with me. Talk, talk, Harry.

HARRY. Sarah! (*He stops, chokes, and then stares wildly around him.*) Mamma. Mamma. (*He is having his first stroke.*)

SARAH (*frightened but not hysterical*). Harry! Harry! What is it?

HARRY (*in Yiddish, gently*). Vie iss sie – der mamma?

SARAH. Stop it, Harry.

HARRY. Sie iss dorten – der mamma?

SARAH. Ronnie! Ronnie!

> RONNIE *comes in from the kitchen.*

Doctor Woolfson – quick, quick, get him.

RONNIE. What's happening?

SARAH. I don't know.

38

RONNIE *runs out.*

Harry, it was only a quarrel, you silly man. None of your tricks now, Harry – Harry, you hear me?

HARRY. Vie iss sie? Mamma, mamma.

CURTAIN

SCENE 2

October 1947. We are in the same room. RONNIE *is making a fire in the grate. When this is done he puts on the radio and goes into the kitchen. The 'Egmont' overture comes over the radio.* RONNIE *comes out of the kitchen with a cup of tea. On hearing the music he lays down the cup and picks up a pencil and proceeds to conduct an imaginary orchestra, until* CISSIE *is seen moving along the balcony. She lets herself in and surprises* RONNIE. *She is carrying a brief-case.*

RONNIE. Aunt!

CISSIE. Hello, Junior. I've come to see your father.

RONNIE. Not back from work yet. Just in time for a cuppa.
    Goes off to make one.

CISSIE. He still has that job, then?

RONNIE (*from kitchen*). Can't hear you.

CISSIE. Turn this bloody wireless down. (*Does so.*)

RONNIE. Aunty! Please! Beethoven!

CISSIE. I know, I know. Some other time. I'm not feeling so good. (*Takes cigarette from handbag.*)

RONNIE (*entering with tea*). What price partition in Palestine, Aunt?

CISSIE. Russia's backing the plan.

RONNIE. Yes – and haven't the Arabs got upset over that.

39

They're taking it to the high courts. They expected Russia to attack the United Nations plan if only to upset the West. Power politics!

CISSIE. Has your father still got that job?

RONNIE. No, he's a store-keeper in a sweet factory now. Look. (*Shows her a biscuit tin full of sweets.*) Jelly babies. Can't help himself. Doesn't do it on a large scale, mind, just a handful each night. Everyone does it.

CISSIE. How long has he been there?

RONNIE. Three weeks. You know he can't stay long at a job – and now he has got what he always wanted – a legitimate excuse.

CISSIE. He can *walk*, can't he?

RONNIE. He walks – slowly and stooped – with his head sunk into his shoulders, hands in his pockets. (*Imitates his father.*) His step isn't sure – frightened to exert him-self in case he should suddenly drop dead. You ought to see him in a strong wind – (*moves drunkenly round the room*) like an autumn leaf. He seems to have given up the fight, as though *thank God* he was no longer respon-sible for himself. You know, Aunt, I don't suppose there is anything more terrifying to a man than his own sense of failure, and your brother Harry is really a very sensitive man. No one knows more than he does how he's failed. Now that's tragedy for you: having the ability to see what is happening to yourself and yet not being able to do anything about it. Like a long nightmare. God! fancy being born just to live a long nightmare. He gets around. But who knows how sick he is? Now we can't tell his lethargy from his illness.

CISSIE. It sounds just like Mother. Mother was bed-ridden for years. He seems to be moving that way—

RONNIE. Almost deliberately. Here! (*Goes to a drawer and takes out a notebook.*) Did you know he once started to write his autobiography? Listen. (*Reads.*) 'Of me, the dummy and my family.' How's that for a poetic title! 'Sitting at my work in the shop one day my attention was drawn to the dummy that we all try the work on. The rhythm of the machines and my constant looking at the dummy rocked me off into a kind of sleepy daze. And to my surprise the dummy began to take the shape of a human, it began to speak. Softly at first, so softly I could hardly hear it. And then louder and still louder, and it seemed to raise its eyebrows and with a challenge asked: Your life, what of your life? My life? I had never thought, and I began to take my mind back, way back to the time when I was a little boy.' There, a whole note-book full, and then one day he stopped! Just like that! God knows why a man stops doing the one thing that can keep him together.

CISSIE. How's Ada and Dave?

RONNIE. Struggling in a cottage in the country. Ada suckles a beautiful baby, Dave lays concrete floors in the day-time and makes furniture by hand in the evening.

CISSIE. Lunatics!

RONNIE. They're happy. Two Jews in the Fens. They had to get a Rabbi from King's Lynn to circumcize the baby. A Rabbi from King's Lynn! Who'd ever think there were Rabbis in King's Lynn?

CISSIE. And you?

RONNIE. A bookshop.

CISSIE. Same one?

RONNIE. Same one.

CISSIE. You're also crazy and mixed up, I suppose?

RONNIE (*highly indignant*). Don't call me that! God in heaven, don't call me that! I'm a poet.

CISSIE. Another one!

RONNIE. A socialist poet.

CISSIE. A socialist poet!

RONNIE. I have all the world at my fingertips. Nothing is

mixed up. I have so much life that I don't know who to give it to first. I see beyond the coloured curtains of *my* eyes to a world – say, how do you like that line? Beyond the coloured curtains of *my* eyes, waiting for time and timing nothing but the slow hours, lay the thoughts in the mind. Past the pool of *my* smile . . .

CISSIE. What does that mean?

RONNIE. What, the pool of my smile? It's a metaphor – the pool of my smile – a very lovely metaphor. How's trade-union activity?

CISSIE. We've got a strike on. Dillingers are probably going to lock out its workers.

RONNIE. Ah, Dillingers! 'Dillingers styles gets all the men's smiles, this is the wear for everywhere!' No wonder the workers don't like poetry.

CISSIE. The old boy wants to reduce their wages because they're doing sale work.

RONNIE. What's that?

CISSIE. You know – sale work – specially made-up clothes for the big West End sales.

RONNIE. You mean a sale is not what is left over from the season before?

CISSIE. Oh, grow up, Ronnie. You should know that by now. It's cheaper stuff, inferior quality.

RONNIE. And the union doesn't protest? (*Jumping on a chair and waving his arms in the air*) Capitalist exploiters! The bastards – if you'll excuse the expression. I'll write a book about them! I'll expose them in their true light. What a novel, Aunt – set in a clothing factory, the sweat shops, the—

CISSIE. Look, you want to hear about this strike or you don't want to hear about this strike?

 RONNIE *sits down*.

So because it's sale work Dillinger wants to cut the women's wages by ten per cent and the men's by twelve and a half

42

per cent. So what does he plan to do? I'll tell you what he plans to do – he plans to pay all thirty of them for one full week, sack them, and then re-employ them, which would mean they were new employees and only entitled to Board of Trade rate, which is considerably less.

RONNIE. But can he do that?

CISSIE. He did it! He did it! The girls told me. But this year the shop stewards got together and asked me to go down and negotiate. They didn't all want it, mind you. One wagged his finger at me and cried: 'We're not taking your advice, we're not taking your advice!' I gave them – you know me. First I read the Riot Act to them and then I lashed out. You ought to be ashamed of yourselves, I told them, after the union struggled hard, tooth and nail, for every penny you get and at the first sign of intimidation you want to give in. For shame! I yelled at them – for shame! I tell you, Ronnie – a boss you can always handle because he always wants to bribe you, and that gives you the upper hand – but the worker . . .

> HARRY *has by this time entered through the front door, and he shuffles down the passage into the front room. He is slightly paralysed down one side but is still very able to move around. The first stroke has just made him age prematurely.*

HARRY. Hello, Cissie, what are you doing here?

CISSIE. I've come to see you. Well, how are you?

HARRY. I'm all right, Cissie, I'm fine.

CISSIE. Can you work all right?

HARRY. I can't move my left hand very well. Lost its grip or something. (*Clutches and unclutches fist to prove the point.*)

RONNIE (*gripping* HARRY'S *hand in a shake*). Strong as an ox. You're a sham, Harry boy. Want some tea?

HARRY. Yes please, son.

CISSIE. What do the doctors say is wrong with you.

HARRY. I had a stroke – that's all they know. They don't tell you anything in the hospitals these days. Sarah's gone to the doctor's now to find out if I can go back again for observation.

CISSIE. More observation?

HARRY. Ach! Don't talk to me about them, they make me sick.

CISSIE. All those blood tests they took and they still don't know – after a year. I'm surprised you had that much blood. Well, I'm going. Here, smoke yourself to death.

Hands him forty cigarettes.

RONNIE (*bringing in the tea*). Going?

CISSIE. I've got a strike meeting.

RONNIE. In the evening?

CISSIE. Any time. So long, Junior.

She kisses HARRY and RONNIE and goes out. On the landing she meets SARAH.

Hello, Sarah. I just come to see Harry. Sorry I must go. How are you?

SARAH. I'm all right. Why don't you stay for supper?

CISSIE (*out of sight by now*). I've got a strike meeting. I'll be seeing you.

HARRY (*to SARAH as she comes in*). Did you go to the doctor's?

SARAH (*wearily*). I've been, I've been. Oh, those stairs will kill me.

HARRY. What does he say?

SARAH (*taking out a letter from her bag and placing it on the mantelpiece*). He gave me a letter: you should take it to the hospital.

HARRY. What does it say; show me.

SARAH. It's sealed; you mustn't open it.

HARRY. Show me it.

SARAH. What can you see? It's sealed.

HARRY (*irritably*). Oh, I want to see who it's addressed to.

Too tired to cope with him she hands him the letter and then goes to the kitchen.

SARAH (*from the kitchen*). Did anybody make supper?

RONNIE. We've not long come in. (*To* HARRY, *taking away the envelope he is trying to open*) Uh-uh. Mustn't open. It's for the hospital.

SARAH (*entering with a cup of tea and sitting down*). I've got a branch meeting tonight. Ronnie, you can take your own supper. It's fried fish from yesterday. You want to come with me, Harry?

HARRY. I don't feel like going to any branch meeting.

SARAH. You want to get well, don't you? You don't want to become an invalid, do you? So come to a meeting tonight. Mix with people. They're your comrades, aren't they?

HARRY. Yes my comrades.

SARAH. Nothing is sacred for him. Ach! Why should I worry whether you come or not. What are you doing, Ronnie?

RONNIE. An evening in. I want to write a novel tonight.

SARAH. What, all in one night? Ronnie, do you think you'll ever publish anything? I mean, don't you have to be famous or be able to write or something? There must be such a lot of people writing novels.

RONNIE. Not socialist novels. Faith, Mother, faith! I am one of the sons of the working class, one of its own artists.

HARRY. You mean a political writer like Winston Churchill?

SARAH. What, does he write novels as well? I thought he was only a politician.

RONNIE. Well, he's both – *and* he paints pictures.

SARAH. A painter? He paints pictures? Landscapes and things?

RONNIE. Of course! And in his spare time he—

SARAH. What, he has spare time also?

45

RONNIE. In his spare time he builds walls at the bottom of his garden.

SARAH (*in admiration*). A bricklayer! Ronnie, I told you you should take up a trade! Why don't you? Go to evening classes. Why should you waste your time in a bookshop? If I were young, oh, what wouldn't I study! All the world I would study. How properly to talk and to write and make sentences. You'll be sorry – don't be like your father, don't be unsettled. Learn a good trade and then you have something to fall back on. You can always write – and when you work then you'll have something to write about.

RONNIE. Give me a chance, Ma. I only left school a year ago.

SARAH. That's what he kept on saying. Give me a chance! Everybody had to give him a chance: now look at him. Harry – you're not working in the sweet factory any more, are you?

HARRY. Who said I'm not?

RONNIE. Well, isn't he?

SARAH. Well, ask him, he knows.

RONNIE *inclines his head inquiringly.*

HARRY. Of course I'm still working there.

SARAH (*wearily, for the time has gone for violent rows*). Harry, answer me. What do you gain by telling me this lie? Tell me, I want to know. All my life I've wanted to know what you've gained by a lie. *I* know you're not working because I saw the foreman. You're not even a good liar. I've always known when you've lied. For twenty-five years it's been the same and all the time I've not known what it's about. But *you* know – no one else knows, but you do. I'm asking you, Harry – let me be your doctor, let me try and help you. What is it that makes you what you are? Tell me – only tell me. Don't sit there and say nothing. I'm entitled to know – after all this time, I'm entitled to know. Well, aren't I, Ronnie?

Nobody answers her. HARRY *avoids her gaze,*
RONNIE *waits till it's all over.*

So look at him. He sits and he sits and he sits and all his
life goes away from him. (*To* RONNIE) You won't be like
that, will you?

RONNIE. I shall never take up a trade I hate as he did – if
that's what you mean; and I shall never marry – at least
not until I'm real and healthy. (*Cheerfully*) But what's
there to grumble about, little Sarah? You have two splendid children, a fine son-in-law and a grandson.

SARAH. I haven't seen my grandson yet. My daughter lives
two hundred miles away from me and my husband is a
sick man. That's my family. Well, it's a family, I suppose.
(*She rises to go.*)

RONNIE. What about me? (*He regards himself in a mirror.*)
Young, good-looking, hopeful, talented . . . hopeful, anyway.

SARAH (*sadly*). You? I'll wait and see what happens to you.
Please God you don't make a mess of your life, please God.
Did you ask for that rise?

RONNIE. I did ask for that rise. 'Mr Randolph,' I said – he's
the manager of that branch – 'Mr Randolph, I know that
the less wages you pay us bookshop assistants the more you
get in your salary. But don't you think I've sold enough
books for long enough time to warrant you foregoing some
of your commission?'

SARAH. So what did he say, you liar?

RONNIE. 'You're our best salesman,' he said, 'but I've got to
keep head office happy.'

SARAH. So what did you say, you liar?

RONNIE. So I said, 'It's not head office, it's your wife.'

SARAH. So what did he say, you liar?

RONNIE. He said, 'Kahn,' he said, 'as you're so frank and
you know too much I'll give you a two-pound rise.'

SARAH. Ronnie, did you get a rise, I asked you?

RONNIE (*kissing her*). No, I did not get a rise.

SARAH. Mad boy, you! I'm going to the meeting.

RONNIE. That's it, Mother. You go to the meeting. At least if you keep on fighting then there's hope for me. (*He helps her on with a coat as he speaks, then she goes. Returning to room*) You want supper, Dad? It's the old dead fish again. I'll lay it for you. (*Moves to kitchen.*)

HARRY. Aren't you going to eat?

RONNIE (*from kitchen*). I'm not hungry. I'll eat later. I must work now. You want me to read the first chapter to you, Dad?

HARRY. Oh, leave me alone, Ronnie – I'm tired.

RONNIE. Tired! You're not tired, Harry – you're just drowning with heritage, mate! (*Re-enters with an assortment of plates, which he lays on the table.*) There, you can wash up after you. I'm going to my room now.

> RONNIE *goes to his room.* HARRY *moves the table and begins to eat. He eats in silence for a few seconds, then stretches out for a newspaper. After glancing through this he turns to the mantelpiece and sees the letter. He looks to* RONNIE'S *room to make sure he is not coming and then moves slowly across to get the letter. First of all he tries to prise it open without tearing anything. Then not succeeding in this he moves to the table to get a knife. As he picks up the knife* RONNIE *enters again.*

RONNIE. Christ! It's bloody cold in that room: I – now then, Harry – (*as though playfully scolding a child*) you know you must not read the letter, remember what Mummykins said. (*He moves to take it.*)

HARRY (*retaining it*). I want to see it; it's about me, isn't what's in it.

RONNIE (*making another bid for it*). Use some will-power, Dad; you know the letter is not for you. Now leave it be, there's a good boy.

HARRY (*still retaining it*). I want to see it; it's about me, isn't it? Now leave off, Ronnie.

RONNIE (*snatching it from his father's hand*). No!

HARRY (*banging his hand on the table in rapid succession with the words, like a child in anger, hating to be like a child, and shrieking*). GIVE ME THAT LETTER. GIMME. S'mine. S'mine. I WAN' THAT ENVELOPE. Now. This instant. I – wan' – that – envelope!

> RONNIE *stands there trembling. He had not meant to provoke such anger, and now, having done so, is upset. He is not quite sure what to do. Almost involuntarily he hands over the envelope, and when he has done so he goes to a wall and cries. He is still a boy – he has been frightened.* HARRY *picks up envelope, himself distraught. He does not bother to open it now. Seeing that* RONNIE *is crying he goes over to him and clasps him.*

HARRY. You shouldn't do these things. I'm a sick man. If I want to open the envelope you shouldn't stop me. You've got no right to stop me. Now you've upset me and yourself – you silly boy.

RONNIE. Can't you see that I can't bear what you are. I don't want to hear your lies all my life. Your weakness frightens me, Harry – did you ever think about that? I watch you and I see myself and I'm terrified.

HARRY (*wandering away from him; he does not know what to say*). What I am – I am. I will never alter. Neither you nor your mother will change me. It's too late now; I'm an old man and if I've been the same all my life so I will always be. You can't alter people, Ronnie. You can only give them some love and hope they'll take it. I'm sorry. It's too late now. I can't help you. (*He shuffles miserably to his room, perceptibly older.*) Don't forget to have supper. Good night.

CURTAIN

49

Act Three

November 1955.

HARRY *has had his second stroke, and now paralysis has made him completely unfit for work. He can only just move around, has difficulty in talking, and is sometimes senile.* SARAH *retains much of her energy but shows signs of age and her troubles – her tone of speaking is compassionate now.*

Evening, in the same L.C.C. flat. HARRY *sits in a chair – huddled by the fireplace, listening to Ravel's 'La Valse' on the radio. He smokes more than ever, it is his one comfort.* SARAH *is sitting by the table struggling to fill out an official Government form – she talks a lot to herself.*

SARAH (*reading form*). Have you an insurance policy for life or death? Name of company. Amount issued for. Annual payments. How should I know the annual payments? I pay one and a penny a week – that's fifty-two shillings and fifty-two pennies. (*Makes mental reckoning.*)
The music on the radio has by this time reached a climax and is too loud. SARAH *goes to turn it off.*
Oh, shut that off! Classical music! All of a sudden it starts shouting at you.

HARRY. No, no, no, no, I was – I was listening.

SARAH. You *liked* it?

HARRY. I liked it. It reminds me of – of – of – of – it reminds me of Blackfriars Bridge in a fog.

SARAH. Blackfriars Bridge in a fog it reminds you of? Why a fog?

HARRY. Oh, I don't know why a fog. Why a fog?

SARAH. And why Blackfriars Bridge?

HARRY. Because I said so! Och, you're such a silly woman sometimes, Sarah.

SARAH (*playing with him*). But if it's in a fog so what dif-

ference whether it's Blackfriars Bridge or London Bridge?
Ach, I must get these forms done before Bessie and Monty
arrive. You remember Bessie and Monty are coming tonight? (SARAH *continues to complete forms*.) If Ronnie
were here I'd get him to fill it in for me ... as if they don't
know how many times I was at work this year. Forms!
You tell the National Insurance office that you started
work on such and such a day so they tell the National
Assistance and the National Assistance tells the Income
Tax and then there's forms, forms, forms, forms. Oi – such
forms. They can't get enough of them into one envelope.
(*Writing*) No, I haven't got any property, I haven't got
any lodgers, I haven't got a housekeeper. A housekeeper!
A housekeeper wouldn't do what I do for you, Harry –
washing all those sheets.

    MONTY BLATT *and his wife* BESSIE *appear on
    the balcony. They knock.* SARAH *jumps up.*

They're here already. Now Harry, sit up. Do your flies up
and brush that cigarette ash off you. And remember –
don't let me down – you promised. You want to go now?

    She takes HARRY'S *arm but he pushes her away;
    he doesn't want to go.* SARAH *opens the door to
    her visitors. Both are richly dressed – over-dressed –
    and full of bounce and property.*

MONTY. Sarah – little Sarah. How are you, sweetheart? You
remember Bessie?

    They all shake hands and enter the front room.

Harry boy! How's Harry? You're looking well. You feeling well? They haven't changed a bit. Neither of them.

SARAH. Sit down, both of you; I'll get the kettle on. (*Goes
off to kitchen.*)

MONTY (*to* BESSIE). Always put the kettle on – that was
the first thing Sarah always did. Am I right, Harry? I'm
right, aren't I? (*Shouting to* SARAH) Remember, Sarah?
It was always a cup of tea first.

SARAH (*coming in*). I remember, I remember.

MONTY (*to* BESSIE). We used to *live* in their old place in the East End, all the boys. Remember Prince and your brother Hymie? How is Hymie? Since we moved to Manchester I've lost contact with everybody, everyeee-body!

SARAH. Hymie's all right. He's got a business. His children are married and he stays at home all the time. Prince works in a second-hand shop.

MONTY. A second-hand shop? But I thought – and Cissie?

SARAH. The union members retired her. She lives on a pension, visits the relatives – you know . . .

MONTY. It's all broken up, then?

SARAH. What's broken up about it? They couldn't keep up with the Party – so? The *fight* still goes on.

MONTY (*hastily changing the subject*). And Ada and Dave and Ronnie? Where are they all? Tell me everything. Tell me all the news. I haven't seen you for so long, Sarah – it's so good to see you – isn't it good to see them, Bessie?

SARAH. Ada and Dave are still in the country. They've got two children. Dave is still making furniture by hand—

MONTY. He makes a living?

SARAH. They live! They're not prosperous, but they live.

MONTY. And Ronnie? Ronnie had such ambitions; what's he doing?

SARAH. My Ronnie? He's in Paris.

MONTY. There, I told you he'd go far.

SARAH. As a cook.

MONTY (*not so enthusiastically*). A cook? Ronnie?

BESSIE (*helping them out*). A cook makes good money.

MONTY (*reviving*). Sure a cook makes good money. Ronnie is a smart boy, isn't he, Sarah? Didn't I always say Ronnie was a smart boy? Nobody could understand how an East End boy could speak with such a posh accent. But cooking! He likes it? I mean he's happy?

SARAH. I tell you something, Monty. People ask me what

is Ronnie doing and, believe me, I don't know what to answer. He used to throw his arms up in the air and say 'I want to do something worth while, I want to create.' Create! So, he's a cook in Paris.

MONTY. Please God he'll be a hotel manager one day.

SARAH. Please God.

MONTY. And Harry? (*He indicates with his head that* HARRY *has dozed off.*)

SARAH. Poor Harry. He's had two strokes. He won't get any better. Paralysed down one side. He can't control his bowels, you know.

BESSIE. Poor man.

SARAH. You think *he* likes it? It's ach a nebish Harry now. It's not easy for him. But he won't do anything to help himself. I don't know, other men get ill but they fight. Harry's never fought. Funny thing. There were three men like this in the flats, all had strokes. And all three of them seemed to look the same. They walked the same, stooped the same, and all needing a shave. They used to sit outside together and talk for hours on end and smoke. Sit and talk and smoke. That was their life. Then one day one of them decided he wanted to live so he gets up and finds himself a job – running a small shoe-mender's – and he's earning money now. A miracle! Just like that. But the other one – he wanted to die. I used to see him standing outside in the rain, the pouring rain, getting all wet so that he could catch a cold and die. Well, it happened: last week he died. Influenza! He just didn't want to live. But Harry was not like either of them. He didn't want to die but he doesn't seem to care about living. So! What can you do to help a man like that? I make his food and I buy him cigarettes and he's happy. My only dread is that he will mess himself. When that happens I go mad – I just don't know what I'm doing.

MONTY. It's like that, is it?

53

SARAH. It's like that. That's life. But how about you, Monty? You still in the Party?

MONTY. No, Sarah – I'm not still in the Party, and I'll tell you why if you want to know—

BESSIE. Now, Monty, don't get on to politics. Sarah, do me a favour and don't get him on to politics.

MONTY. Don't worry, I won't say much—

SARAH. Politics is living, Bessie. I mean everything that happens in the world has got to do with politics.

BESSIE. Listen, Sarah. Monty's got a nice little greengrocer's business in Manchester, no one knows he was ever a member of the Party and we're all happy. It's better he forgets it.

MONTY. No, no – I'll tell her, let me tell her.

BESSIE. I'm warning you, Monty, if you get involved in a political argument I shan't stay. No political argument, you hear me?

MONTY. Listen, Sarah. Remember Spain? Remember how we were proud of Dave and the other boys who answered the call? But did Dave ever tell you the way some of the Party members refused to fight alongside the Trotskyists? And one or two of the Trotskyists didn't come back and they weren't killed in the fighting either? And remember Itzack Pheffer – the Soviet Yiddish writer? We used to laugh because Itzack Pheffer was a funny name – ha, ha. Where's Itzack Pheffer? everyone used to say. Well, we know now, don't we. The great 'leader' is dead now, and we know. The whole committee of the Jewish Anti-Fascist League were shot! Shot, Sarah! In our land of socialism. That was *our* land – what a land that was for us! We didn't believe the stories then; it wasn't possible that it could happen in our one-sixth of the world.

SARAH. And you believe the stories now, Monty?

MONTY (*incredulously*). You don't—

BESSIE. Now, Monty—

MONTY. You don't believe it, Sarah? You won't believe it!

54

SARAH. And supposing it's true, Monty? So? What should we do, bring back the old days? Is that what you want?

MONTY. I don't know, sweetheart. I haven't got any solutions any more. I've got a little shop up north – I'm not a capitalist by any means – I just make a comfortable living and I'm happy. Bessie – bless her – is having a baby. (*Taps* BESSIE'S *belly.*) I'm going to give him all that I can, pay for his education, university if he likes, and then I shall be satisfied. A man can't do anything more, Sarah, believe me. There's nothing more to life than a house, some friends, and a family – take my word.

SARAH. And when someone drops an atom bomb on your family?

MONTY (*pleading*). So what can I do – tell me? There's nothing I can do any more. I'm too small; who can I trust? It's a big, lousy world of mad politicians – I can't trust them, Sarah.

SARAH. The kettle's boiling – I'll make some tea. (*Goes to kitchen.*)

BESSIE. Enough now, Monty, enough.

MONTY (*he has upset himself*). All right, all right. I didn't tell her anything she doesn't know. She's a fine woman is Sarah. She's a fighter. All that worry and she's still going strong. But she has one fault. For her the world is black and white. If you're not white so you must be black. She can't see shades in character – know what I mean? She can't see people in the round. 'They' are all the same bunch. The authorities, the governments, the police, the Post Office – even the shopkeepers. She's never trusted any of them, always fighting them. It was all so simple. The only thing that mattered was to be happy and eat. Anything that made you unhappy or stopped you from eating was the fault of capitalism. Do you think she ever read a book on political economy in her life? Bless her! Someone told her socialism was happiness so she joined the Party. You don't find many left like Sarah Kahn. I wish you'd have known us in the old days. Harry there used to have a lovely tenor voice. All the songs we sang together, and the strikes and the rallies. I used to carry Ronnie shoulder high to the May Day demonstrations. Everyone in the East End was going somewhere. It was a slum, there was misery, but we were going somewhere. The East End was a big mother.

SARAH *comes in with the tea.*

We'll talk about the good times now, shall we, Sarah? Blimey, sweetheart, it's not often that I come to London for a week-end. Here, remember the stall I used to have in Petticoat Lane? I'll take you there tomorrow, Bessie. And Manny the Corn King? Him and his wife used to go to Norwich, to sell phoney corn cures. His wife used to dress up as a nurse and they'd hang letters round the stall from people who were supposed to have been cured.

SARAH. And what about Barney?

MONTY. And Barney, that's it! He used to sell all the old farmers a lucky charm to bring them fortune. Sixpence each he'd sell them for and you know what they were? Haricot beans! Haricot beans dropped in dye to colour them. You could get them for threepence a pound in a grocer's shop and Barney sold them for sixpence each! Sixpence! A pound of beans used to last him for months.

SARAH. Ach! Horrible times! Horrible times – dirty, unclean, cheating!

MONTY. But friendly.

SARAH. Friendly, you call it? You think it was friendly to swindle people?

MONTY. Sweetheart, you take life too seriously. Believe me, those farmers knew very well what they were buying. Nobody swindled anybody because everyone knew.

SARAH. You think so, Monty?

HARRY *wakes up with a jerk. Something has happened. He tries hurriedly to rise.*

HARRY. Sarah, quick, help me.

SARAH. What! It's happened? (*She moves quickly to him.*)

MONTY. What is it, Harry boy?

SARAH. It's happened, Harry? Well, quickly then, quickly.
HARRY, *crippled by paralysis and this attack of incontinence, shuffles, painfully, towards the toilet, with* SARAH *almost dragging him along. He whines and groans pathetically.*

In front of Monty and Bessie. I'm so ashamed.
MONTY *attempts to help* HARRY *move.*

(*Abruptly*) No, leave him. It's all right. I'll manage. Leave him, Monty.
They struggle out and into the passage. When they have left the front room, BESSIE *turns her head away and shudders.*

BESSIE. Oh, good God!

MONTY. Poor Sarah and Harry. Jesus! It's all come to this?

CURTAIN

SCENE 2

December 1956.
The Kahns' room, late one evening. SARAH, PRINCE, HYMIE *and* CISSIE *are sitting round the table playing solo.* HARRY *is by the fire, gazing into it, quite oblivious of what is going on. The cards have just been dealt for a round. Everyone is evaluating his cards in silence. After some seconds:*

PRINCE (*studying his cards*). What time you expecting Ronnie, Sarah?

SARAH (*studying her cards*). He's supposed to arrive at nine thirty tonight.

Again silence.

HYMIE (*to* CISSIE). Nu? Call!

CISSIE. Misère.

SARAH. How can you call a misère when I want to call a misère?

CISSIE. Please, Sarah – don't give the game away.

PRINCE. Wait a minute, not everybody has passed.

CISSIE. All right then, call!

SARAH. Pass.

PRINCE. Pass.

HYMIE. Pass.

CISSIE. Thank you. Can I start now?

SARAH. Is it your lead? I thought Prince dealt the cards.

CISSIE. What's the matter with you, Sarah? – Hymie dealt them.

PRINCE. I could have sworn Sarah dealt them.

CISSIE. Hymie, who dealt the cards?

HYMIE. We've been so long deciding what to call that I don't know any more. Did I deal them? I don't remember.

There is a general discussion as to who dealt them.

CISSIE. Now quiet, everybody. Quiet! Every time I come to this house to play solo there's the same confusion. Why don't you pay attention to the game? Now then, what was laid on the table for trumps?

SARAH. The two of spades.

HYMIE. That was the last round. It was the six of diamonds.

SARAH. But I saw it with my own eyes, it was the—

HYMIE. You aren't wearing your glasses, Sarah.

PRINCE. It was the six of hearts, I remember now.

CISSIE. Ah, thank God! We've got two people to agree. I also saw the six of hearts on the table. Who's got the six of hearts?

HYMIE. I have.

CISSIE. Which means that you dealt and if you dealt that means that I lead. Everybody happy now? There!

> CISSIE *throws down a card. The others follow. It's* HYMIE'S *trick. He lays down a card and the others follow, but* SARAH *realizes she has made a mistake.*

SARAH. Wait a minute, wait a minute. I didn't mean to play that card.

CISSIE. Too late; you should watch the game.

SARAH. Ach! fool that I am. But you can see I shouldn't have played that card.

CISSIE. Of course I can see, but I'm glad that you did!

SARAH. Now, Hymie, would I normally play that card?

HYMIE. You aren't wearing your glasses, Sarah: I told you. We can still catch her. Now play.

SARAH. A second, a second. Let me get my glasses. (*Finds her bag, takes out her glasses and proceeds to puff on them and clean them.*) I don't know what's happened to my eyes lately. I went to have my glasses changed the other day – the rims were too big for me, kept slipping into my mouth – so I went to have them changed. The man said he couldn't change them because they were National Health glasses. So you know me, I tell him what for and he says, 'Madam,' he says, 'you want your money back?' So I say, 'Sure I want my money back.' And then I go up to the National Health offices – now listen to this – I go up to the National Health offices and I complain about the small allowance they make me for Harry. So the chap behind the desk – may he wake up dead – he says, 'What do you want, madam, ten pounds a week?' Did you ever hear? So I said, 'Son,' I said, 'when you were still peeing all over the floor I was on strike for better conditions, and don't you be cheeky.' 'Oh dear, you mustn't talk to me like that per, per, per, per!'

PRINCE. Come on, Sarah, the game.

> *It is* PRINCE'S *lead. The others follow; it is his*

trick again. Again he leads and the others follow.
Now it is for SARAH *to lead, and she does so.*

What did you play hearts for? Couldn't you see what suit I was showing you?

SARAH. Prince, let me play my own game. Don't I know what I'm doing?

PRINCE. Well, it doesn't look like it, Sarah, so help me it doesn't. You can't be watching the game. Couldn't you guess she was going to throw off on hearts?

CISSIE. What is this! In the middle of the game!

SARAH. Of course I could see, but how do you know that I can't put anything else?

CISSIE. Are you going to play solo or aren't you going to play solo? No inquests, please.

HYMIE. Prince, play your game.

CISSIE. It's always the same. You can't even get a good game of solo these days!

PRINCE *plays his card and they all follow.*

SARAH. Look at him! Now he comes out diamonds and he wants to teach me how to play solo.

SARAH *leads next time, and after that* CISSIE *lays down her cards and shows that she can't be caught.*

CISSIE. There! Three-halfpence from everybody, please.
Now everybody looks at everybody else's hand to see where everybody else went wrong.

SARAH. Well, of course I couldn't catch her, not with my hand.

PRINCE. Why did you come out with hearts when you knew she might be throwing off on them?

SARAH. Because I wanted to give the lead away – *I* couldn't do anything.

HYMIE. But why give the lead away with hearts when you knew she might not have any?

SARAH. How was I to know? It was my smallest card.

CISSIE. You never could play a good game of solo, Sarah.

60

SARAH. But do me a favour—
CISSIE. Spades! That was the suit to play.
SARAH. Spades? Never!

Again everybody starts to speak at once until a loud
scream brings them to silence. It comes from the
playground below and is followed by a young girl's
voice crying.

GIRL'S VOICE. Philip! Philip! I want my Philip. Leave i
alone – go away.

MAN'S VOICE. Go 'ome, I tell you, 'ome, you silly co\
'Ome!

GIRL'S VOICE. I won't go till I see Philip. I love him!
love him!

CISSIE. They making a film out there or something?

They all go out to the balcony and look down.
SARAH *walks along it off-stage to see what the com-*
motion is all about.

Can't see a thing. There's always something happening in
these flats. Last week a woman tried to gas herself. Come
on, let's go in.

They return to room.

HARRY. What happened?

PRINCE. Your neighbours are having a party. Sarah's gone
to see who's dead.

HYMIE. Why did the woman want to commit suicide?

CISSIE (*raising her skirt to warm her behind*). Who knows
why a woman of thirty-two wants to commit suicide? These
flats are a world on their own. You live a whole lifetime
here and not know your next-door neighbour.

HARRY. I don' – I don' – I don' –

CISSIE. Do you want to write it down?

HARRY. I don' know the woman downstairs yet.

Everyone smiles for him, and having said his piece
he returns to gazing at the fire. SARAH *re-enters.*

SARAH. Children! They don't know what to do with them-

selves. Seems she'd just spent the evening watching television with Philip and it was a horror film or something and he kept frightening her. Frightening her! That's all they can do to each other! She got home late and her father started on her so she ran back and started screaming for Philip. The great lover! He came out in his pyjamas to soothe her.

CISSIE (*going to get her coat*). Well, Sarah, I had a nice supper, a nice game of solo, and I'm going before the washing up. It doesn't look as though Ronnie caught that train anyway.

SARAH. I can't understand it. He wrote he was leaving Paris at eight this morning.

HYMIE. Well, it's nearly ten thirty and I must be going as well.

PRINCE. Me, too, Sarah.

SARAH. Won't you stay for a cup of tea at least? It's so long since we've played a game of solo. Harry and I don't see many people these days.

HYMIE. It's been a nice evening, Sarah. Why don't you come up to *us* sometimes? I'm always at home.

SARAH. What chance do I get to leave Harry now?

CISSIE. Good night, Sarah.

> HYMIE *kisses* SARAH *and* CISSIE *kisses* HARRY, *and all leave.* SARAH *waves to them from the balcony and returns to the room. She collects the cards and tidies up.*

SARAH. Harry, you want a cup of tea?

HARRY (*slowly rising*). I'm going to bed.

SARAH. You won't wait up for Ronnie?

HARRY. I'll – I'll – I'll—

SARAH. You'll what?

HARRY. See him in the morning.

> SARAH *helps* HARRY *shuffle away to bed, and then settles down in the armchair to read. But she is*

tired now and lets the paper fall, and dozes. RONNIE
*appears on the balcony with his cases. He gently
opens the door and lets himself in. He tiptoes over
to* SARAH *and stands looking at her. It is no longer
an enthusiastic* RONNIE. *She opens her eyes and
after a second of looking at him she jumps up into
his arms.*

SARAH. I fell asleep.

RONNIE. So I saw.

SARAH. I thought you were a dream.

RONNIE. Perhaps I am.

SARAH (*pushing him away to look at him*). I hope not,
Ronnie. Oh God, I hope not. Don't go away again. It's
been so lonely without you and your friends. I don't mind
not having any money, we can always eat, you know that,
but I can't bear being on my own. (*Begins to cry.*)

RONNIE. I've only once ever seen you cry.

SARAH. What's the good of crying?

RONNIE. I wish I could cry sometimes. Perhaps if you'd
have cried more often it would have been easier.

SARAH. It's just that I can't cope any longer, that's all.
Three times a week Daddy has that accident and it gets
too much. I'm an old woman now.

RONNIE. What makes you think I shall be able to cope?

SARAH. You? What are you talking about? Of course you'll
be able to cope. You're young, aren't you? Your going to
settle down.

RONNIE. I – I'm sick, Sarah.

SARAH. Sick?

RONNIE. Oh, not physically. That's why I came home.

SARAH. Didn't you like the place where you worked? You
always wrote how happy you were – what an experience
it was.

RONNIE. I hated the kitchen.

SARAH. But—

63

RONNIE. I – hated – the – kitchen! People coming and going and not staying long enough to understand each other. Do you know what I finally discovered – it's all my eye! This notion of earning an honest penny is all my eye. A man can work a whole lifetime and when he is sixty-five he considers himself rich if he has saved a thousand pounds. Rich! A whole lifetime of working in a good, steady, settled, enterprising, fascinating job! For every manager in a restaurant there must be twenty chefs terrified of old age. That's all we are – people terrified of old age, hoping for the football pools to come home. It's all my eye, Sarah.

SARAH. I'll make you some tea. Are you hungry?

RONNIE. No, I don't want anything to eat, thank you – I want to talk to you about something.

SARAH. But you must have to eat, you've been travelling all day.

RONNIE (*categorically*). I do not want to eat – I want to talk.

SARAH. I'll just make some tea, then; the water's boiled. You sit and relax and then you'll go straight to sleep. You'll see, by the morning you'll feel much better. (*Goes to the kitchen.*)

RONNIE. Still optimistic, Mother. Food and sleep and you can see no reason why a person should be unhappy.

SARAH (*from the kitchen*). I'd have looked blue all these years if I hadn't've been optimistic.

RONNIE. How's Harry?

SARAH (*entering with two cups of tea*). You'll see him to-morrow; he was too tired to wait up. Want some biscuits? Have a piece of cake. Look, cake I made specially for you – your favourite.

RONNIE (*loudly*). Mother, don't fuss. I'm sorry.

SARAH. Is this how you've come home? You start by shouting? Is this a nice homecoming?

RONNIE (*something is obviously boiling in him*). Are you still in the Party?

SARAH (*quizzically*). Yes.

RONNIE (*suddenly*). I don't suppose you've bothered to read what happened in Hungary.

SARAH. Hungary?

RONNIE. Look at me, Mother. Talk to me. Take me by the hand and show me who was right and who was wrong. Point them out. Do it *for* me. I stand here and a thousand different voices are murdering my mind. Do you know, I couldn't wait to come home and accuse you.

SARAH. Accuse me?

RONNIE. You didn't tell me there were any doubts.

SARAH. What doubts? What are you talking about?

RONNIE. Everything has broken up around you and you can't see it.

SARAH (*shouting*). What, what, what, you mad boy? Explain what you mean.

RONNIE. What has happened to all the comrades, Sarah? I even blush when I use that word. Comrade! Why do I blush? Why do I feel ashamed to use words like democracy and freedom and brotherhood? They don't have meaning any more. I have nothing to write about any more. Remember all that writing I did? I was going to be a great socialist writer. I can't make sense of a word, a simple word. You look at me as if I'm talking in a foreign language. Didn't it hurt *you* to read about the murder of the Jewish Anti-Fascist Committee in the Soviet Union?

SARAH. You as well. Monty Blatt came up some months ago and said the same thing. He's also left the Party. He runs a greengrocer shop in Manchester.

RONNIE. And Dave and Ada in Norfolk, and Prince working in the second-hand shop, and Uncle Hymie stuck smugly at home and Auntie Cissie once devoted – once involved – wandering from relative to relative. What's

happened to us? Were we cheated or did we cheat ourselves? I just don't know, God in heaven, I just do not
know! Can you understand what it is suddenly not to
know? (*Collapses into armchair.*) And the terrifying thing
is – I don't care either.

　　They sit in silence for some seconds.

SARAH. Drink your tea, darling.

　　RONNIE *closes his eyes and talks.*

RONNIE. Do you know what the trouble is, Mother? Can't
you guess?

SARAH. You're tired, Ronnie.

RONNIE. You *do* know what the trouble is. You just won't
admit it.

SARAH. In the morning you'll feel better.

RONNIE. Think hard. Look at my face. Look at my nose and
my deep-set eyes; even my forehead is receding.

SARAH. Why don't you listen to me? Go to bed and—

RONNIE. Political institutions, society – they don't really
affect people that much.

SARAH. Ronnie!

RONNIE. Who else was it who hated the jobs he had, who
couldn't bear the discipline imposed by a daily routine,
couldn't make sense of himself and gave up?

SARAH (*frightened*). Are you mad?

RONNIE. I've lost my faith and I've lost my ambition. Now
I understand him perfectly. I wish I hadn't shouted at him
as I used to.

SARAH. Mad boy!

RONNIE (*rising, opens his eyes and shouts*). You know that
I'm right. *You've* never been right about anything. You
wanted everybody to be happy but you wanted them to be
happy your way. It was strawberries and cream for everyone – whether they liked it or not. And now look what's
happened. The family you always wanted has disintegra-
ted, and the great ideal you always cherished has exploded

in front of your eyes. But you won't face it. You just refuse to face it. I don't know how you do it but you do – you just do. (*Louder*) You're a pathological case, Mother – do you know that? You're still a *communist*!

He wants to take back his words but he has lost the power to express anything any more.

SARAH. All right! So I'm still a communist! Shoot me then! I'm a communist! I've always been one – since the time when all the world was a communist. You know that? When you were a baby and there was unemployment and everybody was thinking so – all the world was a communist. But it's different now. Now the people have forgotten. I sometimes think they're not worth fighting for because they forget so easily. You give them a few shillings in the bank and they can buy a television so they think it's all over, there's nothing more to be got, they don't have to think any more! Is that what you want? A world where people don't think any more? Is that what you want me to be satisfied with – a television set? Look at him! My son! He wants to die!

RONNIE. Don't laugh at me, Sarah.

SARAH. You want me to cry again? We should all sit down and cry?

RONNIE. I don't see things in black and white any more. My thoughts keep going pop, like bubbles. That's my life now – you know? – a lot of little bubbles going pop.

SARAH. And he calls me a pathological case! Pop! Pop, pop, pop, pop – shmop! You think it doesn't hurt me – the news about Hungary? You think I know what happened and what didn't happen? Do any of us know? Who do I know who to trust now – God, who are our friends now? But all my life I've fought. With your father and the rotten system that couldn't help him. All my life I worked with a party that meant glory and freedom and brotherhood. You want me to give it up now? You want me to

67

move to Hendon and forget who I am? If the electrician who comes to mend my fuse blows it instead, so I should stop having electricity? I should cut off my light? Socialism is my light, can you understand that? A way of life. A man *can* be beautiful. I hate ugly people – I can't bear meanness and fighting and jealousy – I've got to have light. I'm a simple person, Ronnie, and I've got to have light and love.

RONNIE *looks up at her meaningfully.*

You think I didn't love your father enough, don't you? I'll tell you something. When Ada had diphtheria and I was pregnant I asked Daddy to carry her to the hospital. He wouldn't. We didn't have money because he didn't care to work and I didn't know what to do. He disappeared. It was Mrs Bernstein who saved her – you remember Mrs Bernstein? No, of course not, she died before you were born. It was Mrs Bernstein's soup. Ada still has that taste in her mouth – chicken soup with barley. She says it is a friendly taste – ask her. That saved her. Not even my brothers had money in those days, and a bit of dry crust with a cup of tea – ah! it was wonderful. But Daddy had the relief money. Someone told me they saw him eating salt-beef sandwiches in Bloom's. He didn't care. Maybe it was his illness *then* – who knows! He was never really a bad man. He never beat us or got drunk or gambled – he wasn't vulgar or coarse and he always had friends. So what was wrong? *I* could never understand him. All I did was fight him because he didn't care. Look at him now. He doesn't care to live. He's never cared to fully undress himself and put on pyjamas; never cared to keep shaved or washed; or be time or even turn up! And now he walks around with his fly-buttons and his shoelaces undone because he still doesn't care to fight his illness – and the dirt gathers around him. He doesn't care! And so I fought him because he didn't care. I fought everybody who didn't

care. All the authorities, the shopkeepers, even today –
those stinking assistance officers – I could buy them with
my little finger – even now I'm still fighting them. And
you want to be like them, like your father? I'll fight you
then.

RONNIE. And lose again.

SARAH. But your father was a weak man. Could you do any
of the things he did?

RONNIE. I would not be surprised.

SARAH. Ronnie, your father would never have left his mother
to go abroad as you did. I don't tell you all this now to pull
you down but on the contrary – so you should know, so
you should care. Learn from us, for God's sake learn from
us. What does it matter if your father was a weakling, or
the man you worked with was an imbecile. They're human
beings.

RONNIE. That doesn't mean a thing.

SARAH. There will always be human beings and as long as
there are there will always be the idea of brotherhood.

RONNIE. Doesn't mean a thing.

SARAH. Despite the human beings.

RONNIE. Not a thing.

SARAH. Despise them!

RONNIE. It doesn't mean . . .

SARAH (*exasperated*). All right then! Nothing, then! It all
comes down to nothing! People come and people go, wars
destroy, accidents kill and plagues starve – it's all nothing,
then! Philosophy? You want philosophy? Nothing means
anything! There! Philosophy! I know! So? Nothing! Despair – die then! Will that be achievement? To die? (*Softly*)
You don't want to do that, Ronnie. So what if it all means
nothing? When you know *that* you can start again. Please,
Ronnie, don't let me finish this life thinking I lived for
nothing. We got through, didn't we? We got scars but we
got through. You hear me, Ronnie? (*She clasps him and*

    moans.) You've got to care, you've got to care or you'll die.
    RONNIE *unclasps her and moves away. He tries to
    say something – to explain. He raises his arms and
    some jumbled words come from his lips.*

RONNIE. I – I can't, not now, it's too big, not yet – it's too
    big to care for, I – I . . .
    RONNIE *picks up his case and brokenly moves to
    his room mumbling:* 'Too big, Sarah – too big, too
    big.'

SARAH (*shouting after him*). You'll die, you'll die – if you
    don't care you'll die. (*He pauses at door.*) Ronnie, if you
    don't care you'll die. (*He turns slowly to face her.*)

CURTAIN

Roots

For
Dusty

Characters of the Play

BEATIE BRYANT, *a young woman aged twenty-two, a friend of Ronnie Kahn*
JENNY BEALES, *her sister*
JIMMY BEALES, *her brother-in-law*
MRS BRYANT, *her mother*
MR BRYANT, *her father*
FRANKIE BRYANT, *her brother*
PEARL BRYANT, *her sister-in-law*
STAN MANN, *a neighbour of the Bealeses*
MR HEALEY, *a manager at the farm*

Act I

An isolated cottage in Norfolk, the house of the Bealeses

Act II

SCENE 1: Two days later at the cottage of Mr and Mrs Bryant, in the kitchen
SCENE 2: The same a couple of hours later

Act III

Two weeks later in the front room of the Bryants'

Time: 1958

*First presented at the Belgrade Theatre Coventry
25th May 1959*

Act One

September 1958.

A rather ramshackle house in Norfolk where there is no water laid on, nor electricity, nor gas. Everything rambles and the furniture is cheap and old. If it is untidy it is because there is a child in the house and there are few amenities, so that the mother is too overworked to take much care.

An assortment of clobber lies around: papers and washing, coats and basins, a tin wash-tub with shirts and underwear to be cleaned, tilly lamps and primus stoves. Washing hangs on a line in the room.

JENNY BEALES *is by the sink washing up. She is singing a recent pop song. She is short, fat and friendly, and wears glasses. A child's voice is heard from the bedroom crying* 'Sweet, Mamma, sweet.'

JENNY (*good-naturedly*). Shut you up Daphne and get you to sleep now. (*Moves to get a dishcloth.*)

CHILD'S VOICE. Daphy wan' sweet, sweet, sweet.

JENNY (*going to cupboard to get sweet*). My word child, Father come home and find you awake he'll be after you. (*Disappears to bedroom with sweet.*) There – now sleep, gal, don't wan' you grumpy wi' me in mornin'.

Enter JIMMY BEALES. *Also short, chubby, blond though hardly any hair left, ruddy complexion. He is a garage mechanic. Wears blue dungarees and an army pack slung over his shoulder. He wheels his bike in and lays it by the wall. Seems to be in some sort of pain – around his back.* JENNY *returns.*

Waas matter wi' you then?

JIMMY. I don' know gal. There's a pain in my guts and one a'tween my shoulder blades I can hardly stand up.

JENNY. Sit you down then an' I'll git you your supper on the table.

73

JIMMY. Blust gal! I can't eat yit.

> JIMMY *picks up a pillow from somewhere and lies down on the sofa holding pillow to stomach.* JENNY *watches him a while.*

JENNY. Don't you know what 'tis yit?

JIMMY. Well, how should *I* know what 'tis.

JENNY. I told Mother about the pain and she says it's indigestion.

JIMMY. What the hell's indigestion doin' a'tween my shoulder blades then?

JENNY. She say some people get indigestion so bad it go right through their stomach to the back.

JIMMY. Don't be daft.

JENNY. That's what I say. Blust Mother, I say, you don't git indigestion in the back. Don't you tell me, she say, I hed it!

JIMMY. What hevn't she hed.

> JENNY *returns to washing up while* JIMMY *struggles a while on the sofa.* JENNY *hums. No word. Then—*

JENNY. Who d'you see today?

JIMMY. Only Doctor Gallagher.

JENNY (*wheeling round*). You see who?

JIMMY. Gallagher. His wife driv him up in the ole Armstrong.

JENNY. Well I go t'hell if that ent a rum thing.

JIMMY (*rising and going to table; pain has eased*). What's that then?

JENNY (*moving to get him supper from oven*). We was down at the whist drive in the village and that Judy Maitland say he were dead. 'Cos you know he've hed a cancer this last year and they don't give him no longer'n three weeks don't you?

JIMMY. Ole crows. They don' wan' nothin' less than a death to wake them up.

JENNY. No. No longer'n three weeks.

GIRL'S VOICE (*off*). Yoo-hoo! Yoo-hoo!

JIMMY. There's your sister.

JENNY. That's her.

GIRL'S VOICE (*off*). Yoo-hoo! Anyone home?

JENNY (*calling*). Come you on in gal, don't you worry about yoo-hoo.

> Enter BEATIE BRYANT, *an ample, blonde, healthy-faced young woman of twenty-two years. She is carrying a case.*

JIMMY. Here she is.

JENNY (*with reserve, but pleased*). Hello, Beatrice – how are you?

BEATIE (*with reserve, but pleased*). Hello, Jenny – how are you? What's that lovely smell I smell?

JENNY. Onions for supper and bread for the harvest festival.

BEATIE. Watcha Jimmy Beales, how you doin' bor?

JIMMY. Not so bad gal, how's yourself?

BEATIE. All right you know. When you comin' to London again for a football match?

JIMMY. O blust gal, I don' wanna go to any more o' those things. Ole father Bryant was there in the middle of that crowd and he turn around an' he say (*imitating*), Stop you a-pushin' there, he say, stop you a-pushin'.

JENNY. Where's Ronnie?

BEATIE. He's comin' down at the end of two weeks.

JIMMY. Ent you married yit?

BEATIE. No.

JIMMY. You wanna hurry then gal, a long engagement don't do the ole legs any good.

JENNY. Now shut you up Jimmy Beales and get that food down you. Every time you talk, look, you miss a mouthful! That's why you complain of pain in your shoulder blades.

BEATIE. You bin hevin' pains then Jimmy?

JIMMY. Blust yes! Right a'tween my shoulder blades.

JENNY. Mother says it's indigestion.

BEATIE. What the hell's indigestion doin' a'tween his shoulder blades?

JENNY. Mother reckon some people get indigestion so bad it go right through their stomach to the back.

BEATIE. Don't talk daft!

JENNY. That's what I say. Blust Mother, I say, 'you don' git indigestion in the back. Don't you tell me, she say, I hed it!

BEATIE. What hevn't she hed. How is she?

JENNY. Still the same you know. How long you staying this time?

BEATIE. Two days here – two weeks at home.

JENNY. Hungry gal?

BEATIE. Watcha got?

JENNY. Watcha see.

BEATIE. Liver? I'll hev it!

> BEATIE *makes herself at home. Near by is a pile of comics. She picks one up and reads.*

JENNY. We got some ice-cream after.

BEATIE (*absorbed*). Yearp.

JENNY. Look at her. No sooner she's in than she's at them ole comics. You still read them ole things?

JIMMY. She don't change much do she?

BEATIE. Funny that! Soon ever I'm home again I'm like I always was – it don' even seem I bin away. I do the same lazy things an' I talk the same. Funny that!

JENNY. What do Ronnie say to it?

BEATIE. He don't mind. He don't even know though. He ent never bin here. Not in the three years I known him. But I'll tell you (*she jumps up and moves around as she talks*) I used to read the comics he bought for his nephews and he used to get riled—

> Now BEATIE *begins to quote Ronnie, and when she does she imitates him so well in both manner and*

> *intonation that in fact as the play progresses we see a*
> *picture of him through her.*

'Christ, woman, what can they give you that you can *be*
so absorbed?' So you know what I used to do? I used to get
a copy of the *Manchester Guardian* and sit with that wide
open – and a comic behind!

JIMMY. *Manchester Guardian*? Blimey Joe – he don' believe
in hevin' much fun then?

BEATIE. That's what I used to tell him. 'Fun?' he say, 'fun?
Playing an instrument is fun, painting is fun, reading a
book is fun, talking with friends is fun – but a comic? A
comic? for a young woman of twenty-two?'

JENNY (*handing out meal and sitting down herself*). He
sound a queer bor to me. Sit you down and eat gal.

BEATIE (*enthusiastically*). He's alive though.

JIMMY. Alive? Alive you say? What's alive about someone
who can't read a comic? What's alive about a person that
reads books and looks at paintings and listens to classical
music?

> *There is a silence at this, as though the question*
> *answers itself – reluctantly.*

JIMMY. Well, it's all right for some I suppose.

BEATIE. And then he'd sneak the comic away from me and
read it his-self!

JENNY. Oh, he didn't really mind then?

BEATIE. No – 'cos sometimes I read books as well. 'There's
nothing wrong with comics,' he'd cry – he stand up on
a chair when he want to preach but don't wanna sound too
dramatic.

JIMMY. Eh?

BEATIE. Like this, look. (*Stands on a chair.*) 'There's nothing
wrong with comics only there's something wrong with
comics all the time. There's nothing wrong with football,
only there's something wrong with *only* football. There's
nothing wrong with rock 'n' rolling, only God preserve me

from the girl that can do nothing else!' (*She sits down and then stands up again, remembering something else.*) Oh yes, 'and there's nothing wrong with talking about the weather, only don't talk to me about it!' (*Sits down.*)

> JIMMY *and* JENNY *look at each other as though she, and no doubt Ronnie, is a little barmy.* JIMMY *rises and begins to strap on boots and gaiters ready for going out to an allotment.*

JENNY. He never really row with you then?

BEATIE. We used to. There was a time when he handled all official things for me you know. Once I was in between jobs and I didn't think to ask for my unemployment benefit. *He* told me to. But when I asked they told me I was short on stamps and so I wasn't entitled to benefit. *I* didn't know what to say but he did. He went up and argued for me – he's just like his mother, she argues with everyone – and I got it. I didn't know how to talk see, it was all foreign to me. Think of it! An English girl born and bred and I couldn't talk the language – except for to buy food and clothes. And so sometimes when he were in a black mood he'd start on me. 'What can you talk of?' he'd ask. 'Go on, pick a subject. Talk. Use the language. Do you know what language is?' Well, I'd never thought before – hev you? – it's automatic to you isn't it, like walking? 'Well, language is words,' he'd say, as though he were telling me a secret. 'It's bridges, so that you can get safely from one place to another. And the more bridges you know about the more places you can see!' (*To* JIMMIE) And do *you* know what happens when you can see a place but you don't know where the bridge is?

JIMMY (*angrily*). Blust gal, what the hell are you on about.

BEATIE. Exactly! You see, you hev a row! Still, rows is all right. I like a row. So then he'd say: 'Bridges! bridges! bridges! Use your bridges woman. It took thousands of years to build them, use them!' And that riled me. 'Blust your bridges,' I'd say. 'Blust you and your bridges – I want a row.' Then he'd grin at me. 'You want a row?' he'd ask. 'No bridges this time?' 'No bridges,' I'd say – and we'd row. Sometimes he hurt me but then, slowly, he'd build the bridge up for me – and then we'd make love!

   Innocently continues her meal.

JENNY. You'd what, did you say?

BEATIE. Make love. Love in the afternoon gal. Ever had it? It's the only time *for* it. Go out or entertain in the evenings; sleep at night, study, work and chores in the mornings; but love – alert and fresh, when you got most energy – love in the afternoon.

JIMMY. I suppose you take time off from work every afternoon to do it?

BEATIE. I'm talking about week-ends and holidays – daft.

JENNY. Oh, Beatie, go on wi' you!

BEATIE. Well, go t'hell Jenny Beales, you're blushin'. Ent you never had love in the afternoon? Ask Jimmy then.

JENNY (*rising to get sweet*). Shut you up gal and get on wi' your ice-cream. It's strawberry flavour. Want some more James?

JIMMY (*taking it in the middle of lacing up boots*). Yes please, vanilla please. (*Eating*) Good cream ent it? Made from the white milk of a Jersey cow.

BEATIE. This is good too – made from pint milk ent it?
   Pause.

JIMMY. Yearp! (*Pause.*) Come from a pink cow!
   Pause. They are all enjoying the cream.

JENNY (*eating*). You remember Dickie Smart, Beatie?

BEATIE (*eating*). Who?

JENNY (*eating*). We had a drink wi' him in the Storks when you was down last.

BEATIE (*eating*). Yearp.

JENNY (*eating*). Well, he got gored by a bull last Thursday.

His left ear was nearly off, his knee were gored, his ribs bruised, and the ligaments of his legs torn.

Pause as they finish eating.

BEATIE (*euphemistically*). He had a rough time then!

JENNY. Yearp. (*To* JIMMY) You off now?

JIMMY. Mm.

    JENNIE *collects dishes.*

BEATIE. Still got your allotment Jimmy?

JIMMY. Yearp.

BEATIE. Bit heavy going this weather.

JIMMY. That ent too bad just yit – few more weeks an' the old mowld'll cling.

BEATIE. Watcha got this year?

JIMMY. Had spuds, carrots, cabbages you know. Beetroot, lettuces, onions, and peas. But me runners let me down this year though.

JENNY. I don't go much on them old things.

BEATIE. You got a fair owle turn then?

JIMMY. Yearp.

    JIMMIE *starts to sharpen a reap hook.*

BEATIE (*jumping up*). I'll help you wash.

JENNY. That'se all right gal.

BEATIE. Where's the cloth?

JENNY. Here 'tis.

    BEATIE *helps collect dishes from table and proceeds to help wash up. This is a silence that needs organizing. Throughout the play there is no sign of intense living from any of the characters –* BEATIE's *bursts are the exception. They continue in a routine rural manner. The day comes, one sleeps at night, there is always the winter, the spring, the autumn, and the summer – little amazes them. They talk in fits and starts mainly as a sort of gossip, and they talk quickly too, enacting as though for an audience what they say. Their sense of humour is keen and dry. They*

*show no affection for each other – though this does
not mean they would not be upset were one of them
to die. The silences are important – as important as
the way they speak, if we are to know them.*

JENNY. What about that strike in London? Waas London
like wi'out the buses?

BEATIE. Lovely! No noise – and the streets, you should see
the streets, flowing with people – the city looks human.

JIMMY: They wanna call us Territorials out – we'd soon
break the strike.

BEATIE. That's a soft thing for a worker to say for his mates.

JIMMY. Soft be buggered, soft you say? What they earnin'
those busmen, what they earnin'? And what's the farm
worker's wage? Do you know it gal?

BEATIE. Well, let the farm workers go on strike too then!
It don't help a farm labourer if a busman don't go on
strike do it now?

JENNY. You know they've got a rise though. Father Bryant's
go up by six and six a week as a pigman, and Frank goes
up seven 'n' six a week for driving a tractor.

JIMMY. But you watch the Hall sack some on 'em.

JENNY. Thaas true Beatie. They're such sods, honest to God
they are. Every time there's bin a rise someone get sacked.
Without fail. You watch it – you ask father Bryant
when you get home, ask him who's bin sacked since the
rise.

BEATIE. One person they 'ont sack is him though. They 'ont
find many men 'd tend to pigs seven days a week and stay
up the hours he do.

JENNY. Bloody fool! (*Pause.*) Did Jimmy tell you he've bin
chosen for the Territorials' Jubilee in London this year?

BEATIE. What's this then? What'll you do there?

JIMMY. Demonstrate and parade wi' arms and such like.

BEATIE. Won't do you any good.

JIMMY. Don't you reckon? Gotta show we can defend the

country you know. Demonstrate arms and you prevent war.

BEATIE (*she has finished wiping up*). Won't demonstrate anything bor. (*Goes to undo her case.*) Present for the house! Have a hydrogen bomb fall on you and you'll find them things silly in your hands. (*Searches for other parcels.*)

JIMMY. So you say gal? So you say? That'll frighten them other buggers though.

BEATIE. Frighten yourself y'mean. (*Finds parcels.*) Presents for the kid.

JIMMY. And what do you know about this all of a sudden?

JENNY (*revealing a tablecloth*). Thank you very much Beatie. Just what I need.

BEATIE. You're not interested in defending your country Jimmy, you just enjoy playing soldiers.

JIMMY. What did I do in the last war then – *sing* in the trenches?

BEATIE (*explaining – not trying to get one over on him*). Ever heard of Chaucer, Jimmy?

JIMMY. No.

BEATIE. Do you know the M.P. for this constituency?

JIMMY. What you drivin' at gal – don't give me no riddles.

BEATIE. Do you know how the British Trade Union Movement started? And do you believe in strike action?

JIMMY. No to both those.

BEATIE. What you goin' to war to defend then?

JIMMY (*he is annoyed now*). Beatie – you bin away from us a long time now – you got a boy who's educated an' that and he's taught you a lot maybe. But don't you come pushin' ideas across at us – we're all right as we are. You can come when you like an' welcome but don't bring no discussion of politics in the house wi' you 'cos that'll only cause trouble. I'm telling you. (*He goes off.*)

JENNY. Blust gal, if you hevn't touched him on a sore spot. He live for them Territorials he do – that's half his life.

BEATIE (*she is upset now*). What's he afraid of talking for?

JENNY. He ent afraid of talking Beatie – blust he can do that, gal.

BEATIE. But not talk, not really talk, not use bridges. I sit with Ronnie and his friends sometimes and I listen to them talk about things and you know I've never heard half of the words before.

JENNY. Don't he tell you what they mean?

BEATIE. I get annoyed when he keep tellin' me – and he want me to ask. (*Imitates him half-heartedly now*). 'Always ask, people love to tell you what they know, always ask and people will respect you.'

JENNY. And do you?

BEATIE. No! I don't! An' you know why? Because I'm stubborn, I'm like Mother, I'm stubborn. Somehow I just can't bring myself to ask, and you know what? I go mad when I listen to them. As soon as they start to talk about things I don't know about or I can't understand I get mad. They sit there, casually talking, and suddenly they turn on you, abrupt. 'Don't you think?' they say. Like at school, pick on you and ask a question you ent ready for. Sometimes I don't say anything, sometimes I go to bed or leave the room. Like Jimmy – just like Jimmy.

JENNY. And what do Ronnie say to that then?

BEATIE. He get mad too. 'Why don't you ask me woman, for God's sake why don't you ask me? Aren't I dying to tell you about things? Only ask!'

JENNY. And he's goin' to marry you?

BEATIE. Why not?

JENNY. Well I'm sorry gal, you mustn't mind me saying this, but it don't seem to me like you two got much in common.

BEATIE (*loudly*). It's not true! We're in love!

JENNY. Well, you know.

BEATIE (*softly*). No, I don't know. I won't know till he come here. From the first day I went to work as waitress in the Dell Hotel and saw him working in the kitchen I fell in love – and I thought it was easy. I thought everything was easy. I chased him for three months with compliments and presents until I finally give myself to him. He never said he love me nor I didn't care but once he had taken me he seemed to think he was responsible for me and I told him no different. I'd *make* him love me I thought. I didn't know much about him except he was different and used to write most of the time. And then he went back to London and I followed him there. I've never moved far from home but I did for him and he felt all the time he couldn't leave me and I didn't tell him no different. And then I got to know more about him. He was interested in all the things I never even thought about. About politics and art and all that, and he tried to teach me. He's a socialist and he used to say you couldn't bring socialism to a country by making speeches, but perhaps you could pass it on to someone who was near you. So I pretended I was interested – but I didn't understand much. All the time he's trying to teach me but I can't take it Jenny. And yet, at the same time, I want to show I'm willing. I'm not used to learning. Learning was at school and that's finished with.

JENNY. Blust gal, you don't seem like you're going to be happy then. Like I said.

BEATIE. But I love him.

JENNY. Then you're not right in the head then.

BEATIE. I couldn't have any other life now.

JENNY. Well, I don't know and that's a fact.

BEATIE (*playfully mocking her*). Well I don't know and that's a fact! (*Suddenly*) Come on gal, I'll teach you how to bake some pastries.

JENNY. Pastries?

BEATIE. Ronnie taught me.

JENNY. Oh, you learnt that much then?

BEATIE. But he don't know. I always got annoyed when he tried to teach me to cook as well – Christ! I had to know something – but it sank in all the same.

By this time it has become quite dark and JENNY *proceeds to light a tilly lamp.*

JENNY. You didn't make it easy then?

BEATIE. Oh don't you worry gal, it'll be all right once we're married. Once we're married and I got babies I won't need to be interested in half the things I got to be interested in now.

JENNY. No you won't will you! Don't need no education for babies.

BEATIE. Nope. Babies is babies – you just have 'em.

JENNY. Little sods!

BEATIE. You gonna hev another Jenny?

JENNY. Well, course I am. What you on about? Think Jimmy don't want none of his own?

BEATIE. He's a good man Jenny.

JENNY. Yearp.

BEATIE. Not many men 'd marry you after you had a baby.

JENNY. No.

BEATIE. He didn't ask you any questions? Who was the father? Nor nothing?

JENNY. No.

BEATIE. You hevn't told no one hev you Jenny?

JENNY. No, that I hevn't.

BEATIE. Well, that's it gal, don't you tell me then!

By this time the methylated spirit torch has burned out and JENNY *has finished pumping the tilly lamp and we are in brightness.*

JENNY (*severely*). Now Beatie, stop it. Every time you come home you ask me that question and I hed enough. It's finished with and over. No one don't say nothing and no one know. You hear me?

BEATIE. Are you in love with Jimmy?

JENNY. Love? I don't believe in any of that squit – we just got married, an' that's that.

BEATIE (*suddenly looking around the room at the general chaos*). Jenny Beales, just look at this house. Look at it!

JENNY. I'm looking. What's wrong?

BEATIE. Let's clean it up.

JENNY. Clean what up?

BEATIE. Are you going to live in this house all your life?

JENNY. You gonna buy us another?

BEATIE. Stuck out here in the wilds with only ole Stan Mann and his missus as a neighbour and sand pits all around. Every time it rain look you're stranded.

JENNY. Jimmy don't earn enough for much more'n we got.

BEATIE. But it's so untidy.

JENNY. You don' wan' me bein' like sister Susan do you? 'Cos you know how clean she is don' you – she's so bloody fussy she's gotten to polishing the brass overflow pipe what leads out from the lavatory.

BEATIE. Come on gal, let's make some order anyway – I love tidying up.

JENNY. What about the pastries? Pastries? Oh my sainted aunt, the bread! (*Dashes to the oven and brings out a most beautiful-looking plaited loaf of bread. Admiring it.*) Well, no one wanna complain after that. Isn't that beautiful Beatie?

BEATIE. I could eat it now.

JENNY. You hungry again?

BEATIE (*making an attack upon the clothes that are lying around*). I'm always hungry again. Ronnie say I eat more'n I need. 'If you get fat woman I'll leave you – without even a discussion!'

JENNY (*placing bread on large oval plate to put away*). Well, there ent nothin' wrong in bein' fat.

86

BEATIE. You ent got no choice gal. (*Seeing bike*) A bike!
What's a bike doin' in a livin' room – I'm putting it
outside.

JENNY. Jimmy 'ont know where it is.

BEATIE. Don't be daft, you can't miss a bike. (*Wheels it
outside and calls from there.*) Jenny! Start puttin' the
clothes away.

JENNY. Blust gal, I ent got nowhere to put them.

BEATIE (*from outside*). You got drawers – you got cup-
boards.

JENNY. They're full already.

BEATIE (*entering – energy sparks from her*). Come here –
let's look. (*Looks.*) Oh, go away – you got enough room for
ten families. You just bung it all in with no order, that's
why. Here – help me.

> They drag out all manner of clothes from the cup-
> board and begin to fold them up.

BEATIE. How's my Frankie and Pearl?

JENNY. They're all right. You know she and Mother don't
talk to each other?

BEATIE. What, again? Who's fault is it this time?

JENNY. Well, Mother she say it's Pearl's fault and Pearl she
say it's Mother.

BEATIE. Well, they wanna get together quick and find
whose fault it is 'cos I'm going to call the whole family
together for tea to meet Ronnie.

JENNY. Well, Susan and Mother don't talk neither so you
got a lot of peace-making to do.

BEATIE. Well, go t'hell, what's broken them two up?

JENNY. Susan hev never bin struck on her mother, you
know that don't you – well, it seems that Susan bought
something off the club from Pearl and Pearl give it to
Mother and Mother sent it to Susan through the fish-
monger what live next door her in the council houses. And
of course Susan were riled 'cos she didn't want her neigh-

bours to know that she bought anything off the club. So they don't speak.

BEATIE. Kids! It make me mad.

JENNY. And you know what 'tis with Pearl don't you – it's 'cos Mother hev never thought she was good enough for her son Frankie.

BEATIE. No more she wasn't neither!

JENNY. What's wrong wi' her then? I get on all right.

BEATIE. Nothing's wrong wi' her, she just wasn't good enough for our Frankie, that's all.

JENNY. Who's being small-minded now?

BEATIE. Always wantin' more'n he can give her.

JENNY. An' I know someone else who always wanted more'n she got.

BEATIE (*sulkily*). It's not the same thing.

JENNY. Oh yes 'tis.

BEATIE. 'Tent.

JENNY. 'Tis my gal. (*Mimicking the child* BEATIE) I wan' a 'nan, a 'nana, a 'nana. Frankie's got my 'nana, 'nana, 'nana.

BEATIE. Well, I liked bananas.

JENNY. You liked anything you could get your hands on and Mother used to give in to you 'cos you were the youngest. Me and Susan and Frankie never got nothing 'cos o' you – 'cept a clout round the ear.

BEATIE. 'Tent so likely. You got everything and I got nothing.

JENNY. All we got was what we pinched out the larder and then you used to go and tell tales to Mother.

BEATIE. I never did.

JENNY. Oh, didn't you my gal? Many's the time I'd've willingly strangled you – with no prayers – there you are, no prayers whatsoever. Strangled you till you was dead.

BEATIE. Oh go on wi' you Jenny Beales.

By now they have finished folding the clothes and

*have put away most of the laundry and garments
that have till this moment cluttered up the room.*
BEATIE *says 'There,' stands up and looks around,
finds some coats sprawled helter-skelter, and hangs
them up behind the door.*

BEATIE. I'll buy you some coat hangers.

JENNY. You get me a couple o' coats to hang on 'em first
please.

BEATIE (*looking around*). What next. Bottles, jars, nick-
nacks, saucepans, cups, papers – everything anywhere.
Look at it! Come on!

BEATIE *attempts to get these things either into
their proper places or out of sight.*

JENNY. You hit this place like a bloody whirlwind you do,
like a bloody whirlwind. Jimmy'll think he've come into
the wrong house and I shan't be able to find a thing.

BEATIE. Here, grab a broom. (*She is now gurgling with sort
of animal noises signifying excitement. Her joy is childlike.*) How's Poppy?

JENNY. Tight as ever.

BEATIE. What won't he give you now?

JENNY. 'Tent nothing wi' me gal. Nothing he do don't
affect me. It's Mother I'm referring to.

BEATIE. Don't he still give her much money?

JENNY. Money? She hev to struggle and skint all the time –
all the time. Well it ent never bin no different from when
we was kids hev it?

BEATIE. No.

JENNY. I tell you what. It wouldn't surprise me if Mother
were in debt all the time, that it wouldn't. No. It wouldn't
surprise me at all.

BEATIE. Oh, never.

JENNY. Well, what do you say that for Beatie – do you
know how much he allow her a week look?

BEATIE. Six pounds?

JENNY. Six pound be buggered. Four pounds ten! An' she hev to keep house *an'* buy her own clothes out of that.

BEATIE. Still, there's only two on 'em.

JENNY. You try keepin' two people in food for four pound ten. She pay seven an' six a week into Pearl's club for clothes, two and six she hev on the pools, and a shilling a week on the Labour Tote. (*Suddenly*) Blust! I forgot to say. Pearl won the Tote last week.

BEATIE. A hundred pounds?

JENNY. A hundred pounds! An' ole Mrs Dyson what used to live Startson way, she come up second wi' five pounds and seventy.

BEATIE. Well no one wrote me about it.

JENNY. 'Cos you never wrote no one else.

BEATIE. What she gonna do wi' it – buy a TV?

JENNY. TV? Blust no. You know she hevn't got electricity in that house. No, she say she's gonna get some clothes for the kids.

There is a sound now of a drunk old man approaching, and alongside of it the voice of JIMMY. *The drunk is singing:* 'I come from Bungay Town, I calls I Bungay Johnnie.'

Well I go t'hell if that ent Stan Mann drunk again. And is that Jimmy wi' him? (*Listens.*)

BEATIE. But I thought Stan Mann was paralysed.

JENNY. That don't stop him getting paralytic drunk. (*Listens again.*) That's Jimmy taking him into the house I bet. A fortune that man hev drunk away – a whole bleedin' fortune. Remember the fleet of cars he used to run and all that land he owned, and all them cattle he had and them fowl? Well, he've only got a few acres left and a few ole chickens. He drink it all away. Two strokes he've had from drinking and now he's paralysed down one side. But that don't stop him getting drunk – no it don't.

JIMMY *enters and throws his jacket on the couch,*
takes off his boots and gaiters, and smiles meanwhile.

JIMMY. Silly ole bugger.

JENNY. I was just telling Beatie how he've drunk a fortune
away hevn't he?

JIMMY. He wanna drink a little more often and he'll be
finished for good.

JENNY. Didn't he hev all them cows and cars and land
Jimmy? And didn't he drink it all away bit by bit?

JIMMY. Silly ole sod don't know when to stop.

JENNY. I wished I had half the money he drink.

JIMMY. He messed his pants.

JENNY. He what? Well where was this then?

JIMMY. By the allotment.

JENNY. Well, what did *you* do then?

JIMMY. He come up to me – 'course I knowed he were drunk
the way he walk – he come up to me an' he say, "Evenin'
Jimmy Beales, thaas a fine turnover you got there.' An'
I say, 'Yearp 'tis.' An' then he bent down to pick a carrot
from the ground an' then he cry, 'Oops, I done it again!'
An' 'course, soon ever he say 'done it again' I knowed
what'd happened. So I took his trousers down and ran
the ole hose over him.

BEATIE. Oh, Jimmy, you never did.

JIMMY. I did gal. I put the ole hose over him and brought
him home along the fields with an ole sack around his
waist.

BEATIE. He'll catch his death.

JIMMY. Never – he's strong as an ox.

JENNY. What'd you do with his trousers and things?

JIMMY. Put it on the compost heap – good for the land!

Now STAN MANN *enters. He's not all that drunk.*
The cold water has sobered him a little. He is old
– about seventy-five – and despite his slight stoop
one can see he was a very strong upright man. He

*probably looks like everyman's idea of a farmer –
except that he wears no socks or boots at this moment
and he hobbles on a stick.*

STAN. Sorry about that ole son.

JIMMY. Don't you go worrying about that my manny – get
you along to bed.

JENNY. Get some shoes on you too Stan, or you'll die of
cold *and* booze.

STAN (*screwing up his eyes across the room*). Is that you
Jenny? Hello ole gal. How are you?

JENNY. It's you you wanna worry about now ole matey. I'm
well enough.

STAN. (*screwing his eyes still more*). Who's that next to
you?

JENNY. Don't you recognize her? It's our Beatie, Stan.

STAN. Is that you Beatie? Well blust gal, you gotten fatter
since I seen you last. You gonna be fat as Jenny here?
Come on over an' let's look at you.

BEATIE (*approaching*). Hello Stan Mann, how are you?

STAN (*looking her up and down*). Well enough gal, well
enough. You married yit?

BEATIE. No.

STAN. You bin courtin' three years. Why ent you married
yit?

BEATIE (*slightly embarrassed*). We ent sure yit.

STAN. You ent sure you say? What ent you sure of? You
know how to do it don't you?

JENNY. Go on wi' you to bed Stan Mann.

STAN. Tell your boy he don't wanna waste too much time
or I'll be hevin' yer myself for breakfast – on a plate.

JENNY. Stan Mann, I'm sendin' you to your bed – go on
now, off wi' you, you can see Beatie in the mornin'.

STAN (*as he is ushered out – to* BEATIE). She's fat ent she?
I'm not sayin' she won't do mind, but she's fat. (*As he goes
out*) All right ole sweetheart, I'm goin'. I'm just right for

bed. Did you see the new bridge they're building? It's a
rum ole thing isn't it . . . (*out of sound*)

JIMMY. Well, I'm ready for bed.

BEATIE. I can't bear sick men. They smell.

JIMMY. Ole Stan's all right – do anythin' for you.

BEATIE. I couldn't look after one you know.

JIMMY. Case of hevin' to sometimes.

BEATIE. Ronnie's father's paralysed like that. I can't touch
him.

JIMMY. Who see to him then?

BEATIE. His mother. She wash him, change him, feed him.
Ronnie help sometimes. I couldn't though. Ronnie say,
'Christ, woman, I hope you aren't around when I'm ill.'
(*Shudders.*) Ole age terrify me.

JIMMY. Where you sleepin' tonight gal?

BEATIE. On the couch in the front room I suppose.

JIMMY. You comfortable sleepin' on that ole thing? You
wanna sleep with Jenny while you're here?

BEATIE. No thanks, Jimmy. (*She is quite subdued now.*)
I'm all right on there.

JIMMY. Right, then I'm off. (*Looking around*) Where's the
Evening News I brought in?

JENNY (*entering*). You off to bed?

JIMMY. Yearp. Reckon I've had 'nough of this ole day.
Where's my *News*?

JENNY. Where d'you put it Beatie?

JIMMY (*suddenly seeing the room*). Blust, you movin' out?

BEATIE. Here you are Jimmy Beales. (*Hands him paper.*)
It's all tidy now.

JIMMY. So I see. Won't last long though will it? 'Night.
(*Goes to bed.*)

JENNY. Well I'm ready for my bed too – how about you
Beatie?

BEATIE. Yearp.

JENNY (*taking a candle in a stick and lighting it*). Here, take

93

this with you. Your bed's made. Want a drink before you
turn in?

BEATIE. No thanks gal.

JENNY (*picking up tilly lamp and making towards one door*).
Right then. Sleep well gal.

BEATIE (*going to other door with candle*). Good night
Jenny. (*She pauses at her door. Loud whispers from now
on.*) Hey Jenny.

JENNY. What is it?

BEATIE. I'll bake you some pastries when I get to Mother's.

JENNY. Father won't let you use his electricity for me, don't
talk daft.

BEATIE. I'll get Mother on to him. It'll be all right. Your ole
ovens weren't big 'nough anyways. Good night.

JENNY. Good night.

BEATIE (*an afterthought*). Hey Jenny.

JENNY. What now?

BEATIE. Did I tell you I took up painting?

JENNY. Painting?

BEATIE. Yes – on cardboard and canvases with brushes.

JENNY. What kind of painting?

BEATIE. Abstract painting – designs and patterns and such
like. I can't do nothing else. I sent two on 'em home. Show
you when you come round – if Mother hevn't thrown
them out.

JENNY. You're an artist then?

BEATIE. Yes. Good night.

JENNY. Good night.

> They enter their bedrooms, leaving the room in
> darkness.[1] Perhaps we see only the faint glow of
> moonlight from outside, and then

THE CURTAIN FALLS

[1] It might be better for Jenny to have previously made up Beatie's
bed in the couch on the set. Then Beatie would not have to leave
the stage at all.

Act Two

SCENE I

Two days have passed. BEATIE *will arrive at her own home, the home of her parents. This is a tied cottage on a main road between two large villages. It is neat and ordinary inside. We can see a large kitchen – where most of the living is done – and attached to it is a large larder; also part of the front room and a piece of the garden where some washing is hanging.*

MRS BRYANT *is a short, stout woman of fifty. She spends most of the day on her own, and consequently when she has a chance to speak to anybody she says as much as she can as fast as she can. The only people she sees are the tradesmen, her husband, the family when they pop in occasionally. She speaks very loudly all the time so that her friendliest tone sounds aggressive, and she manages to dramatize the smallest piece of gossip into something significant. Each piece of gossip is a little act done with little looking at the person to whom it is addressed. At the moment she is at the door leading to the garden, looking for the cat.*

MRS BRYANT. Cossie, Cossie, Cossie, Cossie, Cossie, Cossie! Here Cossie! Food Cossie! Cossie, Cossie, Cossie! Blust you cat, where the hell are you. Oh hell on you then, I ent wastin' my time wi' you now.

> *She returns to the kitchen and thence the larder, from which she emerges with some potatoes. These she starts peeling.* STAN MANN *appears round the back door. He has a handkerchief to his nose and is blowing vigorously, as vigorously as his paralysis will allow.* MRS BRYANT *looks up, but continues her peeling.*

STAN. Rum thing to git a cold in summer, what you say Daphne?

95

MRS BRYANT. What'd you have me say my manny. Sit you down bor and rest a bit. Shouldn't wear such daf' clothes.

STAN. Daf' clothes? Blust woman! I got on half a cow's hide, what you sayin'! Where's the gal?

MRS BRYANT. Beatie? She 'ent come yit. Didn't *you* see her?

STAN. Hell, I was up too early for her. She always stay the weekend wi' Jenny 'fore comin' home?

MRS BRYANT. Most times.

    STAN *sneezes*

What you doin' up this way wi' a cold like that then? Get you home to bed.

STAN. Just come this way to look at the vicarage. Stuff's comin' up for sale soon.

MRS BRYANT. You still visit them things then?

STAN. Yearp. Pass the ole time away. Pass the ole time.

MRS BRYANT. Time drag heavy then?

STAN. Yearp. Time drag heavy. She do that. Time drag so slow, I get to thinkin' it's Monday when it's still Sunday. Still, I had my day gal I say. Yearp. I had that all right.

MRS BRYANT. Yearp. You had that an' a bit more ole son. I shant grumble if I last as long as you.

STAN. Yearp. I hed my day. An' I'd do it all the same again, you know that? Do it all the same I would.

MRS BRYANT. Blust! All your drinkin' an' that?

STAN. Hell! Thaas what kep' me goin' look. Almost anyways. None o' them young 'uns'll do it, hell if they will. There ent much life in the young 'uns. Bunch o' weak-kneed ruffians. None on 'em like livin' look, none on 'em! You read in them ole papers what go on look, an' you wonder if they can see. You do! Wonder if they got eyes to look around them. Think they know where they live? 'Course they don't, they don't you know, not one. Blust! the winter go an' the spring come on after an' they don't see

buds an' they don't smell no breeze an' they don't see
gals, an' when they see gals they don't know whatta do
wi' 'em. They don't!

MRS BRYANT. Oh hell, they know *that* all right.

STAN. Gimme my young days an' I'd show 'em. Public
demonstrations I'd give!

MRS BRYANT. Oh shut you up Stan Mann.

STAN. Just gimme young days again Daphne Bryant an'
I'd mount you. But they 'ont come again will they gal?

MRS BRYANT. That they 'ont. My ole days working in the
fields with them other gals, thems 'ont come again,
either.

STAN. No, they 'ont that! Rum ole things the years ent
they? (*Pause.*) Them young 'uns is all right though. Long
as they don't let no one fool them, long as they think it
out theirselves. (*Sneezes and coughs.*)

MRS BRYANT (*moving to help him up*). Now get back home
Stan Mann. (*Good-naturedly*) Blust, I aren't hevin' no dead
'uns on me look. Take a rum bor, take a rum an' a drop
o' hot milk and get to bed. What's Mrs Mann thinking of
lettin' you out like this.

*She pulls the coat round the old man and pushes him
off. He goes off mumbling and she returns, also
mumbling, to her peeling.*

STAN. She's a good gal, she's right 'nough, she don't think I
got it this bad. I'll pull this ole scarf round me. Hed this
scarf a long time, hed it since I started wi' me cars. *She*
bought it me. Lasted a long time. Shouldn't need it this
weather though . . . (*Exits.*)

MRS BRYANT (*mumbling same time as* STAN). Go on,
off you go. Silly ole bugger, runnin' round with a cold like
that. Don't know what 'e's doin' half the time. Poor ole
man. Cossie? Cossie? That you Cossie? (*Looks through
door into front room and out of window at* STAN.) Poor
ole man.

After peeling some seconds she turns the radio on, turning the dial knob through all manner of stations and back again until she finds some very loud dance music which she leaves blaring on. Audible to us, but not to MRS BRYANT, *is the call of* 'Yoo-hoo Mother, yoo-hoo'. BEATIE *appears round the garden and peers into the kitchen.* MRS BRYANT *jumps.*

MRS BRYANT. Blust, you made me jump.

BEATIE (*toning radio down*). Can't you hear it? Hello, Mother. (*Kisses her.*)

MRS BRYANT. Well, you've arrived then.

BEATIE. Didn't you get my card?

MRS BRYANT. Came this morning.

BEATIE. Then you knew I'd arrive.

MRS BRYANT. 'Course I did.

BEATIE. My things come?

MRS BRYANT. One suitcase, one parcel in brown paper—

BEATIE. My paintings.

MRS BRYANT. And one other case.

BEATIE. My pick-up. D'you see it?

MRS BRYANT. I hevn't touched a thing.

BEATIE. Bought myself a pick-up on the H.P.

MRS BRYANT. Don't you go telling that to Pearl.

BEATIE. Why not?

MRS BRYANT. She'll wanna know why you didn't buy off her on the club.

BEATIE. Well, hell, Mother, I weren't gonna hev an ole pick-up sent me from up north somewhere when we lived next door to a gramophone shop.

MRS BRYANT. No. Well, what bus you come on – the half-past-ten one?

BEATIE. Yearp. Picked it up on the ole bridge near Jenny's.

MRS BRYANT. Well I looked for you on the half-past-nine bus and you weren't on that so I thought to myself I bet she come on the half-past-ten and you did. You see ole Stan Mann?

BEATIE. Was that him just going up the road?

MRS BRYANT. Wearin' an ole brown scarf, that was him.

BEATIE. I see him! Just as I were comin' off the bus. Blust! Jimmy Beales give him a real dowsin' down on his allotment 'cos he had an accident.

MRS BRYANT. What, another?

BEATIE. Yearp.

MRS BRYANT. Poor ole man. Thaas what give him that cold then. He come in here sneezin' fit to knock hisself down.

BEATIE. Poor ole bugger. Got any tea Ma? I'm gonna unpack.

> BEATIE *goes into front room with case. We see her take out frocks, which she puts on hangers, and underwear and blouses, which she puts on couch.*

MRS BRYANT. Did you see my flowers as you come in? Got some of my hollyhocks still flowering. Creeping up the wall they are – did you catch a glimpse on 'em? And my asters and geraniums? Poor ole Joe Simonds gimme those afore he died. Lovely geraniums they are.

BEATIE. Yearp.

MRS BRYANT. When's Ronnie coming?

BEATIE. Saturday week – an' Mother, I'm heving all the family along to meet him when he arrive so you patch your rows wi' them.

MRS BRYANT. What you on about gal? What rows wi' them?

BEATIE. You know full well what rows I mean – them ones you hev wi' Pearl and Susan.

MRS BRYANT. 'Tent so likely. They hev a row wi' me gal but I give 'em no heed, that I don't. (*Hears van pass on road.*) There go Sam Martin's fish van. He'll be calling along here in an hour.

BEATIE (*entering with very smart dress*). Like it Mother?

MRS BRYANT. Blust gal, that's a good 'un ent it! Where d'you buy that then?

BEATIE. Swan and Edgar's.

MRS BRYANT. Did Ronnie choose it?

BEATIE. Yearp.

MRS BRYANT. He've got good taste then.

BEATIE. Yearp. Now listen Mother, I don't want any on you to let me down. When Ronnie come I want him to see we're proper. I'll buy you another bowl so's you don't wash up in the same one as you wash your hands in and I'll get some more tea cloths so's you 'ont use the towels. And no swearin'.

MRS BRYANT. Don't he swear then?

BEATIE. He swear all right, only I don't want him to hear *you* swear.

MRS BRYANT. Hev you given it up then?

BEATIE. Mother, I've never swore.

MRS BRYANT. Go to hell, listen to her!

BEATIE. I never did, now! Mother, I'm *telling* you, listen to me. Ronnie's the best thing I've ever had and I've tried hard for three years to keep hold of him. I don't care what you do when he's gone but don't show me up when he's here.

MRS BRYANT. Speak to your father gal.

BEATIE. Father too. I don't want Ronnie to think I come from a small-minded family. 'I can't bear mean people,' he say. 'I don't care about their education, I don't care about their past as long as their minds are large and inquisitive, as long as they're generous.'

MRS BRYANT. Who say that?

BEATIE. Ronnie.

MRS BRYANT. He *talk* like that?

BEATIE. Yearp.

MRS BRYANT. Sounds like a preacher.

BEATIE (*standing on a chair*). 'I don't care if you call me a preacher, I've got something to say and I'm going to say it. I don't care if you don't like being told things – we've come to a time when you've got to say this is right and this is wrong. God in heaven, have we got to be wet all the time? Well, have we? Christ, Mother, you've got them ole wasps still flying around. (*She waves her arms in the air flaying the wasps.*) September and you've still got wasps. Owee! shoo-shoo! (*In the voice of her childhood*) Mammy, Mammy, take them ole things away. I doesn't like the – ooh! Nasty things.

> BEATIE *jumps off chair and picks up a coat hanger. Now both she and her mother move stealthily around the room 'hunting' wasps. Occasionally* MRS BRYANT *strikes one dead or* BEATIE *spears one against the wall.* MRS BRYANT *conducts herself matter-of-fact-like but* BEATIE *makes a fiendish game of it.*

MRS BRYANT. They're after them apples on that tree outside. Go on! Off wi' you! Outside now! There – that's got 'em out, but I bet the buggers'll be back in a jiffy look.

BEATIE. Oh yes, an' I want to have a bath.

MRS BRYANT. When d'you want that then?

BEATIE. This morning.

MRS BRYANT. You can't hev no bath this morning, that copper won't heat up till after lunch.

BEATIE. Then I'll bake the pastries for Jenny this morning and you can put me water on now. (*She returns to sort her clothes.*)

MRS BRYANT. I'll do that now then. I'll get you the soft water from the tank.

> MRS BRYANT *now proceeds to collect bucket and move back and forth between the garden out of view and the copper in the kitchen. She fills the copper with about three buckets of water and then*

lights the fire underneath it. In between buckets she chats.

(*Off – as she hears lorry go by*) There go Danny Oakley to market. (*She returns with first bucket.*)

BEATIE. Mother! I dreamt I died last night and heaven were at the bottom of a pond. You had to jump in and sink and you know how afeared I am of water. It was full of film stars and soldiers and there were two rooms. In one room they was playing skiffle and – and – I can't remember what were goin' on in the other. Now who was God? I can't remember. It was someone we knew, a she. (*Returns to unpacking.*)

MRS BRYANT (*entering with second bucket; automatically*). Yearp. (*Pause.*) You hear what happened to the headache doctor's patient? You know what they say about him – if you've got a headache you're all right but if you've got something more you've had it! Well he told a woman not to worry about a lump she complained of under her breast and you know what that were? That turned out to be thrombosis! There! Thrombosis! She had that breast off. Yes, she did. Had to hev it cut off. (*Goes for next bucket.*)

BEATIE (*automatically*). Yearp. (*She appears from front room with two framed paintings. She sets them up and admires them. They are primitive designs in bold masses, rather well-balanced shapes and bright poster colours – red, black, and yellow – see Dusty Bicker's work.*) Mother! Did I write and tell you I've took up painting? I started five months ago. Working in gouache. Ronnie says I'm good. Says I should carry on and maybe I can sell them for curtain designs. 'Paint girl,' he say. 'Paint! The world is ful of people who don't do the things they want so you paint and give us all hope!'

MRS BRYANT *enters.*

BEATIE. Like 'em?

MRS BRYANT (*looks at them a second*). Good colours ent

they. (*She is unmoved and continues to empty a third bucket while* BEATIE *returns paintings to other room.*) Yes gal, I ent got no row wi' Pearl but I ask her to change my Labour Tote man 'cos I wanted to give the commission to Charlie Gorleston and she didn't do it. Well, if she can be like that I can be like that too. You gonna do some baking you say?

BEATIE (*enters from front room putting on a pinafore and carrying a parcel*). Right now. Here y'are Daphne Bryant, present for you. I want eggs, flour, sugar, and marg. I'm gonna bake a sponge and give it frilling. (*Goes to larder to collect things.*)

MRS BRYANT (*unpacking parcel; it is a pinafore*). We both got one now.

> MRS BRYANT *continues to peel potatoes as* BEATIE *proceeds to separate four eggs, the yolks of which she starts whipping with sugar. She sings meanwhile a ringing folk song.*

BEATIE

> Oh a dialogue I'll sing you as true as me life.
> Between a coal owner and a poor pitman's wife
> As she was a-walking along the highway
> She met a coal owner and to him did say
>> Derry down, down, down Derry down.
> Whip the eggs till they're light yellow he says.

MRS BRYANT. Who says?

BEATIE. Ronnie.

> Good morning Lord Firedamp the good woman said
> I'll do you no harm sir so don't be afraid
> If you'd been where I'd been for most of my life
> You wouldn't turn pale at a poor pitman's wife
>> Singing down, down, down Derry down.

MRS BRYANT. What song's that?

BEATIE. A coalmining song.

MRS BRYANT. I tell you what I reckon's a good song,

that 'I'll wait for you in the heavens blue'. I reckon that's
a lovely song I do. Jimmy Samson he sing that.

BEATIE. It's like twenty other songs, it don't mean anything
and it's sloshy and sickly.

MRS BRYANT. Yes, I reckon that's a good song that.

BEATIE (*suddenly*). Listen Mother, let me see if I can explain something to you. Ronnie always say that's the point
of knowing people. 'It's no good having friends who scratch
each other's back,' he say. 'The excitement in knowing
people is to hand on what you know and to learn what
you don't know. Learn from me,' he say, 'I don't know
much but learn what I know.' So let me try and explain
to you what he explain to me.

MRS BRYANT (*on hearing a bus*). There go the half-past-
eleven bus to Diss – blust that's early. (*Puts spuds in saucepan on oven and goes to collect runner beans, which she
prepares.*)

BEATIE. Mother, I'm *talking* to you. Blust woman it's not
often we get together and really talk, it's nearly always me
listening to you telling who's dead. Just listen a second.

MRS BRYANT. Well go on gal, but you always take so long
to say it.

BEATIE. What are the words of that song?

MRS BRYANT. I don't know all the words.

BEATIE. I'll tell you.

Recites them.

I'll wait for you in the heavens blue
As my arms are waiting now.
Please come to me and I'll be true
My love shall not turn sour.
I hunger, I hunger, I cannot wait longer,
My love shall not turn sour.

There! Now what do that mean?

MRS BRYANT (*surprised*). Well, don't you know what that
mean?

BEATIE. I mean what do they do to you? How do the words affect you? Are you moved? Do you find them beautiful?

MRS BRYANT. Them's as good words as any.

BEATIE. But do they make you feel better?

MRS BRYANT. Blust gal! That ent meant to be a laxative!

BEATIE. I must be mad to talk with you.

MRS BRYANT. Besides it's the tune I like. Words never mean anything.

BEATIE. All right, the tune then! What does *that* do to you? Make your belly go gooey, your heart throb, make your head spin with passion? Yes, passion, Mother, know what it is? Because you won't find passion in that third-rate song, no you won't!

MRS BRYANT. Well all right gal, so it's third-rate you say. Can you say why? What make that third-rate and them frilly bits of opera and concert first-rate? 'Sides, did I write that song? Beatie Bryant, you do go up and down in your spirits, and I don't know what's gotten into you gal, no I don't.

BEATIE. I don't know either, Mother. I'm worried about Ronnie I suppose. I have that same row with him. I ask him exactly the same questions – what make a pop song third-rate. And he answer and I don't know what he talk about. Something about registers, something about commercial world blunting our responses. 'Give yourself time woman,' he say. 'Time! You can't learn how to live overnight. *I* don't even know,' he say, 'and half the world don't know but we got to try. Try,' he say, "cos we're still suffering from the shock of two world wars and we don't know it. Talk,' he say, 'and look and listen and think and ask questions.' But Jesus! I don't know what questions to ask or *how* to talk. And he gets so riled – and yet sometimes so nice. 'It's all going up in flames,' he say, 'but I'm going to make bloody sure I save someone from the fire.'

MRS BRYANT. Well I'm sure *I* don't know what he's on

about. Turn to your baking gal look and get you done, Father'll be home for his lunch in an hour.

A faint sound of an ambulance is heard. MRS BRYANT *looks up but says nothing.* BEATIE *turns to whipping the eggs again and* MRS BRYANT *to cleaning up the runner beans. Out of this pause* MRS BRYANT *begins to sing 'I'll wait for you in the heavens blue', but on the second line she hums the tune incorrectly.*

BEATIE (*laughs*). No, no, hell Mother, it don't go like that. It's—

BEATIE corrects her and in helping her mother she ends by singing the song, with some enthusiasm, to the end.

MRS BRYANT. Thank God you come home sometimes gal – you do bring a little life with you anyway.

BEATIE. Mother, I ent never heard you express a feeling like that.

MRS BRYANT (*she is embarrassed*). The world don't want no feelings gal. (*Footsteps are heard.*) Is that your father home already?

MR BRYANT *appears at the back door and lays a bicycle against the wall. He is a small shrivelled man wearing denims, a peaked cap, boots, and gaiters. He appears to be in some pain.*

BEATIE. Hello poppy Bryant.

MR BRYANT. Hello Beatie. You're here then.

MRS BRYANT. What are you home so early for?

MR BRYANT. The ole guts ache again. (*Sits in armchair and grimaces.*)

MRS BRYANT. Well, what is it?

MR BRYANT. Blust woman, I don't know what 'tis n'more'n you, do I?

MRS BRYANT. Go to the doctor man I keep telling you.

BEATIE. What is it father Bryant?

MRS BRYANT. He got guts ache.

BEATIE. But what's it from?

MR BRYANT. I've just said I don't know.

MRS BRYANT. Get to a doctor man, don't be so soft. You don't want to be kept from work do you?

MR BRYANT. That I don't, no I don't. Hell, I just see ole Stan Mann picked up an' thaas upset me enough.

MRS BRYANT. Picked up you say?

MR BRYANT. Well, didn't you hear the ambulance?

MRS BRYANT. There! I hear it but I didn't say narthin.' Was that for Stan Mann then?

MR BRYANT. I was cycling along wi' Jack Stones and we see this here figure on the side o' the road there an' I say, thaas a rum shape in the road Jack, and he say, blust, that's ole Stan Mann from Heybrid, an' 'twere. 'Course soon ever he see what 'twere, he rushed off for 'n ambulance and I waited alongside Stan.

BEATIE. But he just left here.

MRS BRYANT. I see it comin'. He come in here an' I shoved him off home. Get you to bed and take some rum an' a drop o' hot milk, I tell him.

BEATIE. Is he gonna die?

MR BRYANT. Wouldn't surprise me, that it wouldn't. Blust, he look done in.

MRS BRYANT. Poor ole fellah. Shame though ent it.

MR BRYANT. When d'you arrive Beatie?

MRS BRYANT. She come in the half-past-ten bus. I looked for her on the nine-thirty bus and she weren't on that, so I thought to myself I bet she come on the half-past-ten. She did.

MR BRYANT. Yearp.

MRS BRYANT. You gonna stay away all day?

MR BRYANT. No I aren't. I gotta go back 'cos one of the ole sows is piggin'. 'Spect she'll be hevin' them in a

couple of hours. (*To* BEATIE) Got a sow had a litter o'
twenty-two. (*Picks up paper to read.*)

BEATIE. Twenty-two? Oh Pop, can I come see this afternoon.

MR BRYANT. Yearp.

MRS BRYANT. Thought you was hevin' a bath.

BEATIE. Oh yes, I forgot. I'll come tomorrow then.

MR BRYANT. They'll be there. What you doin' gal?

MRS BRYANT. She's baking a sponge, now leave her be.

MR BRYANT. Oh, you learnt something in London then.

BEATIE. Ronnie taught me.

MR BRYANT. Well where *is* Ronnie then?

MRS BRYANT. He's comin' on Saturday a week an' the
family's goin' to be here to greet him.

MR BRYANT. All on 'em?

MRS BRYANT *and* BEATIE. All on 'em!

MR BRYANT. Well that'll be a rum gatherin' then.

MRS BRYANT. And we've to be on our best behaviour.

MR BRYANT. No cussin' and swearin'?

MRS BRYANT *and* BEATIE. No.

MR BRYANT. Blust, I shan't talk then.

A young man, MR HEALEY, *appears round the
garden – he is the farmer's son, and manager of the
estate* BRYANT *works for.*

MRS BRYANT (*seeing him first*). Oh, Mr Healey, yes. Jack!
It's Mr Healey.

MR BRYANT rises and goes to the door. HEALEY
*speaks in a firm, not unkind, but business-is-business
voice. There is that apologetic threat even in his
politeness.*

MR HEALEY. You were taken ill.

MR BRYANT. It's all right, sir, only guts ache, won't be
long goin'. The pigs is all seen to, just waiting for the ole
sow to start.

MR HEALEY. What time you expecting it?

MR BRYANT. Oh, she 'ont come afore two this afternoon, no she 'ont be much afore that.

MR HEALEY. You're sure you're well, Jack? I've been thinking that it's too much for you carting those pails round the yard.

MR BRYANT. No, that ent too heavy, sir, 'course 'tent. You don't wanna worry, I'll be along after lunch. Just an ole guts ache that's all – seein' the doctor tonight – eat too fast probably.

MR HEALEY. If you're sure you're all right, then I'll put young Daniels off. You can manage without him now we've fixed the new pump in.

MR BRYANT. I can manage, sir – 'course I can.

MR HEALEY (*moving off outside*). All right then, Jack. I'll be with you around two o'clock. I want to take the old one out of number three and stick her with the others in seventeen. The little ones won't need her, will they? Then we'll have them sorted out tomorrow.

MR BRYANT. That's right, sir, they *can* go on their own now, they can. I'll see to it tomorrow.

MR HEALEY. Right then, Jack. Oh – you hear Stan Mann died?

MR BRYANT. He died already? But I saw him off in the ambulance no more'n half-hour ago.

MR HEALEY. Died on the way to hospital. Jack Stones told me. Lived in Heybrid, didn't he?

MR BRYANT. Alongside my daughter.

MR HEALEY (*calling*). Well, good morning, Mrs Bryant.

MRS BRYANT (*calling*). Good morning, Mr Healey.

The two men nod to each other. MR HEALEY *goes off.* MR BRYANT *lingers a second.*

MRS BRYANT (*to* BEATIE). That was Mr Healey, the new young manager.

BEATIE. I know it Mother.

MR BRYANT (*returning slowly*). He's dead then.

MRS BRYANT. Who? Not Stan Mann!

MR BRYANT. Young Healey just tell me.

MRS BRYANT. Well I go t'hell. An' he were just here look, just here alongside o' me not more'n hour past.

MR BRYANT. Rum ent it?

BEATIE (*weakly*). Oh hell, I hate dying.

MRS BRYANT. He were a good ole bor though. Yes he was. A good ole stick. There!

BEATIE. Used to ride me round on his horse, always full o' life an' jokes. 'Tell your boy he wanna hurry up and marry you,' he say to me, 'or I'll hev you meself on a plate.'

MRS BRYANT. He were a one for smut though.

BEATIE. I was talkin' with him last night. Only last night he was tellin' me how he caught me pinchin' some goose-berries off his patch an' how he gimme a whole apron full and I went into one o' his fields near by an' ate the lot. 'Blust,' he say, 'you had the ole guts ache,' an' he laugh, sat there laughin' away to hisself.

MRS BRYANT. I can remember that. Hell, Jenny'll miss his – used always to pop in an' out o' theirs.

BEATIE. Seem like the whole world gone suddenly dead don' it?

MR BRYANT. Rum ent it?

(*Silence.*)

MRS BRYANT. You say young Healey tell you that? *He's* a nice man Mr Healey is, yes he is, a good sort, I like him.

BEATIE. Sound like he were threatening to sack Father; don't know about being nice.

MR BRYANT. That's what I say see, get a rise and they start cutting down the men or the overtime.

MRS BRYANT. The Union magazine's come.

MR BRYANT. I don't want that ole thing.

BEATIE. Why can't you do something to stop the sackings?

MR BRYANT. You can't, you can't – that's what I say, you

can't. Sharp as a pig's scream they are – you just *can't* do nothin'.

BEATIE. Mother, where's the bakin' tin?

MR BRYANT. When we gonna eat that?

BEATIE. You ent! It's for Jenny Beales.

MR BRYANT. You aren't making that for Jenny are you?

BEATIE. I promised her.

MR BRYANT. Not with my electricity you aren't.

BEATIE. But I promised, Poppy.

MR BRYANT. That's no matters. I aren't spendin' money on electricity bills so's you can make every Tom, Dick 'n' Harry a sponge cake, that I aren't.

MRS BRYANT. Well, don't be so soft man, it won't take more'n half-hour's bakin'.

MR BRYANT. I don't care what it'll take I say. I aren't lettin' her. Jenny wants cakes, she can make 'em herself. So put that away Beatie and use it for something else.

MRS BRYANT. You wanna watch what you're sayin' of 'cos I live here too.

MR BRYANT. I know all about that but I pay the electricity bill and I says she isn't bakin'.

BEATIE. But Poppy, one cake.

MR BRYANT. No I say.

BEATIE. Well Mummy, do something – how can he be so mean.

MRS BRYANT. Blust me if you ent the meanest ole sod that walks this earth. Your own daughter and you won't let her use your oven. You bloody ole hypercrite.

MR BRYANT. You pay the bills and then you call names.

MRS BRYANT. What I ever seen in you God only knows. Yes! an' he never warn me. Bloody ole hypercrite!

MR BRYANT. You pay the bills and then you call names I say.

MRS BRYANT. On four pounds ten a week? You want me to keep you *and* pay bills? Four pound ten he give me. God knows what he do wi' the rest. I don't know how much he've got. I don't, no I don't. Bloody ole hypercrite.

MR BRYANT. Let's hev grub and not so much o' the lip woman.

> BEATIE *begins to put the things away. She is on the verge of the tears she will soon let fall.*

MRS BRYANT. That's how he talk to me – when he do talk. 'Cos you know he don't ever talk more'n he hev to, and when he do say something it's either 'how much this cost' or 'lend us couple o' bob.' He've got the money but sooner than break into that he borrow off me. Bloody old miser. (*To* BEATIE) What you wanna cry for gal? 'Tent worth it. Blust, you don't wanna let an ole hypercrite like him upset you, no you don't. I'll get my back on you my manny, see if I don't. You won't get away with no tricks on me.

> BEATIE *has gone into the other room and returned with a small packet.*

BEATIE (*throwing parcel in father's lap*). Present for you.

MRS BRYANT. I'd give him presents that I would! I'd walk out and disown him! Beatie, now stop you a-cryin' gal – blust, he ent worth cryin' for, that he ent. Stop it I say and we'll have lunch. Or you lost your appetite gal?

> BEATIE *sniffs a few tears back, pauses, and—*

BEATIE. No – no, that I ent. Hell, I can eat all right!

CURTAIN

SCENE 2

Lunch has been eaten. MR BRYANT *is sitting at the table rolling himself a cigarette.* MRS BRYANT *is collecting the dishes and taking them to a sink to wash up.* BEATIE *is taking things off the table and putting them into the larder*

– jars of sauce, plates of sliced bread and cakes, butter, sugar, condiments, and bowl of tinned fruit.

MRS BRYANT (*to* BEATIE). Ask him what he want for his tea.

MR BRYANT. She don't ever ask me before, what she wanna ask me now for?

MRS BRYANT. Tell him it's his stomach I'm thinking about – I don't want him complaining to me about the food I cook.

MR BRYANT. Tell her it's no matters to me – I ent got no pain now besides.

BEATIE. Mother, is that water ready for my bath?

MRS BRYANT. Where you hevin' it?

BEATIE. In the kitchen of course.

MRS BRYANT. Blust gal, you can't bath in this kitchen during the day, what if someone call at the door?

BEATIE. Put up the curtain then, I shan't be no more'n ten minutes.

MR BRYANT. 'Sides, who want to see her in her dickey suit.

BEATIE. I know men as 'ould pay to see me in my dickey suit. (*Posing her plump outline*) Don't you think I got a nice dickey suit?

MR BRYANT *makes a dive and pinches her bottom.*
Ow! Stoppit Bryants, stoppit!
He persists.
Daddy, stop it now!

MRS BRYANT. Tell him he can go as soon as he like, I want your bath over and done with.

BEATIE. Oh Mother, stop this nonsense do. If you want to tell him something tell him – not me.

MRS BRYANT. *I* don't want to speak to him, hell if I do.

BEATIE. Father, get the bath in for me please. Mother, where's them curtains.

MR BRYANT *goes off to fetch a long tin bath – wide*

at one end, narrow at the other – while MRS
BRYANT *leaves washing up to fish out some curtains
which she hangs from one wall to another concealing
thus a corner of the kitchen. Anything that is in the
way is removed* BEATIE *meanwhile brings out a
change of underwear, her dressing-gown, the new
frock, some soap, powder, and towel. These she lays
within easy reach of the curtain.*

BEATIE. I'm gonna wear my new dress and go across the
fields to see Frankie and Pearl.

MRS BRYANT. Frankie won't be there, what you on about?
He'll be gettin' the harvest in.

BEATIE. You makin' anything for the harvest festival?

MR BRYANT (*entering with bath, places it behind curtain*).
Your mother don't ever do anything for the harvest festival – don't you know that by now.

BEATIE. Get you to work father Bryant, I'm gonna plunge in
water and I'll make a splash.

MRS BRYANT. Tell him we've got kippers for tea and if he
don't want none let him say now.

BEATIE. She says it's kippers for tea.

MR BRYANT. Tell her I'll eat kippers. (*Goes off collecting
bike on the way.*)

BEATIE. He says he'll eat kippers. Right now, Mother, you
get cold water an' I'll pour the hot.

Each now picks up a bucket. MRS BRYANT *goes off
out to collect the cold water and* BEATIE *plunges
bucket into boiler to retrieve hot water. The bath is
prepared with much childlike glee.* BEATIE *loves her
creature comforts and does with unabashed, almost
animal, enthusiasm that which she enjoys. When the
bath is prepared,* BEATIE *slips behind the curtain
to undress and enter.*

MRS BRYANT. You hear about Jimmy Skelton? They say
he've bin arrested for accosting some man in the village.

BEATIE. Jimmy Skelton what own the pub.

MRS BRYANT. That's him. I know all about Jimmy Skelton though. He were a young boy when I were a young girl. I always partner him at whist drives. He's been to law before you know. Yes! An' he won the day too! Won the day he did. I don't take notice though, him and me gets on all right. What do Ronnie's mother do with her time?

BEATIE. She've got a sick husband to look after.

MRS BRYANT. She an educated woman?

BEATIE. Educated? No. She's a foreigner. Nor ent Ronnie educated neither. He's an intellectual, failed all his exams. They read and things.

MRS. BRYANT. Oh, they don't do nothing then?

BEATIE. Do nothing? I'll tell you what Ronnie do, he work till all hours in a hot ole kitchen. An' he teach kids in a club to act and jive and such. And he don't stop at week-ends either 'cos then there's political meetings and such and I get breathless trying to keep up wi' him OOOhh, Mother it's hot . . .

MRS BRYANT. I'll get you some cold then.

BEATIE. No – ohh – it's lovely. The water's so soft Mother.

MRS BRYANT. Yearp.

BEATIE. It's so soft and smooth. I'm in.

MRS BRYANT. Don't you stay in too long gal. There go the twenty-minutes-past-one bus.

BEATIE. Oh Mother, me bath cubes. I forgot me bath cubes. In the little case by me pick-up.

MRS BRYANT *finds bath cubes and hands them to* BEATIE.

MRS BRYANT (*continuing her work*). I shall never forget when I furse heard on it. I was in the village and I was talking to Reggie Fowler. I say to him, there've bin a lot o' talk about Jimmy ent there? Disgustin', I say. Still, there's somebody wanna make some easy money, you'd expect that in a village wouldn't you? Yes, I say to him, a lot of talk.

An' he stood there, an' he were a-lookin' at me an' a-lookin' as I were a-talkin' and then he say, missus, he say, I were one o' the victims! Well, you could've hit me over the head wi' a hammer. I was one o' the victims, he say.

BEATIE. Mother, these bath cubes smell beautiful. I could stay here all day.

MRS BRYANT. Still, Jimmy's a good fellow with it all – do anything for you. I partner him at whist drives; he bin had up scores o' times though.

BEATIE. Mother, what we gonna make Ronnie when he come?

MRS BRYANT. Well, what do he like?

BEATIE. He like trifle and he like steak and kidney pie.

MRS BRYANT. We'll make that then. So long as he don't complain o' the guts ache. Frankie hev it too you know.

BEATIE. Know why? You all eat too much. The Londoners think we live a healthy life but they don't know we stuff ourselves silly till our guts ache.

MRS BRYANT. But you know what's wrong wi' Jimmy Beales? It's indigestion. He eat too fast.

BEATIE. What the hell's indigestion doin' a'tween his shoulder blades?

MRS BRYANT. 'Cos some people get it so bad it go right through their stomach to the back.

BEATIE. You don't get indigestion in the back Mother, what you on about?

MRS BRYANT. Don't you tell me gal, I hed it!

BEATIE. Owee! The soap's in me eyes – Mother, towel, the towel, quickly the towel!

MRS BRYANT *hands in towel to* BEATIE. *The washing up is probably done by now, so* MRS BRYANT *sits in a chair, legs apart and arms folded, thinking what else to say.*

MRS BRYANT. You heard that Ma Buckley hev been taken to Mental Hospital in Norwich? Poor ole dear. If there's one thing I can't abide that's mental cases. They frighten me – they do. Can't face 'em. I'd sooner follow a man to a churchyard than the mental hospital. That's a terrible thing to see a person lose their reason – that 'tis. Well, I tell you what, down where I used to live, down the other side of the Hall, years ago we moved in next to an old woman. I only had Jenny and Frank then – an' this woman she were the sweetest of people. We used to talk and do errands for each other – Oh she was a sweet ole dear. And then one afternoon I was going out to get my washin' in and I saw her. She was standin' in a tub of water up to her neck. She was! Up to her neck. An' her eyes had that glazed, wonderin' look and she stared straight at me she did. Straight at me. Well, do you know what? I was struck *dumb*. I was *struck* dumb wi' shock. What wi' her bein' so nice all this while, the sudden comin' on her like that in the tub fair upset me. It did! And people tell me afterwards that she's bin goin' in an' out o' hospital for years. Blust, that scare me. That scare me so much she nearly took me round the bend wi' her.

> BEATIE *appears from behind the curtain in her dressing-gown, a towel round her head.*

BEATIE. There! I'm gonna hev a bath every day when I'm married.

> BEATIE *starts rubbing her hair with towel and fiddles with radio. She finds a programme playing Mendelssohn's Fourth Symphony, the slow movement, and stands before the mirror, listening and rubbing.*

BEATIE (*looking at her reflection*). Isn't your nose a funny thing, and your ears. And your arms and your legs, aren't they funny things – sticking out of a lump.

MRS BRYANT (*switching off radio*). Turn that squit off!

BEATIE (*turning on her mother violently*). Mother! I could kill you when you do that. No wonder I don't know anything about anything. I never heard nothing but dance music because you always turned off the classics. I never knowed anything about the news because you always switched off after the headlines. I never read any good books 'cos there was never any in the house.

MRS BRYANT. What's gotten into you now, gal?

BEATIE. God in heaven Mother, you live in the country but you got no – no – no majesty. You spend your time among green fields, you grow flowers and you breathe fresh air and you got no majesty. Your mind's cluttered up with nothing and you shut out the world. What kind of a life did you give me?

MRS BRYANT. Blust gal, I weren't no teacher.

BEATIE. But you hindered. You didn't open one door for me. Even *his* mother cared more for me than what you did. Beatie she say, Beatie, why don't you take up evening classes and learn something other than waitressing. Yes, she say, you won't ever regret learnin' things. But did you care what job I took up or whether I learned things? You didn't even think it was necessary.

MRS BRYANT. I fed you. I clothed you. I took you out to the sea. What more d'you want. We're only country folk you know. We en't got no big things here you know.

BEATIE. Squit! Squit! It makes no difference country or town. *All* the town girls I ever worked with were just like me. It makes no difference country or town – that's squit. Do you know when I used to work at the holiday camp and I sat down with the other girls to write a letter we used to sit and discuss what we wrote about. An' we all agreed, all on us, that we started: 'Just a few lines to let you know', and then we get on to the weather and then we get stuck so we write about each other and after a page an' half of big scrawl end up: 'Hoping this finds you as well as it leaves me.' There! We couldn't say any more. Thousands of things happening at this holiday camp and we couldn't

118

find words for them. All of us the same. Hundreds of girls and one day we're gonna be mothers, and you *still* talk to me of Jimmy Skelton and the ole woman in the tub. Do you know I've heard that story a dozen times. A dozen times. Can't you hear yourself Mother? Jesus, how can I bring Ronnie to this house.

MRS BRYANT. Blust gal, if Ronnie don't like us then he—

BEATIE. Oh, he'll like you all right. He like people. He'd've loved ole Stan Mann. Ole Stan Mann would've understood everything Ronnie talk about. Blust! That man liked livin'. Besides, Ronnie say it's too late for the old 'uns to learn. But he says it's up to us young 'uns. And them of us that know hev got to teach them of us as don't know.

MRS BRYANT. I bet he hev a hard time trying to change you gal!

BEATIE. He's *not* trying to change me Mother. You can't change people, he say, you can only give them some love and hope they'll take it. And he's tryin' to teach me and I'm tryin' to understand – do you see that Mother?

MRS BRYANT. I don't see what that's got to do with music though.

BEATIE. Oh my God! (*Suddenly*) I'll show you. (*Goes off to front room to collect pick-up and a record.*) Now sit you down gal and I'll show you. Don't start ironing or reading or nothing, just sit there and be prepared to learn something. (*Appears with pick-up and switches on.*) You aren't too old, just you sit and listen. That's the trouble you see, we ent ever prepared to learn anything, we close our minds the minute anything unfamiliar appear. *I* could never listen to music. I used to like some on it but then I'd lose patience, I'd go to bed in the middle of a symphony, or my mind would wander 'cos the music didn't mean anything to me so I'd go to bed or start talking. 'Sit back woman,' he'd say, 'listen to it. Let it happen to you and you'll grow as big as the music itself.'

MRS BRYANT. Blust he talk like a book.

BEATIE. An' sometimes he talk as though you didn't know where the moon or the stars was. (BEATIE *puts on record of Bizet's 'L'Arlésienne' Suite*.) Now listen. This is a simple piece of music, it's not highbrow but it's full of living. And that's what he say socialism is. 'Christ,' he say. 'Socialism isn't talking all the time, it's living, it's singing, it's dancing, it's being interested in what go on around you, it's being concerned about people and the world.' Listen Mother (*She becomes breathless and excited.*) Listen to it. It's simple isn't it? Can you call that squit?

MRS BRYANT. I don't say it's all squit.

BEATIE. You don't have to frown because it's alive.

MRS BRYANT. No, not all on it's squit.

BEATIE. See the way the other tune comes in? Hear it? Two simple tunes, one after the other.

MRS BRYANT. I aren't saying it's all squit.

BEATIE. And now listen, listen, it goes together, the two tunes together, they knit, they're perfect. Don't it make you want to dance? (*She begins to dance a mixture of a cossack dance and a sailor's hornpipe.*)

> *The music becomes fast and her spirits are young and high.*

Listen to that Mother. Is it difficult? Is it squit? It's light. It make me feel light and confident and happy. God, Mother, we could all be so much more happy and alive. Wheeeee ...

> BEATIE *claps her hands and dances on and her* MOTHER *smiles and claps her hands and—*

THE CURTAIN FALLS

Act Three

Two weeks have passed. It is Saturday, the day Ronnie is to arrive. One of the walls of the kitchen is now pushed aside and the front room is revealed. It is low-ceilinged, and has dark brown wooden beams. The furniture is not typical country farmhouse type. There may be one or two Windsor-type straight-back chairs, but for the rest it is cheap utility stuff. Two armchairs, a table, a small bamboo table, wooden chairs, a small sofa, and a swivel bookcase. There are a lot of flowers around – in pots on the window ledge and in vases on the bamboo table and swivel case.

It is three in the afternoon, the weather is cloudy – it has been raining and is likely to start again. On the table is a spread of food (none of this will be eaten). There are cakes and biscuits on plates and glass stands. Bread and butter, butter in a dish, tomatoes, cheese, jars of pickled onions, sausage rolls, dishes of tinned fruit – it is a spread! Round the table are eight chairs. BEATIE'S *paintings are hanging on the wall. The room is empty because* BEATIE *is upstairs changing and* MRS BRYANT *is in the kitchen.* BEATIE – *until she descends – conducts all her conversation shouting from upstairs.*

BEATIE. Mother! What you on at now?

MRS BRYANT (*from kitchen*). I'm just puttin' these glass cherries on the trifle.

BEATIE. Well come on look, he'll be here at four thirty.

MRS BRYANT (*from kitchen*). Don't you fret gal, it's another hour 'n' half yet, the postman hevn't gone by. (*Enters with an enormous bowl of trifle.*) There! He like trifle you say?

BEATIE. He love it.

MRS BRYANT. Well he need to 'cos there's plenty on it. (*To herself, surveying the table.*) Yes, there is, there's plenty on it. (*It starts to rain.*) Blust, listen to that weather.

BEATIE. Rainin' again!

MRS BRYANT (*looking out of window*). Raining? It's rainin' fit to drowned you. (Sound of bus.) There go the three o'clock.

BEATIE. Mother get you changed, come on, I want us ready in time.

MRS BRYANT. Blust you'd think it were the bloody Prince of Egypt comin'. (*Goes upstairs.*)

The stage is empty again for a few seconds. People are heard taking off their macs and exclaiming at the weather from the kitchen. Enter FRANK *and* PEARL BRYANT. *He is pleasant and dressed in a blue pin-striped suit, is ruddy-faced and blond-haired. An odd sort of shyness make him treat everything as a joke. His wife is a pretty brunette, young, and ordinarily dressed in plain, flowered frock.*

FRANK (*calling*). Well, where are you all? Come on – I'm hungry.

PEARL. Shut you up bor, you only just had lunch.

FRANK. Well I'm hungry again. (*Calling*) Well, where is this article we come to see?

BEATIE. He ent arrived.

FRANK. Well, he want to hurry, 'cos I'm hungry.

BEATIE. You're always hungry.

FRANK. What do you say he is – a strong socialist?

BEATIE. Yes.

FRANK. And a Jew boy?

BEATIE. Yes.

FRANK (*to himself*). Well, that's a queer mixture then.

PEARL (*calling*). I hope he don't talk politics all the time.

FRANK. Have you had a letter from him yet?

PEARL. Stop it Frank, you know she hevn't heard.

FRANK. Well that's a rum boy friend what don't write.

Looks at paintings, pauses before one of them and growls.

PEARL. Watch out or it'll bite you back.

> BEATIE *comes down from upstairs. She is dressed in her new frock and looks happy, healthy, and radiant.*

FRANK. Hail there, sister! I was then contemplating your masterpiece.

BEATIE. Well don't contemplate too long 'cos you aren't hevin' it.

FRANK. Blust! I'd set my ole heart on it.

PEARL. That's a nice frock Beatie.

FRANK. Where's the rest of our mighty clan?

BEATIE. Jenny and Jimmy should be here soon and Susie and Stan mightn't come.

FRANK. What's wrong wi' them?

BEATIE. Don't talk to me about it 'cos I hed enough! Susie won't talk to Mother.

PEARL. That make nearly eighteen months she hevn't spoke.

BEATIE. Why ever did *you* and Mother fall out Pearl?

FRANK. 'Cos Mother's so bloody stubborn that's why.

PEARL. Because one day she said she wanted to change her Labour Tote man, that's why, and she asked me to do it for her. So I said all right, but it'll take a couple of weeks; and then she get riled because she said I didn't want to change it for her. And then I ask her why didn't she change him herself and she say because she was too ill to go all the way to see John Clayton to tell him, and then she say to me, why, don't you think I'm ill? And I say – I know this were tactless o' me – but I say, no Mother, you don't look ill to me. And she didn't speak to me since. I only hope she don't snub me this afternoon.

BEATIE. Well, she tell me a different story.

FRANK. Mother's always quarrelling.

PEARL. Well I reckon there ent much else she *can* do stuck in this ole house on her own all day. And father Bryant he don't say too much when he's home you know.

FRANK. Well blust, she hevn't spoke to her own mother for

three years, not since Granny Dykes took Jenny in when she had that illegitimate gal Daphne.

BEATIE. Hell! What a bloody family!

FRANK. A mighty clan I say.

JIMMY *and* JENNY BEALES *now enter.*

JENNY. Hello Frankie, hello Pearl, hello Beatie.

FRANK. And more of the mighty clan.

JENNY. Mighty clan you say? Mighty bloody daft you mean. Well, where is he?

FRANK. The mysterious stranger has not yet come – we await.

JENNY. Well, I aren't waitin' long 'cos I'm hungry.

PEARL. That's all this family of Bryants ever do is think o' their guts.

FRANK (*to* JIMMY). Have you formed your association yit?

JENNY. What association is this?

FRANK. What! Hevn't he told you?

JIMMY. Shut you up Frank Bryant or you'll get me hung.

FRANK. Oh, a mighty association – a mighty one! I'll tell ye. One day you see we was all sittin' round in the pub – Jimmy, me, Starkie, Johnny Oats, and Bonky Dawson – we'd hed a few drinks and Jimmy was feelin' – well, he was feelin' – you know what, the itch! He hed the itch! He started complaining about ham, ham, ham all the time. So then Bonky Dawson say, blust, he say, there must be women about who feel the same. And Starkie he say, well 'course they are, only how do you tell? And then we was all quiet a while thinkin' on it when suddenly Jimmy says, we ought to start an association of them as need a bit now and then and we all ought to wear a badge he say, and when you see a woman wearin' a badge you know she need a bit too.

JIMMY. Now that's enough Frank or I'll hit you over the skull.

FRANK. Now, not content wi' just that, ole Jimmy then say,

and we ought to have a password to indicate how bad off you are. So listen what he suggest. He suggest you go up to any one o' these women what's wearin' a badge and you say, how many lumps of sugar do you take in your tea? And if she say 'two' then you know she ent too badly off, but she's willin'. But if she say 'four' then you know she's in as bad a state as what you are, see?

Long pause.

JENNY. He'd hev a fit if she said she took sixteen lumps though wouldn't he?

Pause.

PEARL. Where's mother Bryant?

BEATIE. Upstairs changin'.

PEARL. Where's father Bryant?

BEATIE. Tendin' the pigs.

FRANK. You're lucky to hev my presence you know.

BEATIE. Oh?

FRANK. A little more sun and I'd've bin gettin' in the harvest.

PEARL. Well, what did you think of that storm last night? All that thunder 'n' lightnin' and it didn't stop once.

BEATIE. Ronnie love it you know. He sit and watch it for bloody hours.

FRANK. He's a queer article then.

JENNY. He do sound a rum 'un don't he?

BEATIE. Well you'll soon see.

JIMMY. Hev he got any sisters?

BEATIE. One married and she live not far from here.

PEARL. She live in the country? A town girl? Whatever for?

BEATIE. Her husband make furniture by hand.

PEARL. Can't he do that in London?

BEATIE. Ronnie say they think London's an inhuman place.

JIMMY. So 'tis, so 'tis.

BEATIE. Here come father Bryant.

MR BRYANT *enters. He is in denims and raincoat, tired, and stooping slightly.*

FRANK. And this be the male head of the mighty Bryant clan!

MR BRYANT. Blust, you're all here soon then.

BEATIE. Get you changed quick Father – he'll be along any minute look.

MR BRYANT. Shut you up gal, I'll go when I'm ready, I don't want you pushin' me.

MRS BRYANT *comes from upstairs. She looks neat and also wears a flowered frock.*

FRANK. And this be the female head o' the mighty Bryant clan!

MRS BRYANT. Come on Bryant, get you changed – we're all ready look.

MR BRYANT. Blust, there go the other one. Who is he this boy, that's what I wanna know.

MRS BRYANT. He's upset! I can see it! I can tell it in his voice. Come on Bryants, what's the matters.

MR BRYANT. There ent much up wi' me, what you on about woman. (*Makes to go.*) Now leave me be, you want me changed look.

MRS BRYANT. If there ent much up wi' you, I'll marry some other.

FRANK. Healey bin at you Pop?

BEATIE. The pigs dyin'?

MRS BRYANT. It's something serious or he wouldn't be so happy lookin'.

MR BRYANT. I bin put on casual labour.

JENNY. Well isn't that a sod now.

MRS BRYANT. Your guts I suppose.

MR BRYANT. I tell him it's no odds, that there's no pain. That don't matters Jack, he says, I aren't hevin' you break up completely on me. You go on casual, he say, and if you gets better you can come on to the pigs again.

MRS BRYANT. That's half pay then?

BEATIE. Can't you get another job?

FRANK. He've bin wi them for eighteen years.

BEATIE. But you must be able to do something else – what about cowman again?

MR BRYANT. Bill Waddington do that see. He've bin at it this last six 'n' half years.

JENNY. It's no good upsettin' yourself Beatie. It happen all the time gal.

JIMMY. Well, we told her when she was at ours didn't we.

MRS BRYANT (*to* MR BRYANT). All right, get you on up, there ent nothin' we can do. We'll worry on it later. We always manage. It's gettin' late look.

MR BRYANT. Can he swim? 'Cos he bloody need to. It's rainin' fit to drowned you. (*Goes off upstairs.*)

MRS BRYANT. Well, shall we have a little cup o' tea while we're waitin'? I'll go put the kettle on. (*Goes to kitchen.*)
Everyone sits around now. JENNY *takes out some knitting and* JIMMY *picks up a paper to read. There is silence. It is not an awkward silence, just a conversationless room.*

PEARL (*to* JENNY). Who's lookin' after your children?

JENNY. Ole mother Mann next door.

PEARL. Poor ole dear. How's she feelin' now?

JENNY. She took it bad. (*Nodding at* JIMMY) Him too. He think he were to blame.

PEARL. Blust that weren't his fault. Don't be so daft Jimmy Beales. Don't you go fretting yourself or you'll make us all feel queer look. You done nothin' wrong bor – he weren't far off dying 'sides.

FRANK. They weren't even married were they?

JENNY. No, they never were – she started lookin' after him when he had that first stroke and she just stayed.

JIMMY. Lost her job 'cos of it too.

FRANK. Well, yes, she would, wouldn't she – she was a State Registered Nurse or something weren't she? (*To* BEATIE)

Soon ever the authorities got to hear o' that they told her to pack up livin' wi' him or quit her job, see?

JENNY. Bloody daft I reckon. What difference it make whether she married him or not.

PEARL. I reckon you miss him Jenny?

JENNY. Hell yes – that I do. He were a good ole bor – always joking and buying the kid sweets. Well, do you know I cry when I heard it? I did. Blust, that fair shook me – that it did, there!

JIMMY. Who's lookin' after *your* kid then, Pearl?

PEARL. Father.

Pause.

JIMMY (*to* FRANK). Who do you think'll win today?

FRANK. Well Norwich won't.

JIMMY. No.

Pause. MRS BRYANT *enters and sits down.*

MRS BRYANT. Well the kettle's on.

PEARL (*to* BEATIE). Hev his sister got any children?

BEATIE. Two boys.

JIMMY. She wanna get on top one night then they'll hev girls.

JENNY. Oh shut you up Jimmy Beales.

MRS BRYANT. Hed another little win last night.

JENNY. When was this?

MRS BRYANT. The firemen's whist drive. Won seven 'n' six in the knockout.

JENNY. Yearp.

FRANK (*reading the paper*). I see that boy what assaulted the ole woman in London got six years.

MRS BRYANT Blust! He need to! I'd've given him six years and a bit more. Bloody ole hooligans. Do you give me a chance to pass sentence and I'd soon clear the streets of crime, that I would. Yes, that I would.

BEATIE (*springing into activity*). All right Mother – we'll give you a chance. (*Grabs* JIMMY's *hat and umbrella.*

Places hat on mother's head and umbrella in her arms.) There you are, you're a judge. Now sum up and pass judgment.

MRS BRYANT. I'd put him in prison for life.

FRANK. You gotta sum up though. Blust, you can't stick a man in prison and say nothing.

MRS BRYANT. Goodbye, I'd say.

BEATIE. Come on Mother, speak up. Anybody can say 'go to prison', but *you* want to be a judge. Well, you show a judge's understanding. Talk! Come on Mother, talk!

Everyone leans forward eagerly to hear Mother talk.
She looks startled and speechless.

MRS BRYANT. Well I – I – yes I – well I – Oh, don't be so soft.

FRANK. The mighty head is silent.

BEATIE. Well yes, she would be wouldn't she.

MRS BRYANT. What do you mean, I would be? You don't expect me to know what they say in courts do you? I aren't no judge.

BEATIE. Then why do you sit and pass judgment on people? If someone do something wrong you don't stop and think why. No discussin', no questions, just (*snap of fingers*) – off with his head. I mean look at Father getting less money. I don't see the family sittin' together and discussin' it. It's a problem! But which of you said it concerns you?

MRS BRYANT. Nor don't it concern them. I aren't hevin' people mix in my matters.

BEATIE. But they aren't just people – they're your family for hell's sake!

MRS BRYANT. No matters, I aren't hevin' it!

BEATIE. But Mother I—

MRS BRYANT. Now shut you up Beatie Bryant and leave it alone. I shall talk when I hev to and I never shall do, so there!

BEATIE. You're so stubborn.

MRS BRYANT. So you keep saying.

MR BRYANT *enters, he is clean and dressed in blue pin-striped suit.*

MR BRYANT. You brewed up yit?

MRS BRYANT (*jumping up and going to kitchen*). Oh hell, yes – forgot the tea look.

MR BRYANT. Well, now we're all waitin' on him.

JENNY. Don't look as if Susie's comin'.

BEATIE. Stubborn cow!

Silence.

JENNY. Hev you seen Susie's television set yit?

BEATIE. I seen it.

FRANK. Did you know also that when they first hed it they took it up to bed wi' them and lay in bed wi' a dish of chocolate biscuits?

PEARL. But now they don't bother – they say they've had it a year now and all the old programmes they saw in the beginning they're seein' again.

MRS BRYANT (*entering with tea*). Brew's up!

BEATIE. Oh, for Christ's sake let's stop gossiping.

PEARL. I aren't gossiping. I'm making an intelligent observation about the state of television, now then.

MR BRYANT. What's up wi' you now?

BEATIE. You weren't doin' nothin' o' the sort – you was gossiping.

PEARL. Well that's a heap sight better'n quotin' all the time.

BEATIE. I don't quote all the time, I just tell you what Ronnie say.

FRANK. Take it easy gal – he's comin' soon – don't need to go all jumpin' an' frantic.

BEATIE. Listen! Let me set you a problem.

JIMMY. Here we go.

BEATIE. While we're waitin' for him I'll set you a moral problem. You know what a moral problem is? It's a problem about right and wrong. I'll get you buggers thinking

130

if it's the last thing I do. Now listen. There are four huts –

FRANK. What?

BEATIE. Huts. You know – them little things you live in. Now there are two huts on one side of a stream and two huts on the other side. On one side live a girl in one hut and a wise man in the other. On the other side live Tom in one hut and Archie in the other. Also there's a ferryman what run a boat across the river. Now – listen, concentrate – the girl loves Archie but Archie don't love the girl. And Tom love the girl but the girl don't go much on Tom.

JIMMY. Poor bugger.

BEATIE. One day the girl hears that Archie – who don't love her, remember – is going to America, so she decides to try once more to persuade him to take her with him. So listen what she do. She go to the ferryman and ask him to take her across. The ferryman say, I will, but you must take off all your clothes.

MRS BRYANT. Well, whatever do he wanna ask that for?

BEATIE. It don't matter why – he do! Now the girl doesn't know what to do so she ask the wise man for advice, and he say, you must do what you think best.

FRANK. Well that weren't much advice was it!

BEATIE. No matters – he give it. So the girl thinks about it and being so in love she decides to strip.

PEARL. Oh I say!

MR BRYANT. Well, this is a rum ole story ent it?

BEATIE. Shut up Father and listen. Now, er – where was I?

MR BRYANT. She was strippin'.

BEATIE. Oh yes! So, the girl strips and the ferryman takes her over – he don't touch her or nothing – just takes her over and she rushes to Archie's hut to implore him to take her with him and to declare her love again. Now Archie promises to take her with him and so she sleeps with him the night. But when she wake up in the morning he've gone. She's left alone. So she go across to Tom and explain her plight and ask for help. But soon ever he knowed what she've done, he chuck her out see? So there she is. Poor little gal. Left alone with no clothes and no friends and no hope of staying alive. Now – this is the question, think about it, don't answer quick – who is the person most responsible for her plight?

JIMMY. Well, can't she get back?

BEATIE. No, she can't do anything. She's finished. She've hed it! Now, who's to blame?

There is a general air of thought for the moment and
BEATIE looks triumphant and pleased with herself.

MRS BRYANT. Be you a-drinkin' on your tea look. Don't you worry about no naked gals. The gal won't get cold but the tea will.

PEARL. Well I say the girl's most responsible.

BEATIE. Why?

PEARL. Well, she made the choice didn't she?

FRANK. Yes, but the old ferryman made her take off her clothes.

PEARL. But she didn't hev to.

FRANK. Blust woman, she were in love!

BEATIE. Good ole Frank.

JENNY. Hell if I know.

BEATIE. Jimmy?

JIMMY. Don't ask me gal – I follow decisions. I aren't makin' none.

BEATIE. Father?

MR BRYANT. I don't know what you're on about.

BEATIE. Mother?

MRS BRYANT. Drink your tea gal – never you mind what I think.

This is what they're waiting for.

PEARL. Well – what do Ronnie say?

BEATIE. He say the gal is responsible only for makin' the

decision to strip off and go across and that she do that because she's in love. After that she's the victim of two phoney men – one who don't love her but take advantage of her and one who say he love her but don't love her enough to help her, and that the man who say he love her but don't do nothin' to help her is most responsible because he were the last one she could turn to.

JENNY. He've got it all worked out then!

BEATIE (*jumping on a chair thrusting her fist into the air like Ronnie, and glorying in what is the beginning of a hysteric outburst of his quotes*). 'No one do that bad that you can't forgive them.'

PEARL. He's sure of himself then?

BEATIE. 'We can't be sure of everything but certain basic things we must be sure about or we'll die.'

FRANK. He think everyone is gonna listen then?

BEATIE. 'People *must* listen. It's no good talking to the converted. *Everyone* must argue and think or they will stagnate and rot and the rot will spread.'

JENNY. Hark at that then.

BEATIE (*her strange excitement growing; she has a quote for everything*). 'If wanting the best things in life means being a snob then glory hallelujah I'm a snob. But I'm not a snob Beatie, I just believe in human dignity and tolerance and co-operation and equality and—'

JIMMY (*jumping up in terror*). He's a communist!

BEATIE. 'I'm a socialist!'

There is a knock on the front door.

BEATIE (*jumping down joyously as though her excited quotes have been leading to this one moment*). He's here, he's here! (*But at the door it is the* POSTMAN, *from whom she takes a letter and a parcel.*) Oh, the silly fool, the fool. Trust him to write a letter on the day he's coming. Parcel for you Mother.

PEARL. Oh, that'll be your dress from the club.

MRS BRYANT. What dress is this then? I didn't ask for no dress from the club.

PEARL. Yes you did, you did ask me, didn't she ask me Frank? Why, we were looking through the book together Mother.

MRS BRYANT. No matters what we was doin' together I aren't hevin' it.

PEARL. But Mother you distinctly—

MRS BRYANT. I aren't hevin' it so there now!

BEATIE *has read the letter – the contents stun her.*
She cannot move. She stares around speechlessly at
everyone.

MRS BRYANT. Well, what's the matter wi' you gal? Let's have a read. (*Takes the letter and reads contents in a dead flat but loud voice – as though it were a proclamation.*) 'My dear Beatie. It wouldn't really work would it? My ideas about handing on a new kind of life are quite useless and romantic if I'm really honest. If I were a healthy human being it might have been all right but most of us intellectuals are pretty sick and neurotic – as you have often observed – and we couldn't build a world even if we were given the reins of government – not yet any-rate. I don't blame you for being stubborn, I don't blame you for ignoring every suggestion I ever made – I only blame myself for encouraging you to believe we could make a go of it and now two weeks of your not being here has given me the cowardly chance to think about it and decide and I—'

BEATIE (*snatching letter*). Shut up!

MRS BRYANT. Oh – so we know now do we?

MR BRYANT. What's this then – ent he comin'?

MRS BRYANT. Yes, we know now.

MR BRYANT. Ent he comin' I ask?

BEATIE. *No he ent comin'.*

An awful silence ensues. Everyone looks uncomfortable.

JENNY (*softly*). Well blust gal, didn't you know this was going to happen?

BEATIE *shakes her head.*

MRS BRYANT. So *we're* stubborn are we?

JENNY. Shut you up Mother, the girl's upset.

MRS BRYANT. Well I can see that, I can see that, he ent coming, I can see that, and we're here like bloody fools, I can see that.

PEARL. Well did you quarrel all that much Beatie?

BEATIE (*as if discovering this for the first time*). He always wanted me to help him but I never could. Once he tried to teach me to type but soon ever I made a mistake I'd give up. I'd give up every time! I couldn't bear making mistakes. I don't know why, but I couldn't bear making mistakes.

MRS BRYANT. Oh – so we're hearin' the other side o' the story now are we?

BEATIE. He used to suggest I start to copy real objects on to my paintings instead of only abstracts and I never took heed.

MRS BRYANT. Oh, so you never took heed.

JENNY. Shut you up I say.

BEATIE. He gimme a book sometimes and I never bothered to read it.

FRANK (*not maliciously*). What about all this discussion we heard of?

BEATIE. I *never* discussed things. He used to beg me to discuss things but I never saw the point on it.

PEARL. And he got riled because o' that?

BEATIE (*trying to understand*). I didn't have any patience.

MRS BRYANT. Now it's coming out.

BEATIE. I couldn't help him – I never knew patience. Once he looked at me with terrified eyes and said, 'We've been together for three years but you don't know who I am or what I'm trying to say – and you don't care do you?'

135

MRS BRYANT. And there she was tellin' me.

BEATIE. I never knew what he wanted – I didn't think it mattered.

MR BRYANT. And there she were gettin' us to solve the moral problem and now we know she didn't even do it herself. That's a rum 'un, ent it?

MRS BRYANT. The apple don't fall far from the tree – that it don't.

BEATIE (*wearily*). So you're proud on it? You sit there smug and you're proud that a daughter of yours wasn't able to help her boy friend? Look at you. All of you. You can't say anything. You can't even help your own flesh and blood. Your daughter's bin ditched. It's your problem as well isn't it? I'm part of your family aren't I? Well, help me then! Give me words of comfort! Talk to me – for God's sake, someone talk to me. (*She cries at last.*)

MR BRYANT. Well, what do we do now?

MRS BRYANT. We sit down and we eat that's what we do now.

JENNY. Don't be soft Mother, we can't leave the girl crying like that.

MRS BRYANT. Well, blust, 'tent my fault she's cryin'. I did what I could – I prepared all this food, I'd've treated him as my own son if he'd come but he hevn't! We got a whole family gathering specially to greet him, all on us look, but he hevn't come. So what am I supposed to do?

BEATIE. My God, Mother, I hate you – the only thing I ever wanted and I weren't able to keep him, I didn't know how. I hate you, I hate . . .

  MRS BRYANT *slaps* BEATIE'S *face. Everyone is a little shocked at this harsh treatment.*

MRS BRYANT. There! I hed enough!

MR BRYANT. Well what d'you wanna do that for?

MRS BRYANT. I hed enough. All this time she've bin home she've bin tellin' me I didn't do this and I didn't do that

136

and I hevn't understood half what she've said and I've hed
enough. She talk about bein' part o' the family but she've
never lived at home since she've left school look. Then she
go away from here and fill her head wi' high-class squit
and then it turn out she don't understand any on it herself.
It turn out she do just the same things she say I do. (*Into*
BEATIE'S *face*) Well, am I right gal? I'm right ent I?
when you tell me I was stubborn, what you mean was that
he told you *you* was stubborn – eh? When you tell me I
don't understand you mean *you* don't understand isn't it?
When you tell me I don't make no effort you mean *you*
don't make no effort. Well, what you blaming me for?
Blaming me all the time! I haven't bin responsible for
you since you left home – you bin on your own. She think
I like it, she do! Thinks I like it being cooped up in this
house all day. Well I'm telling you my gal – I don't! There!
And if I had a chance to be away working somewhere the
whole lot on you's could go to hell – the lot on you's. All
right so I am a bloody fool – all right! So I know it! A
whole two weeks I've bin told it. Well, so then I can't help
you my gal, no that I can't, and you get used to that once
and for all.

BEATIE. No you can't Mother, I know you can't.

MRS BRYANT. I suppose doin' all those things for him
weren't enough. I suppose he weren't satisfied wi' goodness
only.

BEATIE. Oh, what's the use.

MRS BRYANT. Well, don't you sit there an' sigh gal like
you was Lady Nevershit. I ask you something. Answer me.
You do the talking then. Go on – you say you know something we don't so *you* do the talking. Talk – go on, talk
gal.

BEATIE (*despairingly*). I can't Mother, you're right – the
apple don't fall far from the tree do it? You're right, I'm
like you. Stubborn, empty, wi' no tools for livin'. I got no

roots in nothing. I come from a family o' farm labourers yet I ent got no roots – just like town people – just a mass o' nothin'.

FRANK. Roots, gal? What do you mean, roots?

BEATIE (*impatiently*). Roots, roots, roots! Christ, Frankie, you're in the fields all day, you should know about growing things. Roots! The things you come from, the things that feed you. The things that make you proud of yourself – roots!

MR BRYANT. You got a family ent you?

BEATIE. I am not talking about family roots – I mean – the – I mean – Look! Ever since it begun the world's bin growin' hasn't it? Things hev happened, things have bin discovered, people have bin thinking and improving and inventing but what do we know about it all?

JIMMY. What is she on about?

BEATIE (*various interjections*). What do you mean, what am I on about? I'm talking! Listen to me! I'm tellin' you that the world's bin growing for two thousand years and we hevn't noticed it. I'm telling you that we don't know what we are or where we come from. I'm telling you something's cut us off from the beginning. I'm telling you we've got no roots. Blimey Joe! We've all got large allotments, we all grow things around us so we should know about roots. You know how to keep your flowers alive don't you Mother? Jimmy – you know how to keep the roots of your veges strong and healthy. It's not only the corn that need strong roots, you know, it's us too. But what've we got? Go on, tell me, what've we got? We don't know where we push up from and we don't bother neither.

PEARL. Well, I aren't grumbling.

BEATIE. You say you aren't – oh yes, you say so, but look at you. What've you done since you come in? Hev you said anythin'? I mean really said or done anything to show you're alive? Alive! Blust, what do it mean? Do you know what it mean? Any of you? Shall I tell you what Susie said when I went and saw her? She say she don't care if that ole atom bomb drop and she die – that's what she say. And you know why she say it? I'll tell you why, because if she had to care she'd have to do something about it and she find *that* too much effort. Yes she do. She can't be bothered – she's too bored with it all. That's what we all are – we're all too bored.

MRS BRYANT. Blust woman – bored you say, bored? You say Susie's bored, with a radio and television an' that? I go t'hell if she's bored!

BEATIE. Oh yes, we turn on a radio or a TV set maybe, or we go to the pictures – if them's love stories or gangsters – but isn't that the easiest way out? Anything so long as we don't have to make an effort. Well, am I right? You know I'm right. Education ent only books and music – it's asking questions, all the time. There are millions of us, all over the country, and no one, not one of us, is asking questions, we're all taking the easiest way out. Everyone I ever worked with took the easiest way out. We don't fight for anything, we're so mentally lazy we might as well be dead. Blust, we are dead! And you know what Ronnie say sometimes? He say it serves us right! That's what he say – it's our own bloody fault!

JIMMY. So that's us summed up then – so we know where *we* are then!

MRS BRYANT. Well if he don't reckon we count nor nothin' then it's as well he didn't come. There! It's as well he didn't come.

BEATIE. Oh, *he* thinks we count all right – living in mystic communion with nature. Living in mystic bloody communion with nature (indeed). But us count? Count Mother? I wonder. Do we? Do you think we really count? You don' wanna take any notice of what them ole papers say about the workers bein' all-important these days – that's all squit! 'Cos we aren't. Do you think when the really talented people in the country get to work they get to work for us? Hell if they do! Do you think they don't know we 'ont make the effort? The writers don't write thinkin' we can understand, nor the painters don't paint expecting us to be interested – that they don't, nor don't the composers give out music thinking we can appreciate it. 'Blust,' they say, 'the masses is too stupid for us to come down to them. Blust,' they say, 'if they don't make no effort why should we bother?' So you know who come along? The slop singers and the pop writers and the film makers and women's magazines and the Sunday papers and the picture strip love stories – that's who come along, and you don't have to make no effort for them, it come easy. 'We know where the money lie,' they say, 'hell we do! The workers've got it so let's give them what they want. If they want slop songs and film idols we'll give 'em that then. If they want words of one syllable, we'll give 'em that then. If they want the third-rate, *blust!* We'll give 'em *that* then. Anything's good enough for them 'cos they don't ask for no more!' The whole stinkin' commercial world insults us and we don't care a damn. Well, Ronnie's right – it's our own bloody fault. We want the third-rate – we got it! We got it! We got it! We . . .

Suddenly BEATIE *stops as if listening to herself. She pauses, turns with an ecstatic smile on her face—*

D'you hear that? D'you hear it? Did you listen to me? I'm talking, Jenny, Frankie, Mother – I'm not quoting no more.

MRS BRYANT (*getting up to sit at table*). Oh hell, I hed enough of her – let her talk a while she'll soon get fed up.

The others join her at the table and proceed to eat and murmur.

BEATIE. Listen to me someone. (*As though a vision were revealed to her*) God in heaven, *Ronnie!* It does work, it's

140

happening to me, I can feel it's happened, I'm beginning
on my own two feet – I'm beginning . . .

*The murmur of the family sitting down to eat
grows as* BEATIE'S *last cry is heard. Whatever
she will do they will continue to live as before. As*
BEATIE *stands alone, articulate at last—*

THE CURTAIN FALLS

I'm Talking about Jerusalem

For
Della and Ralph

Characters of the Play

RONNIE KAHN
ADA SIMMONDS, *his sister*
SARAH KAHN, *their mother*
DAVE SIMMONDS, *Ada's husband*
1ST REMOVAL MAN
2ND REMOVAL MAN
LIBBY DOBSON, *wartime friend of Dave*
COLONEL DEWHURST, *Dave's employer*
SAMMY, *Dave's apprentice*
DANNY SIMMONDS
ESTHER KAHN ⎱ *aunts of Ronnie and Ada*
CISSIE KAHN ⎰

Act I

September 1946

Act II

SCENE 1: July 1947
SCENE 2: Autumn 1953

Act III

SCENE 1: Autumn 1956
SCENE 2: 1959

*First presented at the Belgrade Theatre, Coventry, on
4th April 1960*

Act One

September 1946.

Norfolk. A house in the middle of fields. We see the large kitchen of the house, the garden, and the end part of an old barn.

DAVE *and* ADA SIMMONDS *are just moving in. Boxes and cases are strewn around.* DAVE *and two* REMOVAL MEN *are manoeuvring a large wardrobe, 1930 type, from a lorry off stage.* ADA *is unpacking one of the cases.* SARAH KAHN, *her mother, is buttering some bread on a table, and from a portable radio comes a stirring part of Beethoven's Ninth Symphony.* RONNIE KAHN, *Ada's brother, is standing on a box conducting both the music and the movement of people back and forth.* DAVE – *unlike* ADA *and* RONNIE – *speaks with a slight cockney accent.*

RONNIE. Gently now. Don't rush it. You're winning.

DAVE. Instead of standing there and giving orders why don't you give a bloody hand?

RONNIE. You don't need any more hands. I'm organizing you, I'm inspiring you.

DAVE. Jesus Christ it's heavy, it's heavy. Drop it a minute.

RONNIE. Lower it gently – mind the edges, it's a work of art.

DAVE. I'll work of art you. And turn that radio off – I can cope with Beethoven but not both of you.

RONNIE (*turns off radio*). What are you grumbling for? I've been shlapping things to and fro up till now, haven't I? Only as it's the last piece I thought I'd exercise my talents as a foreman. Don't I make a good foreman? (*Calling*) Hey, Mother, don't I make a good foreman?

SARAH (*coming from the kitchen*). What've you lost?

RONNIE. Listen to her! What've you lost! She's just like her daughter, she can't hear a thing straight. Watch this. Hey, Ada! The sea's not far away you know.

145

ADA. You can't have any because I haven't put the kettle on yet.

RONNIE. Lunatic family.

DAVE. Come on. We'll never get done. Ready?

They bend to lift the wardrobe. SARAH *returns to kitchen.*

RONNIE. Heave – slowly – don't strain – heave.

1ST R.M. Where's it going?

DAVE. Through the kitchen and upstairs.

RONNIE. You won't get through the kitchen, go round the back.

DAVE. We'll manage.

RONNIE *goes on ahead and pushes* ADA, *the box and* SARAH *and table out of their path.*

RONNIE. Make way, make way – the army is marching on its stomach. (DAVE *and the two men are bent forward in effort.*) You see, I can't help, there's not enough room for four to get round that door.

They stop at other end of the kitchen and lower the wardrobe.

DAVE. We have to get round here and along the passage.

2ND R.M. Never. You can't bend wardrobes.

1ST R.M. Could saw it in half.

RONNIE (*pretending to be offended*). Good God man! An original twentieth-century piece and you want to saw it in half? Ahhhhhhhhh. (*Weeps upon it.*)

1ST R.M. You still at school?

RONNIE. So?

1ST R.M. Talk a lot don't you.

RONNIE. What's that got to do with school?

1ST R.M. Should've thought they'd have taught you manners.

SARAH (*coming into battle*). Don't you think he's got manners then?

2ND R.M. But he talks so don't he?

146

ADA (*joining battle*). Sooner he talked than he remained silent.

RONNIE. My lunatic family comes to my rescue.

1ST R.M. I'd've clipped him round the ear if he'd've called me lunatic.

DAVE. We'll have to take it back and use the front entrance.

RONNIE. What's the good of me being a foreman if you don't listen to me.

> RONNIE *again pushes back table and box which women had returned.*

RONNIE. Make way, make way. The retreat! (*Opens radio again and conducts them and symphony out of kitchen.*)

SARAH. Everything he makes into a joke.

> *The men raise the wardrobe and struggle back, this time going round the back of the house.* RONNIE *pauses and surveys the scene.*

RONNIE. Nineteen forty-six! The war is really over isn't isn't it, eh, Mother? Aren't you proud that your children are the first to pick up the ruins?

SARAH. I'm proud, yes! (*Pushes radio lid closed*).

RONNIE. Of course proud! We just put a Labour Party in power didn't we? It's right they should be the pioneers – good! Ever-y-bo-dy is building. Out go the slums, whist! And the National Health Service comes in. The millennium's come and you're still grumbling. What's the matter, you don't like strawberries and cream?

SARAH (*looking around*). Strawberries and cream?

RONNIE. All right, so it's shmultz herring and plum pudding for the meanwhile. But it's a great saga you're witnessing. The wandering Jews strike again! None of the easy life for them, none of the comforts of electricity—

SARAH. They're madmen!

RONNIE. They don't need roads, give them a muddy lane—

SARAH. Tell me Ada, how are you going to get to the

147

village? Not even a road here there isn't. Just fields – a
house in the middle of nowhere.

ADA. Ronnie, go and get some water for tea.

RONNIE. And none of the joys of running water for these
brave people, a well! A biblical well. I can see you Ada,
like Miriam at the well and Dave will come like Moses and
drive away the strangers and draw water for you and you
shall love him and marry him, and you shall bear him a
son and he will be called Adam and the son shall grow
strong and the land of Israel shall grow mighty around
him—

SARAH. Yes, here!

    SARAH *moves to throw something on a dustheap out
of hearing.*

ADA. It was Zipporah and Moses anyway.

RONNIE. Zipporah. What a beautiful name. I've always
wanted to write the Bible. Ada, haven't you ever felt
you've wanted to sit down and write something that's
already written? God, how many times I've felt like com-
posing the 'Autumn Journal'.

    SARAH *returns in time to hear this.*

ADA. What?

RONNIE. You know – Louis MacNeice—

    Sleep, my past and all my sins,
    In distant snow or dried roses
    Under the moon for night's cocoon will open
    When day begins.

ADA. I know what you mean.

SARAH (*surprised*). It's wonderful, Ronnie.

RONNIE. Isn't it beautiful Mother? It's a poetry I can talk,
I don't have to recite it.

    As if telling her *something.*

    Sleep to the noise of running water
    Tomorrow to be crossed, however deep;
    This is no river of the dead or Lethe,

    Tonight we sleep
    On the banks of Rubicon – the die is cast;
    There will be time to audit
    The accounts later, there will be sunlight later
    And the equation will come out at last.
My God, I want to write it again and again.

SARAH. But Ronnie, you've never read me that one before. Now that one, *that* one you try and get published.

    At this, ADA *and* RONNIE *break into uncontrollable laughter.* SARAH *cannot understand why.*

SARAH. So what's funny?

RONNIE. Oh, Mother I love you, love you. (*He cuddles her.*)

SARAH (*pushing him away because he tends to smother her*). All right so you love me, love me, but what's funny?

RONNIE (*picking up pail and going to get water*). My mother encourages me – get it published she says! (*Goes off laughing.*)

SARAH. Is he gone mad or something?

ADA. Oh, Mummy, you are funny – he was quoting a poem by a famous poet.

SARAH. How did I get such clever children?

RONNIE (*off*). Hey, Ada! How do I get the water out of this well?

ADA (*shouting*). Lift up the lid and hook the bucket on and just let it down.

RONNIE (*after a second*). Hey Ada! There's no water in this well.

ADA (*shouting*). Of course there is, you idiot.

RONNIE. But I can't see it.

ADA. It's a long way down.

RONNIE. You can die of thirst before you get to the bottom.

SARAH (*sighing*). Ada, Ada. You're both mad.

ADA. Next time you come down, we'll have lots of improvements.

SARAH. I don't understand it, I just don't see why you have

to come out here. Is London so bad? Millions of people
live there!

ADA. Thank you.

SARAH. All of a sudden they pick up and go away.

ADA (*calling*). Dave, where's the paraffin?

DAVE (*off*). I put it in the corner.

ADA. I see it. (*Picks up paraffin and proceeds to fill and light
primus stove.*)

SARAH. A primus stove! What's the point? All this heavy
work. No roads, no electricity, no running water, no proper
lavatory. It's the Middle Ages. Tell me why you want to
go back to the Middle Ages?

ADA. We'll get a Calor gas stove in time.

SARAH. Progress!

ADA. Mummy, please, ple-ease help us. It's not easy this
move, for any of us. Doesn't it occur to you that we
desperately need your blessing, please—

SARAH. I'm here aren't I? Silly girl. But how can I bless – ?
I brought up two nice children, and I want to see them
round me – that's wrong? But all right, so you want to go
away, so you want to build a life of your own, but here?
Why here? Explain it to me, maybe I'll be happier. Why
here?

RONNIE (*off, shouting*). Hey Dave – how you managing?

DAVE (*off*). We're managing. Just a few more stairs.

RONNIE. That's right boys – heave, heave!

DAVE. I'll heave this bloody thing on top of your head if
you don't shut up. Go away and make some tea.

RONNIE (*entering*). The men want tea. Feed the workers.
Hey Addie – you know what I discovered by the well? You
can shout! It's marvellous. You can shout and no one can
hear you.

ADA (*triumphantly*). Of course!

SARAH (*derisively*). Of course.

RONNIE. Of course – listen. (*Goes into garden and stands*

on a tea chest and shouts.) *Down with capitalism! Long
live the workers' revolution!* You see? *And long live Ronnie
Kahn too!* (*Waits for a reply.*) No one argues with you. No
one says anything. Freedom! You can jump about. (*Jumps
off chest.*) You can spin in the air. (*Jumps and spins with
arms akimbo.*) You can do somersaults . . . (*He rolls on the
grass shouting 'wheeeee'.*) You can bang the earth. (*He
thumps the ground with his fists with utter joy.*) My God –
it's wonderful – you can go mad all on your own and no
one'll say anything. (*Sits up wide-eyed.*)

SARAH. He's not my son. I'll swear he's not my son.

RONNIE (*crawling on all fours up to the kitchen door*). Of
course I'm not your son. My real mother was a gipsy and
lived in a caravan, and one day she came to your door and
instead of buying flowers from her you bought me. And
everyone believed us. They used to look at you, and then
at me and say no – no, it's true, he doesn't look like you
does he?

SARAH. Make the tea.

RONNIE (*springing up*). Where's the kettle?

ADA. In one of the boxes.

RONNIE. It's like camping.

SARAH. Camping!

ADA. Finished the bread Mummy?

SARAH. I've finished the bread. What about the soup?

ADA. Soup?

RONNIE. She made a chicken soup last night and put it in
bottles. She puts everything in bottles. (*Looks in Sarah's
bag.*)

SARAH. And a meat pie too I made.

ADA. Oh Mummy, you shouldn't have.

SARAH. I shouldn't have, I shouldn't have! Everything I
shouldn't have. Did *you* think about what you were going
to eat when you came here?

ADA. I brought bread and tomatoes and fruit and cheese.

RONNIE. Cheese!

SARAH. As if I didn't know what you'd bring!

RONNIE. She always offers me cheese when I'm hungry.

ADA. You're both mad.

SARAH. *We're* mad! My children and they still don't know how to organize their lives.

RONNIE (*holding up jar*). Bottled Chicken Soup. It looks like – er – hum – yes, well, I hope it tastes different.

ADA. We've only one primus so you'll have to wait until the water's boiled. Get out a table-cloth Ronnie.

RONNIE. A table-cloth? What, here? Now?

ADA. This place may be a shambles but I don't intend living as though it's one.

> DAVE *and the* REMOVAL MEN *have returned by this time and* RONNIE *throws out a cloth assisted by* SARAH.

1ST R.M. Got a problem living here haven't you?

2ND R.M. Ain't very modern is it, Jim?

RONNIE. Got the wardrobe in place?

2ND R.M. We got it through the door.

DAVE. You can help me manoeuvre it later, Ronnie.

1ST R.M. What made you move here, mate? Not being nosey or anything, but you can't say it's everybody's choice of a new home.

DAVE. It's a long story.

2ND R.M. Couldn't you find a better place? More convenience? I mean it's not very sanitary, is it?

DAVE. Not easy to find the right place with little cash. Saw the job advertised, a cheap house for sale near by – grabbed it!

SARAH. Hard! Everything has to be hard for them.

1ST R.M. Still, they're young, missus, ain't they? Gotta admit it's fresh out here.

2ND R.M. Too bleedin' fresh if you ask me.

RONNIE. Come on, Dave. Give them an answer. It's a

golden opportunity this. The world has asked you why you've come here. There stands the world (*To* R. MEN) and here stand you two. You're on trial comrade.

ADA. Don't arse around Ronnie, the men want their tea.

RONNIE. But I'm serious, girl. I want to know too. You've always been my heroes, now you've changed course. You've left communism behind – what now?

1ST R.M. Communist, are you?

2ND R.M. That's a dirty word, ain't it?

1ST R.M. Not during the war it wasn't.

RONNIE. The world is waiting, Dave.

DAVE. I'm not going to make speeches, Ronnie.

SARAH. Is a reason a speech?

DAVE. You can't talk about reasons, Sarah, just like that. A decision grows, slowly – you discover it.

RONNIE. But where did this one start?

ADA. Ceylon—

DAVE. – When I was stationed out there. I was with Air Sea Rescue, boat building.

1ST R.M. We was in India. That's where Ted and me met. Decided on this game out there.

DAVE. I was in India for a bit. Where were you?

2ND R.M. Bombay.

DAVE. Karachi, me. That's where I met Libby Dobson, Ada – remember? I always wrote to you about Libby Dobson? Me and him were going to do everything together when we got back to Civvy Street. Like you two. But *that* was a ship in the night.

ADA. He made a great impression on you, though.

DAVE. Taught me a lot. When we get straight we'll have him down here – shouldn't be difficult to trace him. He always wanted to do something like this with me. This'll please him this move, old Libby Dobson'd get a kick out of coming here.

1ST R.M. What was Ceylon like?

DAVE. Beautiful island. Being a carpenter I used to watch the local carpenters at work. They used to make their own tools and sometimes they'd show me. They'd sit out on the beach fashioning the boats or outside their houses planing and chiselling away at their timber, and they let me sit with them once they knew I was also building boats. And you know, one day, as I watched, I made a discovery – the kind of discovery you discover two or three times in a lifetime. I discovered an old truth: that a man is made to work and that when he works he's giving away something of himself, something very precious—

2ND R.M. We didn't see anything precious about living in mud huts and working in disease.

DAVE. No, no. You miss the point – I'm talking about the *way* they worked, not the conditions. I know about disease, I know about the mud huts, but what I was trying to say—

ADA. It's no good trying to explain. We're here and let's—

SARAH (*angrily*). Ada stop it! Stop it! Impatience! What's the matter with you all of a sudden. Don't explain! Nothing she wants to explain. No more talking. Just a cold, English you-go-your-way-and-I'll-go-mine! Why?

ADA. Because language isn't any use! Because we talk about one thing and you hear another that's why.

RONNIE. Come on, Dave, you haven't said enough. The world doesn't believe you—

ADA. The world!

RONNIE. Explain more.

ADA. Explain what? We've moved house, what's there to explain? What's so exceptional?

SARAH (*posing the real question*). What's wrong with socialism that you have to run to an ivory tower?

DAVE. Nothing's wrong with socialism Sarah, only we want to live it – not talk about it.

SARAH. Live it? Here?

ADA. Oh the city is paradise I suppose!

SARAH. The city is human beings. What's socialism without human beings tell me?

DAVE. I know the city Sarah. Believe me sweetheart! Since being demobbed I've worked in a factory turning out doors and window frames and I've seen men hating themselves while they were doing it. Morning after morning they've come in with a cold hatred in their eyes, brutalized! All their humanity gone. These you call men? All their life they're going to drain their energy into something that will give them nothing in return. Why do you think these two (*the* R.M.s) decided to set up on their own? Eh? I'll tell you—

SARAH. But this isn't a socialist society yet—

ADA. What the hell difference do you think that'll make? All anyone talks about is taking over capitalist society, but no one talks about really changing it.

2ND R.M. And you're going to change it?

1ST R.M. On your own, cock?

DAVE. No of course we can't change it. But you see that barn out there? I'll work as a chippy on the Colonel's farm here for a year and then in a year's time that barn'll be my workshop. There I shall work and here, ten yards from me, where I can see and hear them, will be my family. And they will share in my work and I shall share in their lives. I don't want to be married to strangers. I've seen the city make strangers of husbands and wives, but not me, not me and my wife.

SARAH. Words, words.

ADA. *Not* words. At last something more than just words.

Pause. Their defiance sinks in.

RONNIE (*to the* R.M.s). So now *you* (*to* ADA *and* DAVE) and now the *world* knows. And the world – will watch you.

1ST R.M. Come on China. It's time to set off. These socialists can't even make us a cup of tea.

At which point the whole Kahn family swing into

*action with regrets and apologies and thrust sand-
wiches and fruit into the arms of the startled lorry
drivers.*

2ND R.M. Oi, oi! Whoa! Merry Christmas!

1ST R.M. Think of us poor city sods won't you? Good luck!

*The R.M.s go off to the lorry. We hear the lorry start,
it revs and slowly moves off in gear. The family
stands and watches, and waves and calls 'Goodbye,'
listening till the sound dies away.*

Silence.

*Each feels that with the going of the lorry has gone
the last of the old life.*

It is getting dark.

RONNIE. Well – you're here. You've come. Welcome to the
Shambles.

*DAVE moves to ADA and kisses her. RONNIE
watches. SARAH sits unhappily in a chair away
from them all.*

DAVE. We've got a house.

ADA. We've got a house.

DAVE. Tired darling?

ADA. A bit.

DAVE. It's not *such* a mess.

ADA. I know.

DAVE. It looks it but it's not such a mess.

ADA. I know, angel.

DAVE. Are you in control?

ADA. I'm in control.

DAVE. I love you very much.

ADA. I love you very much.

RONNIE (*moving to SARAH*). And I love you too sweetheart.
(*His arm round her*) Look at my sister – (*with mock passion*) isn't she beautiful?

SARAH. I don't understand what went wrong, I don't understand how she can be like that.

ADA (*breaking away from* DAVE). I'm not like anything Mummy, only like your daughter. (*Kisses* SARAH.) You can come and visit us. Look – (*waving arms around with mock majesty*) a country house. Aren't you pleased your daughter's got a country house? We can entertain in grand style! Everyone can come for a holiday – we'll have the maiden aunts down! Aunt Cissy and Aunt Esther can come and pull up weeds for us.

RONNIE. They're really very bourgeois these idealists you know.

SARAH. So far away.

ADA. Only a hundred miles.

SARAH. A hundred miles! You can say it easily. And what if Harry gets worse? It doesn't stop at one stroke, your father's never been very strong.

DAVE. I'm going to unpack some of the things upstairs.

ADA. Light the tilly lamp for me darling before you go up. Supper won't be long. (DAVE *does so.*)

RONNIE. I'm going to look over the district. I bet there are hidden treasures and secret hideouts.

SARAH. Take your raincoat. (RONNIE *does so.*)

DAVE. I suppose *I'll* have to take a candle up with me.

ADA. Come on Mummy. Let's get some supper ready.

SARAH. Do you have to work any more Dave? Can't you rest a little?

DAVE. I'll prepare some beds and take out some of the clothes and hang them. We'll get straight bit by bit. No sense in rushing it. They're good things these lamps. There! It's alight. (*A soft glow covers part of the kitchen.*)

ADA. A lovely light.

SARAH. It took someone all this time to discover electricity – he shouldn't have bothered!

> DAVE *smiles, shakes his head and goes off upstairs. The women busy themselves. They tidy the general mess and then lay plates and knives and forks on the*

table. ADA'S *movements are slow and calm.* SARAH
is volatile and urgent, though somehow she manages
to speak slowly and with deliberation – softly. The
atmosphere sinks in. Then—

SARAH. And Dave doesn't like me – you know that?

ADA *doesn't reply. Silence. They continue moving*
around.

I don't know why it should be that he doesn't like me.
I don't think I've ever done anything to hurt him (*Pause.*)
Perhaps that's why he's taking you away, because he
doesn't like me. Who knows!

Still ADA *does not reply – instead she very softly*
starts humming.

He's changed you. Dave's changed a lot from the old days,
Ada. (*Pause.*) Or perhaps he hasn't, perhaps it's me. Who
knows. I know he fought in Spain, he's really a wonderful
boy but – Ach! children! You bring them up, you teach
them this you teach them that, you do what you think is
right and still it's no good. They grow up and they grow
away and you're left with – with – ! Where do their
madnesses come from? Who knows. *I* don't know why
Dave doesn't like me.

Still no word from ADA. *She hums perhaps a little*
louder.

SARAH. What you humming for? Humming! All of a sudden she does this humming when I talk to her. A new
madness. Stop it Ada. Stop it! Silly girl.

An elderly gentleman appears. He is COLONEL
DEWHURST, *the farmer for whom* DAVE *will be*
working. He comes from the path and knocks on
the kitchen door just as SARAH *finishes.*

COLONEL (*as the door is opened to him*). Mrs Simmonds?
I'm Colonel Dewhurst.

ADA. Oh hello, come in please, we're still unpacking so
forgive—

COLONEL. But I understand, ma'am. I just thought—

ADA. This is my mother. Mother, Colonel Dewhurst, Dave's employer.

COLONEL (*shaking hands*). How do you do, ma'am. You must be very tired. Come a long way today, haven't you?

ADA (*calling*). Dave! Dave! Colonel Dewhurst.

DAVE. I'm coming down, a second.

ADA. Do sit down please.

COLONEL. I was telling your mother you've come a long way today.

ADA. Yes, we have.

COLONEL. It must seem strange.

SARAH. It seems very strange.

ADA. My mother thinks we're mad Colonel.

COLONEL. To come to the country? A fine life, a fine life.

SARAH. With no sanitation or electricity?

COLONEL. Thousands of places like that, thousands! But it's a large house, fresh air—

SARAH. There are parks in London.

COLONEL. *I* wouldn't change now.

SARAH. Maybe you've got some amenities my children haven't?

COLONEL. But they're young, aren't they? It's good they start off with a struggle, makes them appreciate life—

SARAH (*to* ADA). We brought you up with riches I suppose?

DAVE (*appearing and shaking hands*). Hello Colonel Dewhurst.

COLONEL. I thought I'd drop over and see you were arriving safely.

DAVE. That's very good of you.

COLONEL. It won't take you long to get used to it. It's a bracing life in the country.

DAVE. We're not rushing things. I think we'll manage.

COLONEL. Of course you will, yes, I'm sure. When do you

think you'll be able to start – er – you know, when can
I expect—

DAVE. Well I hoped you wouldn't mind giving us a few
days to settle in and get our bearings.

COLONEL. Yes, well, there's no need to come in tomorrow, I
think that'll be all right, yes, that'll be all right. But my
foreman is waiting to start some fencing – want to get a
few more sows in. He's been waiting a long time for a
carpenter. No, no need to come in tomorrow – early start
the next day'll do, do perfectly.

DAVE. Thanks.

COLONEL. Yes, well, thought I'd pop over and see you were
arriving safely. Come at a good time – we've had some
rain but it's gone. Doesn't do to have too much rain.

ADA (*not really knowing the reply*). No it doesn't does it?

COLONEL. Talking of rain, Simmonds, I'd advise you to
buy yourself a tank to catch the soft water. Good stuff,
that. Save you work, too. Not so much to pull up from the
well. Buy one with a tap – easier. Don't drink it, though.
Use it for washing and things.

DAVE. Thank you for telling us.

COLONEL. I'll see you right. (*Walks out into the garden.
DAVE and ADA follow to doorway.*) You'll learn lots of
things as you go along. (*Looks around.*) Good garden here.
Grow your own veges. Apple tree there. Prune it a bit.
Sturdy barn too, couple hundred years old. Use it for
chickens, build a run inside it. You could do that, couldn't
you? Build yourself a chicken run?

DAVE. I expect so. A little bit of intelligence can build you
anything.

COLONEL (*suddenly becoming the employer*). Eight o'clock
on Wednesday morning, then, Simmonds. Good night to
you both. (*Goes off.*)

DAVE and ADA *stand a second and look at each
other.*

160

SARAH. That's the man you're working for?

ADA (*to* DAVE). He didn't give you much time to settle in did he?

DAVE. No, he didn't did he?

SARAH. You won't have time to scratch yourself, I'm telling you.

ADA. Well perhaps he needs you.

DAVE (*certain*). I'm sure he does. (*Not so certain*) But I reckon he could have given us a couple of days to settle in.

ADA. Yes he could have.

DAVE. We're still rushing—

ADA. Seems like it.

They are disappointed. SARAH *watches them sadly.*

SARAH. Oh my children, children! Straight away they want to walk into paradise. Perhaps it's a good thing you should start work so soon, you'll settle in the house gradually and working will get you into a stride, a routine. Always have a routine.

ADA (*brightening at this*). Perhaps Mum is right darling. Perhaps it's better to get stuck in straight away.

DAVE. No moping you mean?

ADA. I mean have no time to think we've done the wrong thing.

DAVE. *You* don't think we've done the wrong thing do you darling.

ADA. No – I do not.

DAVE. I do love you. (*Kisses her briefly.*)

ADA. Come on, let's get this food over with. Where's Ronnie?

SARAH. Looking for hidden treasure.

DAVE. He's what?

SARAH. He's gone out exploring – in the mountains there. *Waves vaguely.*

ADA. There aren't any mountains in Norfolk Mother.

SARAH. I'm very surprised.

DAVE. What's that fire there?

*They all look at a red glow coming from behind the
barn.* DAVE *and* ADA *rush off to one side of the barn.*

DAVE. I hope the bloody fool hasn't been up to any of his
tricks.

SARAH *stands looking in the direction they've gone.
After a few seconds* RONNIE *strolls in from the
other side of the barn. He walks in a kind of daze,
clutching a branch, gazing into space.*

RONNIE. You can build fires under the night sky.

SARAH. What've you been up to you mad boy?

RONNIE. There's bracken in every hedge and you can make
fires with them.

SARAH. Have you set the barn on fire?

RONNIE. It's beautiful.

SARAH. For God's sake stop playing the fool and answer me.

RONNIE. (*looking around him*). It's all very beautiful.

ADA *and* DAVE *appear.*

ADA. Ronnie, you are a nitwit, you could have set the whole
place alight.

RONNIE. Oh no. I know about these things.

SARAH. What did he do? I can't get any sense out of him.

DAVE. It's all right – he made a camp fire, don't panic,
nothing's burning. Let's eat.

They settle down to eat except RONNIE, *who for
the moment leans against a box, still enraptured.*

SARAH. He's so mad. I get so angry sometimes. Look at him,
in a daze. Take your raincoat off and sit down and eat.

RONNIE *sits down at the table but doesn't take off
his raincoat.*

ADA. What are you sitting down in your raincoat for?

RONNIE. Somehow I feel, I feel – I . . . (*unable to explain*)

ADA. Yes, yes, but why are you eating with your raincoat on?

SARAH. Another madness! Every so often he gets a madness into his head and you can't shake him out of it. I get so
annoyed. Ronnie, take your raincoat off!

DAVE. What are you getting upset for, both of you. The boy
wants to eat in his raincoat let him eat in his raincoat.

ADA. He's not normal!

DAVE. All right so he's not normal, why should you worry?

ADA. I do worry. I'm not going to sit at the table with him
while he's wearing a raincoat. Ronnie take your raincoat
off!

RONNIE *continues eating.*

SARAH. I don't know what makes him like this. Ronnie take
your raincoat off!

ADA. He's so bloody stubborn. *Ronnie!*

DAVE. You and your mother, you're both the same. Why
don't you leave the boy alone. What harm is he doing in
a raincoat.

ADA. Because it annoys me that's why! (*to* DAVE) Don't side
with him Dave because if you side with him he knows he
can get away with it.

SARAH *rises at this point and goes to a corner of the
room where she finds an umbrella.*

DAVE. Now look at us! Here we are quarrelling among ourselves just because your brother is sitting down at the table
wearing a macintosh. Have you ever heard such lunacy?
What's your mother up to?

SARAH *sits at the table and opens the umbrella over
her and proceeds to eat. Everyone looks at her in
amazement. Suddenly* RONNIE *bursts out laughing,
jumps up from the chair, kisses her, and takes off
his raincoat.* DAVE *sees what has happened and
laughs also. There is great merriment.*

DAVE. Well if you Kahns aren't the most lunatic family I
know.

*They all begin to eat. Sarah twists the umbrella once
on her shoulders, sticks her hand out to see if the
'rain' has finished, and then folds up the umbrella
and eats.*

SARAH. Don't I know my children!

DAVE. You're all so much alike, that's why.

They eat on in silence for a moment until suddenly
SARAH *gets up from the table and moves quickly out*
from the kitchen to the garden where she takes a
handkerchief from her apron. She weeps a little.
RONNIE *rises and goes to the door.*

RONNIE. Sarah?

SARAH. It's all right, I'm all right, leave me, go back inside and finish eating.

RONNIE *returns.*

RONNIE. Tears again.

ADA. I guessed this might happen. Perhaps she shouldn't have come.

DAVE. Can you blame her darling? Ronnie, sit down and let's finish this food.

RONNIE. I'm not really hungry. (*Half annoyed*) She always makes it seem like the end of the world when she cries.

SARAH (*from the garden*). You know, it reminds me of Hungary, where I was born—

ADA. There, she's better again.

SARAH. There used to be high mountains and a river and a waterfall; my brother Hymie once fell into the river and I saved him. He nearly drowned. The mountains had snow on them.

RONNIE (*calling to her*). But there aren't any mountains or waterfalls here Mother.

SARAH (*after a pause, petulantly*). It still reminds me of Hungary.

ADA. Everything reminds her of Hungary. We were listening to Beethoven the other night and she swore black and blue it was based on a Hungarian folk song.

RONNIE. I'll wash up.

DAVE. Come on, let's finish unpacking.

RONNIE *takes what remains of the water in the*

kettle and pours it into a basin, shakes some soap powder into it and begins to wash up. ADA *and* DAVE *stand by one of the boxes, take out the contents one by one, unwrap them and lay them aside.* SARAH *enters, takes a dishcloth and begins to wipe up what* RONNIE *washes. As they do this* SARAH *begins to sing a soft and melodic Yiddish folk song. She can't remember past the first line.* RONNIE *picks up and reminds her. They sing together.* RONNIE *indicates to* ADA *to join in, she does so and in turn brings in* DAVE. *The new life has started and some of the old has come with them, and –*

THE CURTAIN FALLS

Act Two

July 1947.

Everything is more in order now. Twelve months have passed and with it their first winter.

A signpost saying 'Y.H.A.', with an arrow, leans against a wall, waiting to be knocked into the ground.

The stage is empty. DAVE *appears singing 'Linden Lea' and carrying a roll of linoleum, which he lays down by the back door. He has just returned from work. At the door he pauses and looks out, surveying the countryside. From a room upstairs,* ADA *calls out.*

ADA. Dave?

DAVE. Yes, sweetheart.

ADA. My God, what time is it?

DAVE. About five fifteen. Is Libby here?

ADA. No, he'll be back soon. I'm just finishing this letter.

DAVE. It's all right, don't rush.

ADA. Dave – when did we arrive here?

DAVE. Roughly twelve months ago.

> DAVE *stays by door and begins to unbutton his tall boots. After some seconds* ADA *appears. She is pregnant. She greets* DAVE *with a kiss and then he nods his head towards the view. They both gaze at it a while and inhale deeply.*

ADA. The corn is yellow now.

DAVE. Colours for each season. The children will love it.

ADA. We'll teach the children to look at things won't we Dave? I shall make it into a sort of game for them. Teach them to take notice. (*With mock pomp*) Don't let the world pass you by, I shall tell them – (*breathing deeply*) breathe, I shall say, breathe deeply and fill your lungs and open your eyes. For the sun, I shall say, open your eyes for that laaaarge sun.

DAVE. Not long ago that field was brown. What does Libby say to it all, now he's had a chance to look around? We didn't get much of a chance to talk last night because he arrived so late.

ADA. A very strange fish your friend Libby Dobson. He doesn't quite fit the picture you painted of him does he?

DAVE. No he doesn't does he? What's he been up to all day?

ADA. I packed him up some sandwiches and he went out for a day's walking. God knows where. He stood out here and he looked around and he said 'It's all sky isn't it?' and then he stalked off with a 'see you'.

DAVE. He looked very sad and worn old Libby – never thought he'd end up a – what does he call himself?

ADA. A business consultant.

DAVE. He was a bloody fine mechanic in the RAF.

ADA. You're disappointed aren't you darling?

DAVE. Yes I am – daft, but I am. You know there's always one person you want to show your life to – show what you've done – and I've thought Libby Dobson was the bloke – should've thought he'd've understood. Blimey! the man had a hand in shaping my ideas – people! Well that's people I suppose.

ADA. Maybe he'll be better after a day's walk. Get me some water look or he'll come and nothing'll be ready and then he will be riled.

DAVE. Riled! You're a real Norfolk girl already. (*Holding her*) Let's pretend he's not here and let's go to bed and just lie there.

ADA. Let's get this one over first.

DAVE. We'll leave a note for old Dobson and he can get his own supper.

ADA. Darling the water.

DAVE. He's a big boy – he can look to himself.

ADA. Besides *I'm* – we're – hungry.

DAVE. Water.

He goes off singing 'Linden Lea' and ADA *goes in to lay a salad.* DAVE *begins to talk to her from the back of the house.*

DAVE (*off*). Darling we must start making new plans.

ADA. I'm making a salad for supper.

DAVE. What?

ADA. Salad!

DAVE. Plans!

ADA. What?

DAVE. Plans!

ADA. No, salad!

DAVE *appears at window to kitchen.*

DAVE. Let's get together – what are you talking about?

ADA. I said I'm making a salad for supper.

DAVE. Oh. And I said we must start making new plans. We'll start again. (*Returns to well.*)

ADA (*waits, then calls*). What plans?

DAVE (*off*). I want to build a chicken hut—

ADA. Lovely—

DAVE. And then I want to start laying a concrete floor in the barn so that I can build a proper workshop.

ADA. Have you ever laid a concrete floor before?

DAVE. I hadn't ever made a piece of furniture before had I? You learn. You think about it and you learn. How many more buckets of water do you want for Christ's sake?

ADA. Just fill the copper.

DAVE. But I filled it this morning.

ADA. And I used it this morning.

DAVE *enters, puffed out, carrying a bucket of water.*

ADA. Here, put the spare one in the jug.

ADA *draws a jug from under the sink.*

DAVE. And that's another thing. I've got to take a pipe from the sink to the well and run it into a drain outside.

ADA. A plumber too.

DAVE. And then we must start thinking about buying a soft water tank, that'll save arms at the well.

ADA. Darling, I need storage space. The one cupboard you built there isn't enough.

DAVE. In time my darling, all in good time. We've made our garden grow haven't we? We've made our garden grow and we've stopped our roof from leaking. I've boarded the old stables up and laid by timber ready to work. The rooms are painted white and nearly all the windows have curtains, and in three months' time I reckon I can start on my own. Look, only the hedges are wild. All in good time my darling.

ADA. And Mummy asks us what we do with our time. They're mad.

DAVE. Think we'll stick it out?

ADA. What the hell kind of question is that—

DAVE. Relax Ada – you've gone all tense – you'll give birth to a poker.

ADA. Dave, and that's another thing. I'm worried about the baby. I've been reading that—

DAVE. Whatever you've been reading forget it! Look at you, you're so healthy. Your belly is high and the baby is probably so big that's he bored with it all. (*Puts his ear to her stomach and has a conversation with the baby*.) Listen, he's talking.

ADA. You're mad darling.

DAVE. I tell you he's talking. Yes. Yes, I can hear you – sounds like a dozen drains emptying – what's that? You don't want to come out? But you've got to come out, I don't care how comfortable it is you'll get cramp. No. I'm not going to send a bloody taxi for you – you'll walk. Now listen to me, you come out when you're told or I'll plug you in there for life – you hear me?

ADA. Dave, for God's sake, don't be crude.

DAVE (*snuggling up to her*). Yes, let's be crude.

ADA. Right in the middle of fields?

DAVE. Right in the middle of fields, one night, at full moon.

At this moment LIBBY DOBSON *appears. He's stocky, about 30 years old, and looks as though he wants to be a fisherman and can only be one on holidays.*

DOBSON. Quite a hideout you've got here, haven't you?

DAVE (*hopefully*). What do you think of now you've seen it Libby?

DOBSON. You're going to turn it into a youth hostel?

DAVE. Got to make some spare cash somehow mate.

DOBSON. These places really do cater for the hale and bloody hearty, don't they? There – (*puts two bottles on the table*) wine for the table and the whisky's for me. I'm going up to change. (*Goes off.*)

DAVE. Well, I wonder what sort of evening this is going to be?

ADA (*picking up a bucket of waste from under sink and throwing it outside back door*). It'll be all right Dave. People aren't ever as you remember them – you'll just have to get to know each other again.

Outside ADA *notices the rolls of linoleum. Puts down bucket and undoes them.*

ADA. What's this darling?

DAVE. Some old lino the Colonel threw away. We can use that in the hallway.

ADA. Threw away?

DAVE. Well I saw it lying around in the shed. It's been there for months.

ADA. Did you ask him?

DAVE. But it's been lying around for ages.

ADA. Dave I'm not very moral about taking odd things from employers but I'd hate to have him—

DAVE. It's all right sweetheart I tell you.

ADA. You say it's all right but—

DAVE. Ada, the supper. Libby's hungry and so am I. I want to wash. (*Pours himself water into bowl and strips to the waist to wash, as* ADA *proceeds to lay the table.*)

ADA. Shall I bring out the wine glasses?

DAVE. Bring out the wine glasses.

ADA. Darling don't be cross.

DAVE. But you go on so.

ADA. I don't want things to go wrong.

DAVE. Well a lot will go wrong – so? Are you going to get upset each time?

ADA. Will you light the lamp when you've finished please?

DAVE. I mean a lot *is* going to go wrong isn't it?

ADA. This is different, I—

> DOBSON *returns at this point and sits down, waiting for the next move. Remember, he has already caught them embracing.* DAVE *and* ADA *glance at each other,* DAVE *shrugs his shoulders.* ADA *proceeds to lay out a clean shirt for* DAVE, *he is drying himself. The rest of this scene happens while* ADA *prepares a salad. They never get round to eating it.*

ADA. Don't forget the lamp when you've done please Dave.

DOBSON. Tilly lamps – the lot. You two have really taken your backward march seriously, eh? Dead serious—cor!

DAVE. Libby – what is it mate, come on, out with it – what's nettled you?

DOBSON. Oh no, Simmonds, please No old chums and their war memories – I'm on holiday. I'll help you chop your wood – I'll even dance round the may-pole with you – but no heart-searching, I'm a tired man.

> *Throughout an awkward silence the lamp is lit. During this next scene* DOBSON *drinks his whisky, becoming more and more tipsy; just now he stares at the sky.*

DOBSON. The countryside smells like a cow with diarrhoea.

171

ADA. Perhaps your nose is still full of smoke and petrol fumes.

DOBSON. Jesus! I could've recognized that remark a mile off. If I hadn't known, it would have told me your whole story. Our horrible industrial civilization. We hate the large, inhuman cities. Eh? Back to nature, boys.

An embarrassed silence.

ADA (*to* DAVE). I had a letter from Ronnie today.

DAVE. What does your mad brother say?

ADA. You remember his girl friend Jacqueline? The one he told us knew it all? Well he's come to the dramatic conclusion that people who are similar aren't much good to each other so he's going to marry a prostitute!

DOBSON. Oh God! I bet your mother's in the Salvation Army. (ADA *and* DAVE *laugh uproariously at this.*)

ADA. Can you imagine Sarah in the Salvation Army? 'Comrades, Jesus Christ was the first communist to be born among us.'

DOBSON. Now the picture is complete. Two ex-communists! There's nothing more pathetic than the laughter of people who have lost their pet faith.

The laughter is dead. That was a bomb.

DAVE. What the hell *is* the matter with you Libby? Within a few minutes you've called us idealists as if you were swearing at us, and then you express disgust because you think we've lost our faiths.

ADA. Let's have some of your wine shall we?

DOBSON. Yes, let's.

DAVE. You're being offensive Libby.

DOBSON (*wearily*). Oh, come off it! I'm a cynic. You can recognize a cynic, can't you? You should be using me, sharpening your ideas on me. The more sceptical I become the higher your ideals should soar, shouldn't they? Eh? Well, soar then – soar! Be heroic! There's nothing wrong with idealism, only when it's soft and flabby. The smell of petrol in my nose! So what! You can't change the world because it smells of petrol.

ADA. Who's talking about changing the world?

DOBSON. Then go home. Be good children and go home, because you'll never make the beautiful, rustic estate.

ADA. My God darling – it's come to something when we're sneered at for wanting beautiful things.

DOBSON. Because it's a lie. Outdated! Because it's not new!

DAVE. New! New! Everything has to be new! Contemporary! You could walk around on your hands all day – that's new – but it wouldn't be achieving much would it?

DOBSON. That's better – you're bristling, you're bristling. Soon you'll be able to devour me. That's what a cynic's for, Davey mate, to be devoured, gobbled up.

DAVE (*to* ADA). I don't understand it darling. Everyone accuses us of something or other – rustics, escapists, softheaded. (*To* DOBSON) You think there aren't problems here?

ADA. There isn't a servant to draw our water, you know?

DAVE. Or a gardener to grow our vegetables.

ADA. Do you think I'm going to have a nanny to see to my child?

DAVE. Or that there's a private income somewhere?

ADA. In London you waste your time solving the wrong problems.

DAVE. Leaving early to catch the bus! Is that living?

ADA. But God forbid we should ever imagine that we're changing that world by living here.

DOBSON. Then there's not much point in doing this sort of thing, is there?

DAVE Not even on an individual level?

DOBSON. What do you mean, 'an individual level'?

DAVE. For God's sake stop asking us what we mean by perfectly simple phrases.

DOBSON. That's just it! They are simple phrases. Simple.

inane and irresponsible! Individual level! Have you ever taken your ideas to their logical conclusion? Well, have you? Hasn't a worker in a factory ever looked at you as though you were mad – a little potty, you know? Would you have the world do without cars, planes, electricity, houses, roads? Because *that's* the logical conclusion. If no man should be tied to turning out screws all his life, then that's what it means. No screws – no transport! No labourers – no roads! No banks or offices – no commercial market! No humdrum jobs, then no anything! There you are, solve it! Go on. Think about it. Reorganize the world so's everyone's doing a job he enjoys, so everyone's 'expressing' himself. Go on. Universal happiness? Get it!

DAVE. Now who's being wet? Happiness? (*Mimicking*) What do you mean by happiness? It's the *doing*, the doing! Do you think we care that the city was large or smelt of petrol? It was the boredom man – the sheer boredom. Nine to five! Mass production! Remember? It numbed us, made us soggy and soft. There! *That's* being soggy and soft! Happiness! My God, you cynics are the soggiest.

DOBSON. Nicely, nicely, Davey. Look, only my head and arms are left.

ADA. You sound as though you really believe in Jerusalem.

DOBSON. Shrewd girl. Of course I believe in Jerusalem, only *I* personally can't measure up to it.

ADA. Because your type always tries to win with words that's why – but you never *do* anything, you're never at peace long enough.

DOBSON (*the harshness gone*). The idyll was really broken, wasn't it? I could see it in your faces. Dave's old blood brother has sold his soul. But what do you really know about me, that you think you can say that?

DAVE. We hadn't much of a chance had we comrade? You weren't exactly inviting were you?

DOBSON. I've tried it, Dave – listen to me and go home –

I've tried it and failed. Socialism? I didn't sell out that easily. You've gone back to William Morris, but I went back to old Robert Owen. Five thousand pound my old man left me, and I blushed when I heard it. But I still hung on. It's not mine, I decided – the profits of exploitation, I said. Right! Give it back! So I worked out a plan. I found four other young men who were bright mechanics like myself and who were wasting their talents earning ten pounds a week in other men's garages, and I said 'Here's a thousand pounds for each of you – no strings, no loans, it's yours! Now let's open our own garage and exploit no one but ourselves. There's only one provision, I said, 'only one: as soon as there is an excess profit of another thousand pounds, we find someone else to inherit it and we expand that way!' See the plan? A chain of garages owned and run by the workers themselves, the real thing, and I will build it myself. Can you imagine what a bloody fool they must have thought me? Can you guess the hell of a time they had planning to buy me out? Democracy, mate? I spit it! Benevolent dictatorship for me. You want Jerusalem? Order it with an iron hand – no questions, no speeches for and against – bang! It's there! You don't understand it? You don't want it? Tough luck, comrade – your children will (*To* ADA) No peace? You're right, Mrs Simmonds. I'm dirtied up. Listen to me, Dave, and go home before you're dirtied up.

ADA. You've nearly finished that whisky Libby.

DOBSON. Is that all you can say? I've just related a modern tragedy and you're warning me against alcohol. She's a real woman this Ada of yours. A woman dirties you up as well, you know. She and the world – they change you, they bruise you, they dirty you up – between them, you'll see.

DAVE. And you call the idealist soft and flabby do you?

ADA. Let's drop it Dave – I think Libby's had enough.

DOBSON. Oh no, you mean you've had enough. The little woman senses danger – marvellous instinct for self-preservation. I suppose you two consider you are happily married for ever and ever and ever. (*Pause.*) I was married once. God knows how it happened – just after demob. I used to watch her as the weeks and months went by; I used to sit and watch fascinated and horrified as – as she changed. This was before the old man died and we both went out to work. After supper we'd wash up and she'd sit by the fire and fall asleep. Just fall asleep – like that. She might glance at a newspaper or do a bit of knitting, but nothing else – nothing that might remind me she was alive. And her face would go red in front of the fire and she'd droop around and be slovenly. And I just watched her. She chewed food all the time, you know. Don't believe me? I watched her! Chewing all the time. Even in bed, before she went to sleep – an apple or a piece of gateau – as though terrified she wasn't getting enough into her for that day. And she became so gross, so undelicate, so unfeeling about everything. All the grace she had was going, and instead there was flesh growing all around her. I used to sit and watch it grow. How does one ever know, for Christ's sake, that a woman carries the seeds of such disintegration? Then I tried what your brother wants to do – take a simple girl, a girl from an office, lively, uncluttered. Wife number two! Just about the time I inherited my five thousand pounds. A real socialist enterprise and a simple wife. Ironic, really. There was I putting a vision into practice, and there was she watching me in case I looked at other women – making me feel lecherous and guilty. She's the kind that dirties you up. There was I sharing out my wealth and there was she – always wanting to possess things, terrified of being on her own. She marries a man in order to have something to attach to herself, a possession! The man provides a home – bang! She's got another possession. *Her* furniture, *her* saucepans, *her* kitchen – bang! bang! bang! And then she has a baby – bang again! All possessions! And this is the way she grows. She grows and she grows and she grows and she takes from a man all the things she once loved him for – so that no one else can have them. Because, you see, the more she grows, ah! the more she needs to protect herself. Clever? Bloody clever! I think I hate women because they have no vision. Remember that, Davey – they haven't really got vision – only a sense of self-preservation, and you will get smaller and smaller and she will grow and grow and you will be able, to explain nothing because everything else will be a foreign language to her. You know? Those innocent I-don't-know-what-you're-talking-about eyes?

DAVE. Make an early night Libby, yes?

> DOBSON *rises, suddenly, furious at being told to go to bed. But his own terrible honesty defies him. He shrinks, looks at them for a sort of forgiveness, and then shrugging his shoulders turns and goes, taking maybe something to chew from the table.*

ADA. Do you realize he was talking about what I might become darling?

DAVE. Are you worried?

ADA. Do we really appear like that to you men?

DAVE. You *are* worried aren't you?

ADA. I suddenly feel unclean.

DAVE. A cynic works that way darling. Perhaps he's right when he says we should use him, sharpen ourself on him. I don't know what to say – the man's certainly been bruised hasn't he? Does that make him more reliable or less – I never know.

ADA. The futile pursuit of an ideal. Suddenly it all makes me sick. Like eating too many good things.

DAVE. Right! Then enough now. We're not going to be dragged into this discussion again. We are not going to go around apologizing for the way we live. Listen to people and we'll go mad. Enough now!

Someone is coming from the lane. A torchlight appears. A voice calls. It is COLONEL DEWHURST.

COLONEL. Is anyone at home? Hello there, Simmonds.

ADA. It's Dewhurst. At this hour! (*Opens door to him.*) In here Colonel. Come in.

COLONEL. Good evening.

DAVE. Good evening Colonel Dewhurst. Have a seat. Would you like some wine?

COLONEL. This is not a social visit Simmonds.

DAVE. This sounds very ominous.

ADA. Do have wine Colonel – it's very good.

COLONEL. Please, Mrs Simmonds. You're making it very difficult for me.

DAVE. Difficult?

COLONEL. I've treated you well, Simmonds, haven't I?

DAVE (*not knowing how it's coming*). Ye-es.

COLONEL. That's right, I have. Helped you when you started. Gave you advice.

DAVE. I'm very grateful Colonel, but—

COLONEL. Well, you don't show it!

DAVE. I'm sorry but I don't know what you're talking about.

COLONEL. The lino, the lino! That's what I'm talking about, and you know that's what I'm talking about. Look, Simmonds, you're an intelligent man – you're not the usual sort who works for me, and I didn't expect you to lie. Still, I didn't expect you to steal from me, but you did. Now don't waste time, just tell me and we'll see what we can do: did you or didn't you take two rolls of lino from the shed near the workshop?

DAVE. Those rolls you threw away and said were no use?

ADA. Dave—

DAVE. Darling – let *me*. No Colonel, I did not.

COLONEL. But I don't understand why you're lying. In fact

178

I don't understand you at all, Simmonds. What did you come to the country for? It's a different way of life here, y'know. They're slow people, the country people – slow, but sound. I know where I am with them, and they know their place with me. But with you I could never—

DAVE. Never get the right sort of master-servant relationship?

COLONEL. Yes, if you like. But you didn't like, did you? You spoke to me as if I were a – a—

DAVE. An equal.

COLONEL. I don't like it, Simmonds. I'm not a slave driver, but I believe each person has his place.

DAVE. You're decent like, but it's a favour like?

COLONEL. Are you talking to me about decency, Simmonds?

DAVE. You didn't come all the way up that lane just to find out whether I stole two rolls of lino did you Colonel?

ADA. For God's sake Dave—

DAVE. Now Ada!

COLONEL. Yes I did come all the way up that lane, and I'm damn well furious that I had to. Listen Simmonds, I've got to sack you, because by now all my other men know you took the rolls, and they know I know, and if I don't sack you they'll all think they can get away with pilfering. But thinking you were a decent chap, I thought I'd come here and just tell you what a fool you'd been, and discuss what we could do about it. Now I find you're a petty liar and I'm furious, and I don't care what you do. Good night.

DAVE. But you haven't even any proof – I mean—

COLONEL. You must be insane. And what's outside your back door? (*Silence.*) Well, what is it?

DAVE (*weakly*). You said you didn't want it.

COLONEL. Of course I didn't. Junk! Two and sixpence worth of junk – but that isn't the point.

ADA. What is the point Colonel?

COLONEL. You don't really know the point, do you? We

179

'ask' Simmonds: in my sort of society we ask. That's all. It's twenty-four hours' notice I'm giving, but there is no need to turn up tomorrow. (*He leaves.*)

ADA. You bring the habits of factory life with you? What got into you?

DAVE. Oh God. What a bloody fool I am.

ADA. But I don't understand. Didn't you *know* the lino was outside and that he might see it?

DAVE. I took a chance that it might be dark—

ADA. Oh my God!

DAVE (*surprised*). I feel so ashamed.

ADA. It was so humiliating – if only you'd admitted it—

DAVE. To be caught for something so petty—

ADA. To be doubly caught for lying as well.

DAVE. Jesus! I feel so ashamed.

> *For some seconds* DAVE *sits, thoroughly crushed.*
> ADA *is appalled and uncertain what to do.*

ADA. Well we're not going back to London because of this ridiculous blunder. You're so bloody soft sometimes.

DAVE. Ada I'm sorry.

ADA. You'll have to start your workshop earlier that's all.

DAVE. But we can't afford it.

ADA. Well we'll *have* to afford it. I'm *not* giving up. We'll eat less, we'll buy less, we'll do something but I'm not going away from all this. Thank God the house is still ours anyway. By Christ, Dave – your ideals have got some pretty big leaks in places haven't they?

> DAVE *is deeply hurt by this and* ADA *realizes she has struck deeply. Perhaps this is the first time she has ever hurt him so deeply. They wander round the room in silence now, clearing up the table.*

DAVE. Could you really see me leaving?

> *More silence – the battle dies in silence and the wounds heal quietly. The meal is being finally set.*

ADA. I can help mix cement for the workshop floor you

know – I've developed big muscles from drawing water up the well.

DAVE (*looks at her gratefully*). Oh God I feel such a fool.
Then after a second DAVE *lays his hands on* ADA'S
*shoulders, takes her to a chair, sits her gently on it,
places a stool under her feet, takes an olive branch
from out of the pot and, first offering it to her, lays it
on her lap. Then he looks around and finds a large
red towel which he shrouds on her head and
shoulders. Then he steps back and kneels in homage.
There he remains for a moment till gently he
laughs and gradually* ADA *laughs too. And on
their laughter—*

THE CURTAIN FALLS

SCENE 2

*Late autumn afternoon, 1953. Six years have passed.
The front wall of the barn has been raised, revealing a
furniture-maker's workshop.*

DAVE *is just stepping out of the barn carrying, triumphantly, a chair that he and* SAMMY *have just made.* SAMMY
is DAVE'S *apprentice.* DAVE *is singing (pom-pom) 'Land
of Hope and Glory' while* SAMMY *is on his knees applauding
and bowing at the spectacle. As* DAVE *majestically lays chair
on the 'horse'* SAMMY *speaks. It is fine craftsmanship.*

SAMMY. Looks as though it's sitting down don't it!

DAVE. When a chair does that, it works. (*Pause.*) But there's
something wrong with this one.

SAMMY. Shall us have it apart?

DAVE. No, no. Leave it a while. Pour us out another cuppa.
We'll look at it. (*Walks round chair.*) The legs are too big.

SAMMY. Hell! Have 'em any smaller and you'll be sitting on the floor.

DAVE. True, true. (*Thinks.*) A wrinkle! A little wrinkle! Old Dave's learnt a lot in six years. Give 'em a slight curf with the saw *in between* the joints. Won't need much. Now then, let's have a little clear up shall we? Get the glue on!

SAMMY. When's he coming to see his chair?

DAVE. Who, Selby? Shortly, shortly.

SAMMY. I don't go much on him you know. He run a seed sorting factory. Selby's seeds! Old compost! And they reckon he don't pay his men too well neither.

DAVE. Bit fly eh?

SAMMY. Yearp, fly. And he started as a farm labourer hisself look.

DAVE. Well we've agreed on a good price for the chair anyway.

SAMMY. And you mind you stick to it too. I'll sharpen your chisels. (*Does so.*)

DAVE. The boy say anything to you when you took him to school this morning?

SAMMY. He jabbers a lot don't he?

DAVE. He's like all the Kahns. A funny kid. Comes home with the strangest stories. He's a smasher. Misses his mummy though.

SAMMY. What time train is Ada catchin' from London?

DAVE. Left about twelve this morning I think.

SAMMY. You heard from her? She say how her father was?

DAVE. Not well at all, not well at all poor Harry. This is his second stroke and it seems to have knocked him quite hard. (*He is looking at the chair now.*) I don't think I will. I'll leave the seat as it is. Once you start taking off a piece here and there it makes it worse. It's not all that out of proportion. What say you bor?

SAMMY. Well listen to you then! What say you bor! A proper Norfolk article you're talking like.

DAVE. You taking the mickey out of me? (*Throws a handful of shavings over Sammy's head*.) Are you? (*Another*.) Are you? Are you? Eh?

    SAMMY *throws back shavings, at which* DAVE *cries 'War!' and picks up a stick. A fencing duel takes place* SAMMY *falls defeated*.

SAMMY. Hey pack it in ole son, Mister what's-his-name'll be here soon to have a look at this here squatting chair of his.

DAVE. Look at this mess you've made. Sweep it up at once. Untidy ole bugger.

    SAMMY *gathers shavings on his hands and knees with brush and pan. He wants to say something to* DAVE, *and is uncertain how to start*.

SAMMY. Dave, it'll be a while before Ada come won't it?

DAVE. Yes.

SAMMY. I want a little word with you then.

DAVE. Go on son. I'm listening, but I must get this ready for glueing.

SAMMY. I want to leave soon.

DAVE. That was a very short word. Leave?

SAMMY. I aren't satisfied Dave.

DAVE. Satisfied?

SAMMY. Well I don't seem to be getting anywhere then.

DAVE. But you're learning something boy, you're learnin' to do something with your hands.

SAMMY. But nothing a factory can't do just as well as what we do.

DAVE (*shocked*). Have you ever seen inside a factory? You want to stand by a machine all day? By a planer or a sander or a saw bench?

SAMMY. They change around all the time.

DAVE. Excitement! You change machines! Big difference! All your life Sammy, think of it, all your life.

SAMMY. But you get more money for it.

DAVE. That I do not have an answer to. (*Pause*.) Sammy,

remember that chair? Remember what you said about it? It looks as though it's sitting down you said. That's poetry boy, poetry! No not poetry, what am I talking about. Er – it's – it's – O Jesus how do you start explaining this thing. Look Sammy, look at this rack you made for your chisels. Not an ordinary rack, not just bits of wood nailed together, but a special one with dove-tail joints here and a mortise and tenon joint there, and look what you put on the side, remember you wanted to decorate it, so you used my carving tools and you worked out a design. For no reason at all you worked out a design on an ordinary chisel rack. But there was a reason really wasn't there? You enjoyed using those tools and making up that design. I can remember watching you – a whole afternoon you spent on it and you used up three pieces of oak before you were satisfied. Twenty-seven and six you owe me.

SAMMY. Hell, that were only messing around.

DAVE. *Not* messing around. Creating! For the sheer enjoyment of it just creating. And what about the fun we had putting up this workshop?

SAMMY. It's not that I don't enjoy myself Dave.

DAVE. But that's not all cocker. It's not only the fun or the work – it's the place. Look at it, the place where we work. The sun reaches us, we get black in the summer. And any time we're fed up we pack up and go swimming. Don't you realize what that means? There's no one climbing on our backs. Free agents Sammy boy, we enjoy our work, we like ourselves.

SAMMY. You think I don't know these things, hell Dave. But I've seen the boys in the village, I know them, they don't care about things and I see them hang around all their lives, with twopence halfpenny between them an' half a dozen dependents. But I want to get on – don't you think I ought to get on?

DAVE. A bait! A trap! Don't take any notice of that claptrap for God's sake boy. For every hundred that are lured only one makes it. One, only one. Factories? Offices? When you're in those mate you're there for good. Can't you see that? (*No answer.*) No, you can't can you? Of course you can't. Jesus, I must be mad to imagine I could fight everyone. Sammy, I'm sorry mate – I just—

   At this moment ADA *appears. She looks pale and weary.*

DAVE. Ada! Sweetheart! (*He doesn't know who to talk to first.*)

SAMMY. I'm away home to my tea now Dave. See you tomorrow. How are you Ada? (*Retires quickly.*)

DAVE. Sammy, think again boy, we'll talk some more tomorrow, we'll talk tomorrow, you hear?

ADA. What's been happening?

DAVE. He wants to leave. Work in a factory. Ada, how ill you look. (*Goes to embrace her, she takes his kiss but does not respond.*)

ADA. I met Selby in the village.

DAVE. And?

ADA. He wants to cancel the order for the chair.

DAVE. Cancel it? But it's made.

ADA. The price is too high he says.

DAVE. High? But we agreed – the bastard. That's the third person's done this on me. Blast them, all of them. Twentieth-century, short-sighted, insolent, philistine-type bastards! And the world depends upon them, you know that Ada? Oh sweetheart, what an awful welcome.

   Again he moves towards her but she moves away to sit on a stool.

What is it Ada? Why don't you let me touch you all of a sudden, so long and – O my God, it's Harry, idiot I am, I didn't ask, he's not . . .

ADA. No, he's not dead.

DAVE. Then how is he?

ADA. He was raving when I got there

DAVE. Raving? Old Harry?

ADA. The second stroke affected his brain. He was in a padded cell.

DAVE. O God, Ada—

> DAVE *stretches to her but she continues to refuse his comfort.*

ADA. He didn't recognize me at first. He was lying on his back. You know how large his eyes are. They couldn't focus on anything. He kept shouting in Yiddish, calling for his mother and his sister Cissie. Mummy told me he was talking about Russia. It seems when they first brought him into the ward he threw everything about – that's why a cell. He looked so frightened and mad, as if he were frightened of his own madness.

DAVE. But what brought it on? I mean don't the doctors know?

ADA. A clot of blood. It's reached the brain. And then he recognized me and he looked at me and I said 'Hello Daddy – it's Ada' and he started screaming in Yiddish 'Dir hasst mir, dir hasst mir, dir host mirch alle mul ger hasst!' You hate me and you've always hated me, (*She breaks down uncontrollably.*) Oh darling I haven't stopped crying and I don't understand it, I don't understand it because it's not true, it's never been true.

> DAVE *holds her tightly as she cries, and smothers her with kisses.*

DAVE. Hush darling, gently, gently. It was a sick man screaming, a sick man, hush – O good God.

> *They stand a while. Then* ADA *pulls away and starts mechanically unpacking her case.*

ADA. He smiled and kissed me a lot before I left, it was an uncanny feeling, but you know Dave (*surprised at the thought*) I feel like a murderer.

DAVE. *Ada!* You gone mad? A murderer? Stop this nonsense, you think you were responsible for his illness?

ADA (*calmly*). No, I don't think I was responsible for his illness and neither did I hate him. But perhaps I didn't tell him I loved him. Useless bloody things words are. Ronnie and his bridges! 'Words are bridges' he wrote, 'to get from one place to another.' Wait till he's older and he learns about silences – they span worlds.

DAVE. No one made any rules about it. Sometimes you use bridges. Sometimes you're silent.

ADA. What bridges? Bridges! Do you think I know what words go to make *me*? Do you think I know why I behave the way I behave? Everybody says I'm cold and hard, people want you to cry and gush over them. (*Pause.*) During the war, when you were overseas, I used to spend nights at home with Sarah and the family. There was never a great deal of money coming in and Mummy sometimes got my shopping and did my ironing. Sometimes she used to sit up late with me while I wrote to you in Ceylon, and she used to chatter away and then – fall asleep. She'd sit, in the chair, straight up, and fall asleep. And every time she did that and I looked at her face it was so sweet, so indescribably sweet – that I'd cry. There! Each time she fell asleep I'd cry. But yet I find it difficult to talk to her! So there! Explain it! Use words and explain that to me.

DAVE. What's going to happen to Sarah, Ada? Do you reckon we ought to think about returning?

ADA (*turning to him, slowly and deliberately*). Dave, listen to me. My mother is a strong woman. She was born to survive every battle that faces her. She doesn't need me. You say I'm like her? You're right. I'm also strong, I shall survive every battle that faces me too, and this place means survival for me. We – are – staying – put!

> DAVE *takes her hands and kisses them, then her lips.*
>
> A child's voice calls: 'Mummy, Ada, Mummy, Ada, Mummy, Ada!'

DAVE. It's the boy. Watch how pleased he'll be, he kept asking when you were coming. I bet you a dollar the first
thing he'll want you to do is play your game with him.

ADA. Danny?

DANNY (*off, assuming a gruff voice*). I'm Daniel the lion
killer.

ADA. You're who?

DANNY. I've come to slay your lions for you.

ADA. How much do you charge?

DAVE (*taking out his pipe*). Mothers!

DANNY. I charge sixpence a lion.

ADA. The last time I saw you you were so small, I don't know
whether I could trust you to slay my lions.

DANNY. I'm as tall as an elephant.

ADA. I can't possibly believe that. Come out and show yourself Daniel the lion killer.

DANNY. I shan't show myself until you play the game with
me.

ADA. Oh! And what is the game today Daniel?

DANNY. It is called 'Look I'm alive!'

DAVE *does a there-I-told-you-so look.*

ADA. Oh that one. All right. Are you ready?

DANNY. Yes. Now you do it with me.

Now ADA *faces us and goes through the same actions
as we must assume* DANNY *does. She starts crouched
down, with her face hidden in her arm – as in the
womb.*

ADA. Are you crouched down?

DANNY (*in his own voice*). Yes Mummy.

DAVE *pulls a face at her so she draws him into the
game too.*

ADA. Do you mind if my friend here plays Mr Life? (DAVE
tries to run away.) Dave!

DANNY. No, hurry up, I'm getting cramp.

What happens from now must have the touch of

    magic and of clowning. The day has gone and now
    the light fades slowly into evening.

DAVE (*bowing first to* ADA, *then to* DANNY). I am – (*pause; to* ADA) what's it?

ADA. You're Mr Life.

DAVE. Oh yes, Mr Life. I am Mr Life. I have spent all day making furniture and now I am going to make a human being. You are clay and I am going to make you into a human being. I am going to breathe the fire of life into you. Hissssss, Hissssss, Hissssss.

    As DAVE *breathes the fire* ADA *unfolds and rises very slowly – this is what* DANNY *is doing unseen – her eyes are closed.*

DAVE. Now you have life and you can breathe.

    ADA *breathes deeply.*

DAVE. Now I will give you sight.

    He snaps his fingers at DANNY *then at* ADA. ADA *opens her eyes. There is wonder and joy at what is revealed.*

DAVE. Now I will give you movement.

    DAVE *beckons to* DANNY *then to* ADA. ADA *raises and lowers her arms twice, moving her head from left to right at the same time, full of curiosity and excitement at what she is doing.*

DAVE. Now I will give you speech. (*He draws something unseen from his mouth and throws it to* DANNY, *then he kisses his finger and places the kiss on* ADA's *lips.*) Tell me, what does it feel like to be a human being?

DANNY (*in his gruff voice*). It's a little strange. But I'm used to it. It's very exciting.

    ADA *relaxes and becomes herself and involved in the questioning.*

ADA. Now that you have eyes and tongue to see and talk and limbs to move – move, and tell me what you see.

DANNY (*in his own voice*). Hedges!

ADA. No no Daniel. That's a name, that's not what you see.

DANNY (*in his own voice from now on*). I see thin pieces of wood. Going all over the place. With bumps on them, and thin slips of green like paper, and some funny soft stuff on them.

ADA. Now you can use names.

DANNY. They're hedges with leaves and berries.

ADA. Any colours?

DANNY. The hedges are brown, the leaves are green and the berries are red and black.

ADA (*becoming excited*). What else can you see O Daniel?

DANNY. A blue sky with white cloud.

ADA. More?

DANNY. Birds with long necks.

ADA. More?

DANNY. Green fields with brown bumps.

ADA. More?

DANNY. A red brick house and that's where I live.

ADA. Now you are a real human being Daniel who can look and think and talk and you can come out and slay the lions.

> *We hear* DANNY *run right across the back of the stage* (*past barn and hedges*) *crying*: 'I'm coming I'm coming I'm coming!' *and* ADA *crouches down with her arms outstretched to receive him as the night and—*

THE CURTAIN FALLS[1]

---

[1] The boy could perhaps rush on to the stage as the lights fade, Director's decision.

Act Three

Autumn, 1956. Three years have passed. The wall in front of the barn is lowered. No one works there now.

Two women are seated in the garden. CISSIE *and* ESTHER KAHN, *maiden aunts of* ADA. *The first is a trade unionist, the other owns a market stall.* CISSIE *is shelling peas.*

ESTHER *is peeling potatoes.*

There is a lovely light in the sky and two deck chairs near the back door. It is a warm day.

ESTHER. A guest house they call it.

CISSIE. Esther, stop grumbling – peel!

ESTHER. Three hundred ditches we had to jump over before we even reached the house – and they advertise in newspapers. For peace and quiet and a modest holiday – the Shambles. A very inviting name. Mind you, for a dirty week-end, this place – you know what I mean?

CISSIE (*not really minding*). Why must you be so bloody crude Esther?

ESTHER. What's the matter – all these years you been my sister and you don't know me yet?

CISSIE. What time does Dave come back for lunch?

ESTHER. One o'clock.

CISSIE. Ada'll come back from shopping with him, I suppose.

ESTHER. They better be on time else that dinner'll be burnt.

CISSIE. What?

ESTHER. Don't say 'what', say 'ah?' Fine bloody holiday this. Only two mad maiden aunts like us would do this. Do you realize that we haven't stopped working since we've been here? Look at that job we did yesterday. Pulling up weeds. Agricultural workers!

191

CISSIE. Stop grumbling. You know you're enjoying yourself.

ESTHER. You think they make all their other guests work like this? No wonder they get so few. Cissie – I think we should tell them.

CISSIE. What?

ESTHER. Don't say 'what', say 'ah?' We should tell them that people when they go on holiday don't like digging gardens and feeding chickens.

CISSIE. Don't be daft woman. It's only us. We spoil her. Both her and Ronnie we spoilt.

ESTHER. A guest house they call it. Not even a bleedin' flush lavatory. Just three hundred ditches.

CISSIE. Hush Esther.

ESTHER. What's the matter for Gawd's sake? You frightened someone'll hear me? (*Shouting*) *Cissie, have you stopped peaing yet?*

CISSIE. So help me you're mad.

ESTHER. I'm keeping in training. Though I must say this ain't the most inspiring place for selling underwear. I mean what do their guests do here? The only sights to see are sixty clucking hens waiting to be slaughtered – poor sods – and a two-hundred-year-old barn. A historical monument!

CISSIE. That used to be Dave's workshop.

ESTHER. What did he leave it for?

CISSIE. Ada was telling me that one day about six months ago, he built a beautiful dressing table for someone and he had a lorry come to collect it, and the driver took no care on the bumpy lane so that by the time they reached the main road they'd knocked all the corners off it. A two-hundred-pound job it was, all his own design, ruined! So he found a new workshop in the village.

ESTHER. And he still can't earn money. Poor sod. He works hard that one – and what for? For peanuts that's what for!

CISSIE. Well today may change all that.

ESTHER. You mean the loan?

CISSIE (*nodding*). If he's managed to persuade the bank to loan him money then he can buy machinery and his work'll be easier.

ESTHER. Now *that's* something I don't understand. I can remember him saying when he first moved here that he wanted to make furniture with his own hands. Now he's buying machinery, he'll be like a factory only not big enough to make their turnover. So where's the ideals gone all of a sudden?

CISSIE. Esther, you're a stall-owner, you don't understand these things.

ESTHER. All right, so I'm a coarse stall-owner. I'm a silly cow. So *I'm* a silly cow and *you're* a clever trade union organizer – you explain it to me.

CISSIE. It's all got to do with the work of another socialist furniture-maker, William Morris.

ESTHER. A yiddisha fellow?

CISSIE. He was a famous person. He used to say 'Machines are all right to relieve dull and dreary work, but man must not become a slave to them.'

ESTHER. So?

CISSIE. So Ada says Dave says if he can buy a machine to saw the wood, and another to plane it, that will save him a lot of unnecessary labour and he can still be a craftsman.

ESTHER. I'll tell you something Cissie? Our nieces and nephews are all mad. Look at Ronnie – working in a kitchen, and that silly arse has fallen in love with a waitress.

CISSIE. So what's wrong with a waitress? Beatie Bryant's a very nice girl, very active, bless her.

ESTHER. I know she's a nice girl but she doesn't know what Ronnie's saying half the time.

CISSIE. If it comes to that neither do I. You know where she comes from? About twenty miles from here. Ronnie met her when he came to work in Norwich.

CISSIE *rises and enters kitchen to put peas in pot.*
ESTHER *follows.*

ESTHER. Another wandering Jew. Another one can't settle himself. Hopping about all over the country from one job to another. I'll tell you something Cissie – it's not a joke. Ronnie worries me. He worries me because his father was just the same. You know Harry? Before he fell ill? The way he couldn't stick at one job? The same thing! All over again. It worries me.

CISSIE. Now Esther don't you ever tell him that – you hear me?

ESTHER. Me? I wouldn't say a word! But it worries me. And he wants to spread socialism. Everybody's busy with socialism. 'Aunty Esther' he says 'I've finished making speeches, I'm going to marry a simple girl and hand it all on to her.' So I says to him 'Ronnie' I says 'be careful. Don't hand it on to her *before* you're married.' The meat!

Turns to oven.

At this point ADA *and* DAVE *appear.*

ADA. What's happened to Aunty Esther?

CISSIE. It's all right darling, she's just gone to look at the meat. She always rushes like that – as if the world was on fire. What's the matter Simmonds? You look all done in.

DAVE. Bank managers. How do you talk to them?

CISSIE. Like I talk to employers when I'm negotiating a strike – as though you're doing them a favour by coming at all.

ESTHER (*coming out of the kitchen*). Fifteen more minutes and we can eat.

ADA. You're bricks, the pair of you.

ESTHER. You mean we got thick skulls?

CISSIE. Stop grumbling.

ESTHER. All she can say to me is 'Esther stop grumbling.' I'm a happy woman, let me grumble. So tell us, what happened? (*Returns to chair in garden.*)

CISSIE. Wait a minute, let me get my knitting. (*Goes to kitchen.*)

ESTHER. Can't you ever sit still and do nothing?

CISSIE. No I bloody can't. The good lord gave me hands and I like using them.

ESTHER. The good lord gave you an arse but you don't have to be sh . . .

CISSIE. *Esther!*

ESTHER. She's so squeamish your aunt.

CISSIE (*returning and sitting on deck chair*). Right, now let's hear what happened – I'm very interested.

ADA. I must go in and lay the table, I can hear from inside.

> DAVE *moves to the barn and cleans some of his tools.*

ESTHER. What's the matter with everybody? No one can sit still for five minutes. This one knits, this one must lay the table, that one mucks about with his tools—

CISSIE. He's cleaning his chisels, Esther.

ESTHER. Don't split hairs with me. It's a bleedin' conspiracy to make me feel guilty – well nuts to yers all, I'm sitting still. I'm a lady. A bleedin' civilized lady on holiday. Fan me somebody!

CISSIE. Esther, maybe the kids don't feel like joking.

ESTHER. Dave Simmonds, are you going to tell us what happened at the bank or not?

DAVE. Nothing much. He said I could have an overdraft of two hundred pounds but no loan.

ESTHER. So what you feeling unhappy for? With an overdraft you can lay down deposit on two machines and pay off over three or five years. Who buys anything outright these days anyway.

DAVE. Yeah.

CISSIE. Hey Addie – what kind of school dinners does Danny get?

ESTHER. A real grasshopper mind you've got. Can't you stick to one subject at a time?

CISSIE. Leave off Esther, can't you see the boy doesn't want to talk about it.

ADA *comes out of the kitchen. She is rubbing her hands and face on a towel very slowly. Although she looks red-eyed from washing, she really has been crying and is covering up with a wash.*

ADA. They're not bad. A little bit dull but he gets plenty of it.

ESTHER. Have you been crying Ada?

CISSIE. Leave off Esther, I tell you.

ESTHER. For crying out loud what's been happening to you two?

DAVE *looks up and sees that, in fact,* ADA *has been crying. He lays down his saw, approaches her and takes her in his arms. After a bewildered moment of looking at them and each other—*

CISSIE *and* } (*between them*). Ah Ada darling. My pet.
ESTHER } Sweetheart. Don't cry love. Ah there pop-
} pet, what is it then?

Both aunts start fussing the couple but are unable to do anything except commiserate and get in each other's way while moving around trying to get in somewhere. They cannot reach either of the two. DAVE *and* ADA *stand locked together and rocking, their own misery being the centre of the aunts' faintly comic and frustrated concern.*

CISSIE (*having tripped over* ESTHER'S *feet*). Get back to your deck chair, I'll handle this.

ESTHER. Cissie, carry on knitting and leave off. You always were heavy-handed with people.

CISSIE. That's how it should be. As soon as *you* start handling people you have them in tears.

ESTHER. And you treat every upset as though it was an industrial dispute.

ADA. Listen to those two. Anyone would think we were still fifteen.

DAVE. Feeling better sweetheart?

ADA. How can anyone feel depressed with those two old hens clucking round you.

ESTHER. Here, let me tell you about the time Ronnie made a supper of rice.

CISSIE. That's it, tell them about the time Ronnie made us a supper of rice.

DAVE. Listen to them darling, don't they sound like a music-hall act?

CISSIE. Ronnie invites himself to supper and says he wants to try out a special pork curry—

ESTHER. A very kosher dish he assures us—

CISSIE. We don't even like curry—

ESTHER. Never mind, we agree. What a mess! A whole pound of rice he puts into a saucepan and he starts to boil it – so you know what happens when you boil rice—

CISSIE. It swells!

ESTHER. The whole pound of rice began to swell. And what does he do when it reaches the top of the saucepan? He puts half of it in another saucepan and sets them both to boil. And do you think it was cooked?

CISSIE. Of course it wasn't! And the two saucepans got full again – so he gets two more saucepans and halves them again. For two hours before we got home he was cooking rice—

ESTHER. And by the time we arrived he had five saucepans and two frying pans filled with rice for a supper of three people.

Everyone is in a paroxysm of laughter until, as they emerge out of it, ESTHER *suddenly remembers—*

ESTHER. Oh yes – there's some mail for you.

DAVE. Thank God – at last!

ESTHER. At last, what?

CISSIE. We thought all you wanted was a loan.

ADA. You have to have people to buy the furniture as well you know.

CISSIE. And there's no people?

ADA. Some, but it's mostly for window sashes.

ESTHER. What's so important with the letter then?

DAVE. The letter is important because three weeks ago I had an inquiry for an originally designed suite of dining-room chairs and table and I sent in an estimate and this should be a reply. If they don't want it, it means I have to carry on doing window sashes.

ESTHER. And what's Ada crying for?

DAVE. She's having a baby.

Cries of joy and surprise and 'muzzeltov' and more fussing from the aunts.

ESTHER. So what's there to cry about? Are you sure?

ADA. Of course I'm sure you silly bitch.

ESTHER. Right, then if you don't mind I'm going to say something.

DAVE. Esther, I think we're going to mind—

ESTHER. I'm still going to say it.

ADA. Aunts, please, we're really very tired.

ESTHER. For Gawd's sake! It's not as though we're strangers. We're your aunts. All your life, till we die.

DAVE. What are you going to tell us? We're mad to stay here? Everyone's told us this. Half our battle here has been against people who for a dozen different reasons have tried to tell us we're mad.

ESTHER. Never mind about madness – but you've changed. You're not the same. Once upon a time we could talk to you. You got troubles? So tell us. What's the matter – you think we're going to laugh?

DAVE. We're tired Esther, leave us alone, yes?

ESTHER. Nice life! Lovely! It's a great pleasure knowing you! Open the letter.

DAVE. *I know* what's in the letter. Dear Mr Simmonds, after having carefully considered your designs and estimate we feel sorry to have to inform you – God! I'm learning to hate people!

ESTHER (*telling a story*). My mother loved her children. You know how I know? The way she used to cook our food. With songs. She used to hum and feed us. Sing and dress us. Coo and scold us. You could tell she loved us from the way she did things for us. You want to be a craftsman? Love us. You want to give us beautiful things? Talk to us. You think Cissie and I fight? You're wrong silly boy. She talks to me. I used to be able to watch everything on television, but she moaned so much I can't even enjoy rubbish any more. She drives me mad with her talk.

DAVE. I talked enough! You bloody Kahns you! You all talk. Sarah, Ronnie, all of you. I talked enough! I wanted to do something. Hands I've got – you see them? I wanted to do something.

ESTHER. Hands is the only thing? I'm a worker too. Haven't I worked? From selling flags at a football match to selling foam cushions in Aylesbury market. From six in the morning till six at night. From pitch to pitch, all hours, all my life! That's not work? It doesn't entitle me to a house? Or a fridge? I shouldn't buy a washing machine? How do you *measure* achievement for Christ's sake? Flower and Dean Street was a prison with iron railings, you remember? And my one ambition was to break away from that prison. 'Buy your flags' I used to yell. 'Rattles at rattling good prices' I used to try to be funny. So I sold rattles and now I've got a house. And if I'd've been pretty I'd've had a husband and children as well and they'd've got pleasure from me. Did money change me? You remember me, tell me, have I changed? I'm still the same Esther Kahn. I got no airs. No airs me. I still say the wrong things and nobody minds me. Look at me – you don't like me or something? That's all that matters. Or no, not that, not even like or dislike – do I harm you? Do I offend you? Is there something about me that offends you?

DAVE (*simply*). You haven't got a vision Esther.

ESTHER. A prophet he is!

DAVE. No! We should turn to *you* for prophecies! With your twopenny halfpenny flags and your foam cushions? With your cheap jewels, your market lies and your jerry houses?

ADA. Dave, sweetheart – there's no point – you'll only upset yourselves – and she doesn't mean—

DAVE. No, no. She can take it. Straight Jane and no nonsense she says. Let's talk back a little. I know we decided not to bother to explain but I'm fed up being on the receiving end. I'll tell them. (*To* ESTHER) Once and for all I'll tell you – you call me a prophet and laugh do you? Well I'll tell you. I *am* a prophet. Me. No one's ever heard of me and no one wants to buy my furniture but I'm a bleedin' prophet and don't anyone forget that. As little as you see me so big I am. Now you look at me. I picked up my spear and I've stuck it deep. Prophet Dave Simmonds, me. With a chisel. Dave Simmonds and Jesus Christ. Two yiddisha boys—

ESTHER. Hatred, Cissie. Look at our nephew-in-law, hatred in every spit.

DAVE. Well, what have you left me for God's sake? You want an angel in me? Ten years I spent here trying to carve out a satisfactory life for my wife and kids and on every side we've had opposition. From the cynics, the locals, the family. Everyone was choking with their experience of life and wanted to hand it on. Who came forward with a word of encouragement? Who said we maybe had a little guts? Who offered one tiny word of praise?

ESTHER. Praise pretty boy.

DAVE. Yes, praise! It would hurt you, any of you? There isn't enough generosity to spare a little pat on the back? You think we're cranks – recluses? Well, I'll surprise you, look – no long hair, no sandals. Just flesh and blood. Of course we need a little praise. (*Dips in his pocket for coins.*) Or maybe you want me to buy it from you! Like in the market! Here, two half-crowns for a half-minute of praise. I'll buy it! You can't afford to give it away? I'll pay for it! Five bob for a few kind words, saying we're not mad. Here y'are – take it! Take it!

CISSIE. There! You satisfied Esther? Now you've upset him, you happy?

ESTHER (*subdued*). I know, I know. I'm just a silly old cow. You want to build Jerusalem? Build it! Only maybe we wanted to share it with you. Now open the letter.

> Dave opens the letter, but before he has had a chance to look at it the CURTAIN comes down so that we do not know what it says.

SCENE 2

Three years later. 1959.

The Simmondses are moving out. SARAH *and* RONNIE *are there helping them. Everyone is that much older.*

SARAH *is sweeping up the kitchen.* ADA *is attending to a third baby, who is in a carry-cot up stage.* DAVE *is just taking a box off stage to where the removal lorry is waiting.* RONNIE *is beside a pile of books that are waiting to be packed away.*

But at this moment they are all listening to the radio.[1]

[1] Alternatively, the words given here as a radio announcement could be read out by Ronnie from a newspaper, in which case instead of switching off the radio at the end of the announcement Ronnie would crumple up the newspaper.

ANNOUNCER. Captain Davies, Conservative, 20,429 J. R. Dalton, Labour, 10,526. L. Shaftesbury, Liberal, 4,291. Conservative majority 9,903. The Liberal candidate forfeits his deposit. These latest results bring the Conservative majority up to 93 and will ensure the return to power in the House of Commons of the Conservative Party for a third time in succession since the end of the war. Mr Gaitskell went to Transport House this morning to confer with other Labour leaders – he looked very tired—

RONNIE (*switching off*). Well – you've chosen the right time to return anyway. You came in with them and you go out with them – whisht. (*Continues looking through books in silence.*) I'm all washed up. I don't know why the hell you asked me to help with this morbid job.

ADA. Go home then dear boy.

DAVE (*returning with an empty tea chest*). Here's the box to put the books in.

RONNIE. I said I'm all washed up. I'm complaining. (*No response.*) No one listens to me now. Funny that, everybody loo-ves me but nobody listens to me. I can't keep a job and I can't keep a girl so everyone thinks what I say doesn't count. Like they used to say of Dad. Poor old Harry – poor old Ronnie. But you forgive me my trespasses don't you Addie? Look at my sister, she's still beautiful.

DAVE. It was good of you to help us cocker.

RONNIE. *That's* all I ever get away with – gestures. You give someone a hand and they think you're a saint. Saint Ronnie Kahn.

All continue with their respective jobs. The removal is in its last stages. DAVE *is going round picking up stray tools to place in a tool box.* RONNIE *sings to himself.*

RONNIE.

Come O my love and fare ye well,
Come O my love and fare ye well,

You slighted me but I wish you well.

The winter is gone and the leaves turn green,
The winter is gone and the leaves turn green,
Your innocent face I wish I never had seen.

You realize you two that having come with explanations
you must leave with explanations.

ADA. Is anyone going to care that much Ronnie?

RONNIE. Yes, me! Jesus, one of us has got to make a success
of something. You can understand the Labour Party losing
the elections again, they change their politics like a suit
of clothing or something, but us – well you two, you put it
into practice, God knows why you lost.

ADA. Let's forget it Ronnie.

RONNIE (*jumping up*). No, don't let's forget it. You can still
change your mind. Let's unpack it all. Pay the removers
and try again. There must be something—

DAVE. Don't go on Ronnie, I keep telling you.

RONNIE. But you can't just pack up—

DAVE. I said shut up!

RONNIE.

The rope is hung and the noose hangs high
The rope is hung and the noose hangs high
An innocent man you have all sent to die.

SARAH. What is it, a funeral here?

DAVE. Any chance of a last cup of tea before we go Mum?

SARAH. Tea I can always make.

RONNIE. Tea she can always make.

There ain't a lady livin' in the land
What makes tea like my dear old mum—
No there ain't a lady livin' in the land
What—

What rhymes with 'mum'?

SARAH. Everything he makes into a joke.

DAVE. Did you ever hear what happened to Beatie Bryant, Ronnie?

RONNIE. No.

DAVE. The girl you wanted to change.

RONNIE. Change! Huh! You know what my father once said to me? 'You can't change people Ronnie' he said, 'you can only give them some love and hope they'll take it.' Well, Beatie Bryant took it but nothing seemed to happen.

DAVE. Three years is a long time to go with a girl.

RONNIE. I don't regret it. Maybe something did happen. After all little Sarah, wasn't it you who was always telling us that you don't know people without something happening?

SARAH. I'm always telling you you can't change the world on your own – only no one listens to me.

RONNIE. We carry bits and pieces of each other, like shrapnel from a war. Ada's like you Sarah, strong! I'm charming, like my father, and weak. O God! Isn't it all terribly, terribly sad. (*Suddenly*) Let's do an Israeli dance before we go – come on, let's dance. (*Starts doing a Zanny Hora on his own.*) The wandering Jews move on – bless 'em. Let there be music, let there be—

ADA. Stop clowning Ronnie, we won't be done in time.

RONNIE. Don't argue! Don't sing! Don't clown!

ADA. You don't have to do anything.

RONNIE. That's right. I don't *have* to do anything – except pack up and go home. We're none of us what you could call 'returning heroes' are we? If only we could squeeze a tiny victory out of it all. God, there must be a small victory somewhere for one of us. Maybe I was a good son eh? Before he died I used to wash Harry and shave him. It took him too long to walk so I used to carry him in my arms, like a cooing baby. Then I'd bounce him on the bed and play with him and he used to laugh, a really full laugh.

Funny that, in the last months he couldn't talk but his laughter was full. Mummy even used to try to play cards with him but he couldn't hold them. Sometimes I laid *my* head in *his* arms to make him feel he could still – (*It is too painful to continue.*) No – I don't have to do anything. Only the old worthies are left biding their time, waiting for the new generation. Look at old Mother there, like a patient old tigress – she's still waiting. Nothing surprised you did it Sarah? You still think it'll come, the great millennium?

SARAH. And you don't?

RONNIE. Well. I haven't brought it about – and they (*of* ADA *and* DAVE) haven't brought it about, and the Monty Blatts and Cissie and Esther Kahns haven't brought it about. But then Dad said it would never happen in our lifetime – 'It'll purify itself' he used to say. The difference between capitalism and socialism he used to say was that capitalism contained the seeds of its own destruction but socialism contained the seeds of its own purification. Maybe that's the victory – maybe by coming here you've purified yourselves, like Jesus in the wilderness. Yes? No? (*No response. Places last three books in box, reading titles out like a list of the dead and softly kissing each one.*) *Mother* by Maxim Gorky. *My Son, My Son* by Howard Spring. *Madame Bovary* by Gustave Flaubert. Lovely sound that – Flaubert. Ronnie de Flaubert.

DAVE. Did you ever finish your novel?

RONNIE. No.

DAVE. You've grown older in these last years, haven't you mate?

RONNIE. Yes.

ADA. I don't think there's anything more to pack away.

RONNIE (*making it up*).

Pull down the blind, put away the stars,

The lovers have left their fond house for the town,

No more leaves will be gathered again
And the last nightingales have gone.

ADA. Come on darling – put away your books and poems and let's be having you.

RONNIE. *You're* still smiling anyway.

ADA. Well, we shall be back for the summer holidays.

DAVE. Anyone would think it's your experiment that failed, you with your long face.

RONNIE. O my God, how near the knuckle that is.

SARAH. Come and have some tea and stop depressing each other.

RONNIE. And Mother says little. Quietly packs and takes her children home with her.

SARAH. I've been lonely for long enough Ronnie. A few more years and I'll be dead. I'm committing no crimes.

RONNIE. I never know whether to say at this point (*melo-dramatically*) 'we're all lonely' or not. As soon as I say something, somehow I don't believe it. Don't you find that with things? As soon as you pronounce something it doesn't seem true?

A cry of 'Any more' comes from off stage.

DAVE. The removal men are waiting. Right! Just this last case. Come on Ronnie. The rest of the stuff we'll leave for the holidays.

RONNIE. The radio too?

DAVE. No, bring the radio.

RONNIE *and* DAVE *pick up packing-case and go off.*

ADA. Let's make it quick Dave, because Danny and Jake'll be waiting up for us. (*To* SARAH) I wonder how the children'll take to London?

SARAH. Are you sure Aunty Esther met them at the station?

ADA. Yes, we had a telegram.

RONNIE *and* DAVE *return.*

RONNIE (*trying to be cheerful*). Righto me hearties. The cheerful side. Let's look at the rainbow. The silver lining.

Because remember – in the words of that immortal American prophet – (*Does an Al Jolson act.*)[1]

> Though April showers may come your way,
> They bring the flowers that bloom in May,
> So if it's raining have no regrets
> Because it isn't raining rain, you know, it's . . .

(*Gives up.*) . . . etcetera, etcetera, et bloody cetera!

DAVE. I've found a basement workshop in London and I'll set up shop there.

RONNIE (*sadly*). A basement! The man who started work singing 'Linden Lea' in the open air returns to a basement.

ADA (*after a silence*). The sun is setting Dave. We really must be moving.

DAVE (*picking up again*). Who knows, maybe people will buy furniture in town. They say you can sell them anything in London.

ADA. We've found a house – a roof over our heads.

RONNIE (*jumping on crate*). Oh bloody marvellous!

> We've got sixpence, jolly jolly sixpence
> Di dum dee da to last us all our life
> Pom-pom to lend
> And pom-pom to spend
> And pom-pom to take home to our wives
> *Hallelujah!*

ADA (*finally unnerved*). Ronnie!

DAVE (*after a second*). I can't make you out cock. Not at all I can't make you out.

RONNIE. I'm crying Dave, I'm bloody crying.

Everyone is unnerved. Everyone is feeling the reality of leaving. A long pained silence.

---

[1] Copyright 1921 by Harms Inc. used by permission. Licence for the performance of *April Showers* in any production of this play, must be obtained from Messrs. Chappell & Co. Limited, 13 St. George Street, London, W.1. for the British Commonwealth (except Canada). Harms Inc., 488 Madison Avenue, New York 22, N.Y., U.S.A. for all other countries.

DAVE. So? We're all crying. But what do you want of us. Miracles?

SARAH. I don't know what's happened to you all. Suddenly you're talking and then you're shouting and then you're crying. Suddenly you start hitting each other with words.

DAVE. Well, why must he put us on pedestals.

SARAH. You were the God that fought in Spain, Dave, remember?

DAVE (*to* RONNIE). Is that it? (*Pause.*) You can't really forgive me because I didn't speak heroically about Spain, can you?

RONNIE (*reflectively*). The war that was every man's war.

DAVE. A useless, useless bloody war because Hitler still made it, didn't he, eh? And out went six million Jews in little puffs of smoke. Am I expected to live in the glory of the nineteen thirties all my life?

SARAH. Sick . . . You're all sick or something. We won the last war didn't we? You forgotten that? We put a Labour Party in power and . . .

RONNIE (*with irony*). Oh, yes, that's right! We put a Labour Party in power. Glory! Hurrah! It wasn't such a useless war after all, was it, Mother? But what did the bleeders do, eh? They sang the Red Flag in Parliament and then started building atom bombs. Lunatics! Raving lunatics! And a whole generation of us laid down our arms and retreated into ourselves, a whole generation! But you two. I don't understand what happened to you two. I used to watch you and boast about you. Well, thank God, I thought, it works! But look at us now, now it's all of us.

SARAH. Did you expect the world to suddenly focus on them and say 'Ah, socialism is beautiful,' did you, silly boy? Since when did we preach this sort of poverty?

ADA (*turning on* SARAH). We were never poor! (*Softer to* RONNIE, *putting an arm round him*) You want reassuring, sweetheart? I'll reassure you, shall I? Remember what you said about carrying bits and pieces of each other? Well it's true . . .

RONNIE. The justifications!

ADA. Will you shut up and listen to me for Christ's sake? The kind of life we lived couldn't be a whole philosophy, could it?

RONNIE. Did it have to be?

ADA. Exactly! Did it have to be. Any more than your life with Beatie Bryant or Sarah's life with Harry. Whose life was ever a complete statement? But they're going to have to turn to us in the end, they're going to . . .

RONNIE. Are you mad? To us?

ADA. Us! Us! Because *we* do the living. We *do* the living.
    Pause.

DAVE. What do you think I am, Ronnie? You think I'm an artist's craftsman? Nothing of that sort. A designer? Not even that. Designers are ten a penny. I don't mind Ronnie – believe me I don't. (*But he does.*) I've reached the point where I can face the fact that I'm not a prophet. Once I had – I don't know – a – a moment of vision, and I yelled at your Aunty Esther that I was a prophet. A prophet! Poor woman, I don't think she understood. All I meant was I was a sort of spokesman. That's all. But it passed. Look, I'm a bright boy. There aren't many flies on me and when I was younger I was even brighter. I was interested and alive to everything, history, anthropology, philosophy, architecture – I had ideas. But not now. Not now Ronnie. I don't know – it's sort of sad this what I'm saying, it's a sad time for both of us – Ada and me – sad, yet – you know – it's not all that sad. We came here, we worked hard, we've loved every minute of it and we're still young. Did you expect anything else? You wanted us to grow to be giants, didn't you? The mighty artist craftsman! Well, now the only things that seem to matter to me are the day-to-day problems of my wife, my kids and my work. Face it – as an essential member of society I don't really count. I'm not saying I'm useless, but machinery and modern techniques have come about to make me the odd man out. Here I've been, comrade citizen, presenting my offerings and the world's rejected them. I don't count, Ronnie, and if I'm not sad about it you mustn't be either. Maybe Sarah's right, maybe you can't build on your own.

RONNIE. Remember your phrase about people choking with their own experience?

DAVE. I remember a lot of things – come on, let's go.

RONNIE. That was your apology for defeat, was it?

DAVE (*wearily*). All right, so I'm defeated. Come on, let's go—

RONNIE (*desperately*). Then where do we look for our new vision?

DAVE (*angrily*). *Don't* moan at me about visions. Don't you know they don't work? You child you – visions don't work.

RONNIE (*desperately*). They *do* work! And even if they don't work then for God's sake let's try and behave as though they do – or else nothing will work.

DAVE. Then nothing will work.

RONNIE (*too hastily*). That's cowardice!

DAVE. *You* call me a coward? You? I know your kind, you go around the world crooning about brotherhood and yet you can't even see a sordid love affair through to the end. I know your bloody kind.

ADA. Dave! This is so silly—

DAVE. Well, I've tried haven't I? Everybody wants explanations and I've tried. Do you think I want to go?

RONNIE. It wasn't sordid, you know Dave. I know I didn't see it through to the end but it wasn't sordid. Beatie Bryant could have been a poem – I gave her words – maybe she became one. But you're right. There isn't anything I've seen through to the end – maybe that's why you two were so

important to me. Isn't that curious? I say all the right
things, I think all the right things, but somewhere, some
bloody where I fail as a human being. Like my father –
just like poor old Harry. O Christ! Look at me.

> RONNIE *sinks to his knees in utter despair.*
> *They stand and watch him a while.*
> ADA *moves to him, but* DAVE *holds her back.*
> SARAH *is about to move to him but* DAVE *stops her*
> *with* 'Sarah!'
> RONNIE *is to receive no more comfort. No one can*
> *help him now but himself.*
> *Slowly, very slowly, he unfolds and they all watch*
> *him.*
> *Slowly, very slowly, he rises to his feet. He knows*
> *what is wanted of him but still cannot do more than*
> *stand in a sort of daze, looking from one to another –*
> *then—*

DAVE (*to* ADA). Darling, did you post those letters off?

ADA (*she understands that they must indicate that they are*
going on). Yes, Dave, and the estimates went off too.

DAVE. Where did you put the drawings?

ADA (*indicating brief-case*). It's all right, they're here. All
those you've decided to keep I've rolled up into one pile.
The rejects I burned last night.

DAVE. Now don't forget, first thing tomorrow morning I
must get in touch with the electricians and tell them to
start wiring the place up. Then there's that appointment
with Mrs What's-her-name for her bloody awful wardrobe.

> ADA *goes over to pick up the carry-cot.*

ADA. When we've finished unpacking tonight we'll make a
list of all the things we must do – just before we go to bed.
(*She and* DAVE *pick up cot.*) Come on Simmonds number
three, we'll soon be back again for your holidays, you can
still grow up here, yes you can, or won't *you* care?

DAVE. Ronnie – lock up and stick the key in your pocket,

there's a good lad. Sarah, you take your daughter's bags,
God knows what she's got in them.

> DAVE *picks up his brief-case and he and* ADA *go off
> with the carry-cot, still talking.*

ADA. Are you sure you turned the Calor gas off properly?

DAVE. Positive. Now look darling – you mustn't let me forget to phone those electricians – Hey! Did we pack my
drawing boards away?

ADA. Yes, yes, Simmonds. In those first boxes, don't you
remember?

DAVE. Funny, I don't remember . . .

ADA (*to* SARAH *and* RONNIE). Come on, you two, the men
are waiting.

> *They have gone off by now.* RONNIE *has locked the
> door and* SARAH *is waiting for him. He takes one of
> the baskets from her and puts an arm on her
> shoulder.*

RONNIE. Well Sarah – your children are coming home now.

SARAH. You finished crying, you fool you?

RONNIE. Cry? We must be bloody mad to cry, Mother.

> SARAH *goes off leaving* RONNIE *to linger and
> glance once more around. Suddenly his eye catches
> a stone, which he picks up and throws high into the
> air. He watches, and waits till it falls. Then he cups
> his hands to his mouth and yells to the sky with
> bitterness and some venom—*

RONNIE. We – must – be – bloody – mad – to cry!

> *The stage is empty.*
> *Soon we hear the sound of the lorry revving up and
> moving off.*
> *A last silence.*
> *Then—*

A LAST SLOW CURTAIN

Introduction and Notes

References in *italics* are to events repo

Political Events	Chicken Soup with Barley
1936 Mosley's British Union of Fascists' march through East End called off (The Battle of Cable Street)	Kahns and their friends jubilant over Communist victory over Fascists in East End *Dave leaves for Spain* *Dave called up, marries Ada*
1939 Outbreak of Second World War	
1945 End of Second World War	
1945 Labour Government under Attlee	Harry's first stroke *Ronnie leaves school*
1947	Ronnie working in London bookshop
1951 Conservative Government under Churchill	
1953 Death of Stalin	
1955 Conservative Government under Eden	Harry senile *Ronnie in Paris learning chef's trade*
1956 Hungarian uprising crushed by Khrushchev	Ronnie returns from Paris
1958	
1959 Conservative Government under Macmillan	*Death of Harry*

than to actual happenings in the plays.

Roots	*I'm Talking About Jerusalem*
	Dave and Ada Simmonds move to Norfolk. Dave starts work on Colonel Dewhurst's estate as a carpenter Ada pregnant with Daniel Libby Dobson visits them Dave loses his job
	Dave making furniture Sam, his apprentice, leaves *Harry's second stroke*
	Cissie and Esther visit Dave's business failing *While working as a cook in Norwich, Ronnie meets Beatie Bryant, a waitress*
Beatie Bryant visits her family in Norfolk. Ronnie is expected to visit them, but instead brings their three-year-long affair to an end by letter	
	Dave realises his limitations The Simmonds return to London

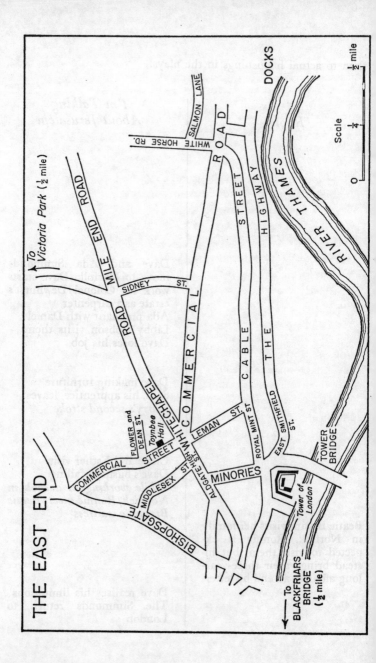

THE EAST END

Introduction

Before we look at the three plays as dramatic texts, we must
glance at their author. It is always distorting to stress too
firmly the links between a literary work and the life of its
creator, for it tempts the reader to forget that a play or novel
should speak for itself, and to hear every voice as the author's
own. We must, therefore, not read the plays as though they
were a dramatized diary, but they, together with *The
Kitchen* (first version 1958, revised 1961) and *Chips with
Everything* (1962), bear the mark of personal experience. All
five plays were written before Arnold Wesker was thirty and
all five are rooted in the author's own life. Clearly no-one
who had not worked in the kitchen of a restaurant could
evoke its pace, its chaos and its ritual as surely as Mr Wesker
does in *The Kitchen*. In fact he worked in kitchens for four
years, in Norwich, Paris and London. *Chips with Everything*
takes place on an R.A.F. 'square-bashing' camp, and it is
written with first-hand knowledge of National Service.

Mr Wesker's East End and his Norfolk are as real as his
kitchen or Royal Air Force billet. He is a highly personal
dramatist and we are aware thoughout *Chicken Soup with
Barley* that the author is Jewish and comes from the East
End, where no such thought would be relevant to the plays
of Harold Pinter, Mr Wesker's contemporary who comes
from a similar background. The plays are infused with the
Jewish sense of apartness, which leads to a passionate identi-
fication with the cause of the dispossessed and exploited. We
are also given in the character of Sarah a strong sense of that
matriarchy which many find typical of Jewish family life. It
is worth emphasizing that anti-Semitism at a private level is
no concern of the author's, however.

Arnold Wesker was born in 1932. His father was a refugee

from Russia, his mother from Hungary. The anti-Semitic 'pogroms' in Eastern Europe brought many such refugees to the East End of London. Since Yiddish was usually their first language and English only their third, such expatriates spoke a bastard tongue, and this Wesker has reproduced in the inversions, the subtly misquoted clichés and the melodic element in the speech of Harry and Sarah. (It is incidentally interesting that Sarah's English becomes more correct and less idiosyncratic in the later scenes of *Chicken Soup with Barley* and *I'm Talking about Jerusalem*, i.e., twenty years after the trilogy opens). Like Ronnie Kahn, Mr Wesker sampled a variety of jobs on leaving school. He worked as a plumber's mate, a kitchen porter, a bookshop assistant. After two years' training as a pastry cook in London, and six months as a chef in Paris, he went to the London School of Film Technique and it was there that he wrote *Chicken Soup with Barley* in 1957. It was first performed in July 1958 at the Belgrade Theatre in Coventry. *Roots* had its first performance there almost a year later, and *I'm Talking about Jerusalem* in April 1960. In the summer of that year all three plays were performed in repertory at the Royal Court Theatre in London, and in the same year were published in a single volume, so that the pattern of the trilogy was clear. They were followed by the simultaneous London presentation of *The Kitchen* as a play and a film.

The Kitchen is an orchestral play and the tempo builds up to the highest pitch. The kitchen passes gradually from relative inactivity to a frenetic battlefield as the restaurant off-stage fills with lunch-time guests. It is a virtuoso piece, full of technical interest, and the kitchen is intended as a microcosm of a grasping society.

Chips with Everything shows us how various recruits react to R.A.F. discipline, and it returns to the theme of class. Here, as in *Roots,* the author is conjuring the working-class to keep its integrity uncorrupted by ties from above. The ritual element is again strong, and one scene consists of a balletic raid on the camp's coke dump by the freezing recruits. The final scene of this play is a parade, where the bandsmen and marching men once more have the quality of a ritual.

Mr Wesker's move away from naturalism is apparent even within the trilogy. The scene that ends Act Two of *I'm Talking about Jerusalem* 'must have the touch of magic and of clowning'. It is part miracle play and part pantomime. Wesker is deliberately striving for a dramatic effect beyond that of the rest of the play. In purely technical terms, we may see such an interlude as the fruit of the author's desire to experiment in stage technique. More important, however, is the reliance on the stage producer that is implicit in the writing of such a scene and in much of *Chips with Everything*. Where everything is stated the director interprets; where the bare words tell little, the director creates.

II BACKGROUND

The world of *Roots* is self-contained, and completely rural. The local town figures not as some centre of civilization, but merely as the home of the football team, Norwich City. The Bryants live in isolated hamlets and their society is feudal. Mr Bryant may not be legally a serf, but he is totally subjected to the law of squire. He accepts without question Mr Healey's decision that after eighteen years work on the farm he should now be put on casual labour and half wages. When the word Union comes up, Beatie demands a stop to unjust sackings, but her father dismally accepts that nothing can be done. The farm life is so totally conservative and circumscribed that the Bryant family could, *mutatis mutandis*, be translated to the nineteenth century. Beatie represents today, her family epitomises yesterday. The Bryants are closed to new ideas but open to new gimmicks. Their very isolation makes them pathetically vulnerable. They are like an obsolescent animal susceptible to every contemporary disease: pop-music, exploitation through advertising, distorting propaganda. The 'mystic communion with nature' for which Dave and Ada strive in *I'm Talking about Jerusalem*, is revealed by Mr Wesker as a life with no mystery and no communication. His recipe, as given by Beatie, is socialism. The Bryants must believe they count, must make a stand against injustice, backwardness and exploitation.

Roots allows us a veiled political message in its last moments; *Chicken Soup with Barley* throws us into a political battle from its first line.

The so-called 'Battle of Cable Street' of October 1936 that plays so important a part in Act 1 of the play is a model of the world's political divisions. Sir Oswald Mosley's British Union of Fascists had become a party of violence. Mosley is the son of a Baronet, and by this time had been a Conservative member of parliament and a Labour Minister. He had left the Labour Party over their failure to solve the issue of unemployment, and had formed his own party, under the influence of Mussolini and Hitler. These two Fascist dictators had swept to power through a ruthless grappling with unsolved economic problems. They believed that Government must be all powerful, which in fact meant that power was centralized in the hands of a dictator. The movement was nationalist, and highly military. Violence broke out at many of the Fascists' meetings. The party was to be Mosley's 'instrument of steel' that would bring a new and Utopian Society to England. This idealism was accompanied by violent anti-Semitic and anti-Communist outbursts. Mosley felt that the country was a prey to the Red threat—creeping international Communism which would destroy liberty and property. Fascists held that Communism emanated from Russia where it had reigned for twenty years, and that it was financed by rich Jewish business interests. As country after country had persecuted and expelled its Jews they had become scattered across the face of the world. Nationalist movements could not forgive them the international links which they enjoyed. The Jewish businessman'could speak to his opposite number in the same language (both literally and metaphorically). It was felt that Jews controlled too much, and the Fascist movements exploited this suppressed jealousy. Hitler's violent revenge against Jewry took the form of concentration camps and the murder of millions of innocents. Mosley's anti-Semitism took the form of whipping up racialist feeling, particularly in the East End. Jews from Eastern Europe, such as Sarah and Harry Kahn, had poured as exiles into this area at the turn of the century. They spoke Yiddish, they formed a community of their own, and they appeared to make money. The Jews were resented by the native East Ender, and Mosley could harness this resentment. Some of the Jewish families had brought Communist beliefs with them, for they had fled just as Russia was waking from feudal sleep and revolution was being born. Families who were Communist and Jewish like the Kahns were doubly threatened by Mosley's political demonstration on their doorsteps. In the Battle of Cable Street, they fought back and eventually the police had to ask Mosley to disband his men. The victory seemed won, although the Fascists counter-attacked a week later in the 'Mile End Road Pogrom', when they threw several people through windows and attacked Jewish property. The Fascists' chief strength was their organization. The East End, a warren of small businesses, was not organized. Hence the Trade Unions could never be strong, as Cissie's eternal battle testifies. Moreover, the traditional Jewish unit is the family, not the wider social group. But Sarah is a fighter and enjoys every moment of the campaign.

The Battle of Cable Street is important to the Kahns and

to Mr Wesker not only for its own sake but because it is a small skirmish in two major battles, the Spanish Civil War and the Second World War.

The Spanish Civil War which broke out in 1936 killed over a million Spaniards and crippled the country, but its importance is not merely Spanish. The Spanish Republican Government had tried to bring reforms to a country which was desperately backward, to attack the archaic civil service, the feudalism, and the supremacy of the Church. The Nationalists, led by General Franco, rebelled against this government, and his fight was backed by Church and Army. The Republican cause excited enormous sympathy abroad. Communists felt sympathetic; Russia gave support. When the International Brigades were formed in Paris in the autumn of 1936, many Party members volunteered for the cause. Here was a clear issue, the Left wing locked in struggle with the Right; Communism versus Capitalism. That the Nationalists' politics were basically Fascist can hardly be denied. They were supported by Hitler's Nazi Party and by Mussolini. The government which emerged victorious from the War and has ruled Spain ever since is based on a dictatorship by General Franco, which depends on suppression both of unions and of the liberty of the press: a rule of the military and the police.

Small wonder that the Republican cause involved Communist and more moderate Left wing parties alike. Liberty, the working class and progress were at stake. Many felt like Dave that the war was a crusade. A number of English writers fought at or at least visited the front: Auden, Orwell, Day Lewis. Britain remained politically neutral but many intellectuals and politicians were committed. The Kahns were deeply involved. Dave was their champion in the crusade, but many other friends and acquaintances are mentioned by name. This was no remote war; it was a personal affair.

Dave expresses the disillusion which later on was felt by many. The Republican cause splintered as one political group squabbled with another. The political distinctions between the various groups may seem slight but there was acrimonious rivalry between so-called allies. The Republicans were beaten in 1939 and Dave with all his contemporaries was almost immediately plunged into the Second World War.

The Battle of Cable Street is also an anticipation of Hitler's War and here lay its second challenge to the Kahns. Mosley's Fascist Party had been founded in 1932, the year before Adolf Hitler became Chancellor of the German Third Reich. Hitler's Nazi party was rabidly racial, and Jewish persecution followed close on its coming to power. Soon Jewish refugees were seeking shelter in countries beyond the German frontiers. To the Kahns, who had themselves been refugees, the situation was all to familiar. The Jews threatened the purity of the German race. Although the nations could not know that the Jews would suffer in their millions in the gas chambers of the Second World War, Europe already showed enough signs of anti-Semitism for the Battle of Cable Street to seem important.

Hitler's power grew and in the two years immediately preceding the outbreak of the Second World War in 1939 he annexed Austria, Czechoslovakia and Poland in turn. England could preserve her uneasy neutrality in the Spanish Civil War, but now she was forced into war with Germany. The Nazi-Soviet pact of 1939 shocked all Communist sympathizers among the Allies. Russia—'our one-sixth of the world' as Monty Blatt calls it, the home of three-million Jews, had made a pact with the Devil, the sworn enemy of Jew and Communist. When Hitler attacked Russia in 1941 Stalin became an Ally, and with Japan's attack on Pearl Harbour, and the entry of America into the war, the whole world was under arms.

The end of the war held two promises for the British Left. They had fought alongside the Russians to a victory over Fascism. Franco's Spain had prospered on neutrality during the war, but Hitler and Mussolini were dead. Internationally the Left was respectable. At home, peace brought a Labour Government, with its assurance of nationalization, social security and fair shares.

Neither promise was kept. The Kahns were let down. The Labour Government 'sang the Red Flag in parliament' and then started building atom bombs; but now the Soviet Union had become the enemy. Social reform was slow and incomplete. The Labour Party failed to obtain a working majority at the next election, and 1951 saw the first of a series of Conservative Governments. Faith in Russia lived longer, but after the death of Stalin in 1953 it became clear to the Left that he had been as ruthless a dictator as his wartime opponent. Particularly shocking to Ronnie Kahn is the news of the anti-Jewish purges under Stalin. The final disillusion came to him as to many European communists when the Hungarian Revolution of 1956 was suppressed.

By 1959, when *I'm Talking about Jerusalem* comes to an end, the pre-war heroic tradition of Communism is dead. Only Sarah continues to fight the battle without realizing that the battleground has shifted and that the enemy has changed his face. Although there is still much that the Left can give to society (in spite of increased social securities and benefits), the present-day Communist in the West is no longer a missionary in a benighted land; he is a sympathizer with an alien power bloc—a mere fellow-traveller.

III THE PRINCIPAL CHARACTERS

At a first reading these plays may seem static and untidy by turns. Nothing very much happens. If we attempt a summary of the plots, we are left with remarkably little. A glance at the time-chart (p. 214) will confirm this. In *Chicken Soup with Barley*, leaving aside the stages of Harry's decline, all that *happens* is that a number of characters are involved in scuffles arising from a political demonstration (which takes place off stage), that Ronnie takes a job in a bookshop, and that Ronnie returns from Paris. There are also visits from neighbours, friends and family. Dave's part in the wars, his marriage, and Ronnie's departure for Paris are all reported by another character before or after the event. Time passes, and is seen to pass. The plays, then, are hardly dramas of events. They are first concerned with human character and ideas; the principal characters being Sarah, Beatie and Ronnie, and Dave and Ada.

Sarah Kahn

Sarah, for all her limitations, is a complete human being. She fights the Left-wing battle, she brings up her children, she struggles against Harry's weakness and withdrawal. Throughout, her confidence is unshaken. She is constant and loyal as a party member, as a mother and as a wife. If circumstance forces her to accept what is at variance with her own cherished beliefs, she has the courage to endure it. Eventually she is unable to see that political problems are not as clearly defined as they were in the early years. With the passing of time she becomes blind to political realities, but never allows herself or her family to indulge in private delusion. The sole person for whom she is a comforter is Ronnie and, as the last act of *I'm Talking about Jerusalem* shows, she can only really help *him* when her maternal sympathy is withheld: 'No-one can help him now but himself'. She can spare little sympathy for Harry. They cannot meet on equal, adult terms. Harry, a mother's son, is driven in upon himself by Sarah's nagging, but he keeps his private world intact, even though this amounts to no more than petty deceit and rebellion. Sarah always acts without thought, while for Harry thought is a substitute for action. His shiftlessness provokes Sarah's frustration and rage, which drive him deeper into lethargy. The wife and her husband become a parody of mother and child. Sarah must nurse the patient she despises, while Harry, cruelly dependent, can no longer rebel. Harry, in saying to Ronnie, 'You can't alter people . . . You can only give them some love and hope they'll take it' is thinking chiefly of Sarah and the life-long struggle between them which defeats them both.

Sarah's instincts may be sure, but her thoughts are invariably muddled. She has no grasp of the progress of events. Such niceties she leaves to others; they are insignificant compared to the bedrock of her faith. This fierce simplicity leaves her unprepared when others come to terms with the very different circumstances of the post-war world, leaving her behind; at forty-seven she is the older generation. When Ada at the age of twenty-five reaches the conclusion that Communism is dead, and that socialism can only be lived at the personal level, her mother protests: '. . . we shouldn't care any more? We must all run away?' When Sarah realizes that her friends Monty and Bessie Blatt have left Communism behind them, she reproaches Bessie with: 'Politics is living'; but Monty comments on Sarah's naivety: '. . . she has one fault. For her the world is black and white . . . She can't see people in the round . . . She's never trusted any of them (those in power of any sort), always fighting them. It was all so simple . . . Someone told her socialism was happiness so she joined the Party'. Sarah cannot refine upon this simple belief, so that when she is nearing sixty we find Ronnie with the ideals he was brought up to tumbling about his ears, saying to his mother: 'You're a pathological case . . . You're still a *communist*!'; and Sarah protests that socalism has been the ideal she has lived for, and why should she all at once cut herself off from it? Her last words to Ronnie at the end of *Chicken Soup with Barley* are 'Ronnie, if you don't care you'll die'. This is Sarah's creed; total involvement with the human beings around you carried to its logical conclusion—the brotherhood of man—socialism. For anyone to forswear this principle is for that person to die, as Harry has died. Sarah is frightened that Ada and Dave have forgotten to care when they bury themselves in Norfolk: 'What's wrong with socialism that you have to run to an ivory tower? . . . What's socialism without human beings?'; and she is more frightened still when Ronnie suffers the negation of disillusion, for she sees him give up the struggle just as Harry did. But Ronnie does finally carry with him his mother's concern, when his own responsibility for Beatie Bryant is awakened. And though that affair lasts only for three years and Ronnie feels that in the last analysis he failed to see it through, he does face the equation (at the end of *I'm Talking about Jerusalem*) that not to care is to fail as a human being and it was Sarah who sowed the seeds of this realization in Ronnie.

Sarah's gospel of love brings out the dissident in both her children. Ada, once she is married, has continually to assert her independence by reminding Sarah that she has a home and a mind of her own. Ronnie's aimlessness and stubbornness persist in spite of his mother's wishes. But ultimately the Kahns cannot resist Sarah's warmth and vitality—it draws them together, and produces a particular brand of happiness which neither Ada nor Ronnie will ever find outside her company. As Monty says: 'The only thing that mattered was to be happy and to eat'. Monty and Bessie arrive from Manchester—at once Sarah gets the kettle on. Ada comes in for an evening—'Supper will soon be ready . . . Barley Soup . . .' When Ronnie returns from Paris and begins to tell Sarah how hateful is the prospect of working life, her immediate reaction is: 'I'll make you some tea. Are you hungry?' But Ronnie recognizes the offering of food as a symbol of that family happiness and solidarity which must not be questioned: the ritual of eating is ordained by the mother as a sign that she is the fount and origin of good things and good times, and acts as a charm against discord or the mutual facing of unpleasant truths. So Ronnie rejects the food, and accuses his mother: 'You didn't tell me there were any doubts'. Here lies the clue to the symbolism of the title 'Chicken Soup with Barley'; it is a way of saying, 'This is Sarah's play'. And in *I'm Talking about Jerusalem* we see even more clearly how much Sarah is hurt by Ada's putting herself out of reach, a hundred miles away. The gesture of bringing Chicken Soup in bottles down from London has a quality of deliberate magic about it: it is telling Ada and Ronnie not to forget their mother, to remember their first and (if the mother could make it so) only family.

Beatie Bryant

If Sarah Kahn is cast in the mould by the age of thirty-seven, Beatie Bryant is at the age of twenty-two shapeless clay. She has not an idea or belief that she can call her own —all her notions about life have been taken on second-hand from Ronnie Kahn, who has been her lover for three years. Beatie has an appetite for life, a bubbling gaiety, and considerable resilience. She is sensual, optimistic, childlike. She has all the frankness and candour of the Bryants, but she contrasts with the rest of her family in wanting to enlarge her experience of life. Yet her energies are impulsive, un-coordinated, and needing direction. What Ronnie gave her in the three years that immediately precede the opening of *Roots* was the desire to question, to evaluate, and to discuss problems. That her time with Ronnie was of life-changing importance to her is shown by her eagerness to share her knowledge of him with her family—hence her continual quoting of him. If she is to make conversation, she cannot get far before Ronnie's words supplant her own. She is deeply in love with him, but she knows that she is out of her

depth. She struggles to be a match for him (the comic con-
cealed behind the *Manchester Guardian*[1] shows how hard a
struggle it is), because he has shown her the limitations of
her earlier life. She has moved on; her family have remained
static. Beatie is converted, and she cannot relapse. Her sister
Jenny sees that the new life does not come naturally; 'You
don't seem like you're going to be happy then'. But Beatie
can only reply, 'I couldn't have any other life now'. Her
curiosity has been distilled and concentrated into the vision
which Ronnie articulates for her, and to which her nature
responds so eagerly: 'God, . . . we could all be so much more
happy and alive!'

   Beatie and Ronnie are together against all the odds. If
Ronnie had arrived as expected, the most Beatie could hope
for from her family would be baffled tolerance; but the evidence is that the Bryants would greet Ronnie with silence—
their only powerful weapon. The Kahns never greet anything with silence, and from isolated remarks it seems clear
that Beatie was regarded as one of Ronnie's failures. Dave
Simmonds probably speaks for all the Kahns when he dis-
misses their relationship as 'a sordid love affair'. Ronnie
defends it, but never knows its effect upon Beatie: she 'could
have been a poem—I gave her words—maybe she became
one'. It is the teacher speaking, and the irony is that it is
only when Beatie forgets her rote-learning that she finds her
own voice. With Ronnie, Beatie would have remained the
eternal disciple, whose faith would always have resided in
him and never in herself. When Ronnie brings the affair to
an abrupt end, Beatie, who has been an emotional and
mental parasite, realizes her own rootlessness. She cannot
finally accept her mother's sententious taunt—'The apple
don't fall far from the tree'. She is *not* back at their level,
'stubborn, empty, wi' no tools for livin''. Ronnie has left her
the tool of words, of communication, and it is in the confi-

[1] See note on p. 253.

dence which this brings her that she can put down roots of her own.

Her family remain quite happy as they are. With gossip to fill the mind and food to fill the belly, they see no cause to change. But Beatie is growing before her own eyes, and she desperately needs words to give her the shape and knowledge of the stages of her growth. Her family cannot understand her, let alone give her any help. 'D'you hear that? D'you hear it? . . . I'm talking . . . I'm beginning, on my own two feet—I'm beginning . . .' The spectacle of Beatie's birth as a person is quite beyond the rest of her family—who sit down at the table and start to eat.

Ronnie Kahn

We have argued that *Chicken Soup with Barley* is Sarah's play, and *Roots* without question belongs to Beatie. The Trilogy is Ronnie's. He is the only character whose part is integral to all three plays. In Act 2 of *Chicken Soup with Barley* we first meet Ronnie at the age of fifteen, in his last year of school. He is already a young communist, working for the party, and shares his mother's dismay at Ada's disenchantment with political activity. Ada and Dave inspired him with the left-wing ideal in the first place, and the success or failure of their lives as socialists is of the greatest importance to him. He is a passionate talker, and a humorist rather than a wit. His humour and his ability to take a detached, ironical look at himself save him from overintensity. His wayward ebullience in this period is seen most clearly in the first act of *I'm Talking about Jerusalem*, when he and Sarah go to Norfolk to help Dave and Ada move in to their cottage. He is immensely excited by the life that Dave and Ada have chosen, and longs for it to be a success, for that would be for him a proof of socialism. As he says to them: 'The world will watch you'.

A year later, 1947, Ronnie is working in a bookshop. He will write—he calls himself a socialist poet, 'young, good-looking, hopeful, talented . . . hopeful, anyway'. He finds the spectacle of his father's failure pathetic and a little frightening. He knows how unhappy Harry is, yet he has little sympathy with his weakness, and like Sarah is impatient with it. He finds it hard to be close to his father because he knows that he himself contains the seeds of a similar spiritual decline—like Harry, he sees clearly his own predicament, without being able to do anything about it (see p. 49).

When we next see Ronnie, in the last act of *Chicken Soup with Barley,* he is twenty-five, and has just returned from Paris after a spell in a kitchen. The kitchen was to him an awful warning of the dehumanizing effect that this kind of work can have on a person. He now sees employment as a gigantic swindle which takes the whole joy out of life and gives you at most a paltry sum of money saved at the end of it. But worse than this is his wretchedness at finding that the socialist ideal is not the answer to the world's problems, which are too complex to admit a clear-cut solution. Russia has proved itself the tyrant by crushing the Hungarian revolt; his relations—even Dave and Ada—have given up the fight; the language of politics has become meaningless. Ronnie is ready to give up the struggle, as his father did before him. Because his disillusion is so painful he blames his mother for it, for she had passed on to him the beliefs which have now collapsed for him. Sarah rallies against his pessimism, and tells him that he must care—if he doesn't care he will die; as long as there are human beings there will always be the idea of brotherhood. Ronnie now gets a job as a cook in Norwich, where he meets Beatie, and then moves to London. All that we learn of him during this period (1956-1958) we hear from Beatie in *Roots.* His despair is over, but it has left behind it a scepticism about the efficacy of action. He no longer works for the party—he *talks* politics. He is writing again, and he is fostering his natural love for art and music. His concern is for humanity, and we feel that he would now put human beings before politics. We gain from Beatie the picture of a young man who is fighting the sordid commercial world which forces him to earn a living at a job he detests, and which offers such a mockery of education to most of its young that twenty-year-olds would rather read a comic than a serious newspaper and would rather exchange gossip than ideas. He is fighting the purveyors of the third-rate, in music, in art, and in ideas. He has evolved a belief in private joy and endeavour which must be shared with other people and passed on to them. In this sense Beatie is his challenge and opportunity. He has a chance with her to test his theory of private socialism; she is his first disciple, yet he never knows how apt and triumphant a pupil Beatie proves to be.

Ronnie passes on his ideas to Beatie, but it is from Dave and Ada that he draws his inspiration. He admires Dave for two things: Dave fought in Spain, and Dave is his own boss, doing the work he loves. Now that Ronnie has tempered his belief in a political solution to the world's ills with an ideal at once more humane and more personal, he can take positive pride and hope in Dave's life. Although *I'm Talking about Jerusalem* is the story of Dave and Ada, Ronnie is with them, aged fifteen, when they move in to their cottage, and he helps them with the move back to London thirteen years later, at the age of twenty-eight. Throughout this play we sense Ronnie's passionate reliance upon the ideal life that Dave and Ada are leading, so that when Dave fails we feel that it is Ronnie's own tragedy. During the removal he is overwrought, hysterical almost. His exaggerated and posturing behaviour is a desperate attempt to keep down his overwhelming sense of disappointment. Finally, 'I'm crying, Dave, I'm bloody crying' brings his feelings into the open.

He realizes that his hopes for Dave and Ada were vicarious hopes. He is wishing them to succeed because they justify to him his best ideas. He himself has failed in jobs and in love seeing neither through to the end, but he could always comfort himself that his thoughts upon how life should be lived were good thoughts, with Dave and Ada a living proof of their validity. Now he is on his own, and must justify *himself*. The constant fear of ending as his father had done he seems finally, with enormous effort, to put behind him. His self-pity gone, he shouts to the sky: 'We must be bloody mad to cry!' Like Beatie, Ronnie finds strength in desolation.

Dave and Ada Simmonds

The war persuaded Dave that international socialism was an illusion and that he and Ada must live their politics at an individual level. As his relatives and Libby Dobson so firmly point out, his disillusionment with an industrial society leads to a negative gesture, the putting back of the clock to nineteenth century socialist experiments. 'The city is human beings. What's socialism without human beings?' challenges Sarah. 'Nothing's wrong with socialism, Sarah, only we want to live it—not talk about it'. For Dave the ten years between 1936 and 1946 are unbridgeable. By volunteering for the International Brigade in Spain, he was talking and living Socialism. A world war has made such idealism hopelessly remote. It has soured Dave and tired him and has sent him into another idealism, only 'it's soft and flabby', far more out of date than the crusading spirit of ten years ago. Dave and Ada's experiment is impractical because it is entirely unrelated to anyone else. In Act 2, Scene 1 of *Chicken Soup with Barley*, Ada turns on her mother and father: 'You have *never* cried against the jungle of an industrial society. You've never wanted to destroy its *values*—simply to own them yourselves'. Her fury suggests that she and Dave are not merely being negative, but want to replace the wrong values with the right. Twelve months after their move to Norfolk, however, Dave denies any sense of mission.

> Libby: You can't change the world because it smells of petrol.
> Dave: Who's talking about changing the world?

Later, he becomes an employer; he is powerless to fight for his apprentice's soul against the lure of money and factory. Socialism ebbs sadly, the Youth Hostel becomes an unsuccessful guest house. Dave as a craftsman furniture maker is not free of commercialism, he is the victim of rich capitalist customers whose bad taste he has to satisfy. When he cries: 'God! I'm learning to hate people!' he is already admitting spiritual defeat, even though the retreat from the country does not come for another three years. Dave is defeated by hatred, where Harry was beaten by his own indifference.

IV THE PLAYS

While each of these plays is a dramatic entity, developing its own theme around a central character, the plays make their fullest impact when seen as a whole. Mr Wesker calls these three plays a trilogy. To the Greeks, 'trilogy' meant a succession of three tragedies on a single subject. The *Oresteia* of Aeschylus is a trilogy, 'Agamemnon', 'Choephoroe', and 'Eumenides'. Each is self-sufficient, but each is the richer for knowledge of the whole. Mr Wesker's trilogy makes similar assumptions. We learn much of Ronnie Kahn from and through Beatie Bryant in *Roots,* but it gives a different light to our enjoyment of *Roots* if we already know Ronnie's story and the nature of his ideals which are given us in *Chicken Soup with Barley* and *I'm Talking about Jerusalem.* Similarly, Ada Simmonds's description of her father Harry's second stroke in *I'm Talking about Jerusalem* becomes more moving and significant if we have already gained the experience of Harry's first stroke, and of the senile incontinence which follows his second stroke, from *Chicken Soup with Barley*. In a sense these plays are more closely knit than any Greek trilogy, for while in the Greek trilogy the plays are in chronological sequence, these plays overlap in time. Passing references to Dave and Ada Simmonds's life in Norfolk occur in *Chicken Soup with Barley*, but it is *I'm Talking about Jerusalem* which tells their story, and in turn fills the gap left in *Chicken Soup with Barley* by giving the account of Harry's second stroke. If you look at the time-chart on p. 214 you will readily see the extent to which these plays cover the same ground; *Roots* is only an apparent exception, for Ronnie's story is relevant to this play, as it is through Ronnie's influence that Beatie attains self-discovery.

These plays are not tragedies however, in the Greek sense. Their characters are *not* trapped by the progress of events larger than themselves, nor are they called upon to serve the will of Fate or God. Mr Wesker's characters—self-determining human beings—act out their own salvation. Sarah has *chosen* Communism, the Left-wing struggle, but no Olympian figure forces her to choose *between* her political faith and, say, her husband. Ronnie makes the decision to bring his three-year long affair with Beatie to an end, but the nature of his decision is hardly tragic nor is its effect on her tragic: they were together for a time, and a short absence gave Ronnie the chance to see that they would never know each other or share the same beliefs.

Having said that these plays are not in the strict sense tragedies, we must emphasize that they are serious plays about people, and that these people are seen in their political and historical context. The principal characters depend for their vigour and significance upon the ideas, human and political, which they hold. Perhaps the element that comes nearest to tragedy lies in our sense that victory for the Left-Wing cause is imminent just before the Second World War; yet in the post-war years Socialism succumbs to Russia's totalitarianism, to the Labour Government's broken promises, and to the defeat of Dave's attempt to work out his private salvation. But if these plays record the sad compromise of the ideals held by various members of the Kahn family, simultaneously they affirm their resilience, their hope, and their humour.

Chicken Soup with Barley

At the opening of *Chicken Soup with Barley* Sarah is thirty-seven, and her children Ada and Ronnie are fourteen and five respectively. Harry, two years younger than his wife, is in retreat from the demands made by his politics and his family, while Sarah throws herself into every battle. She is militant in her quest for an answer. She battles with Harry: 'I want to know why you told me you didn't have tea at Lottie's when you know perfectly well you did'; 'You can still pretend? After you took ten shilling from my bag . . .' To this, Harry offers a passive resistance that hides his chronic spiritual desertion. He is the first of Sarah's lost causes. Indeed, *Chicken Soup with Barley* records a succession of lost causes. The victory in a singe day at the barricades in 1936 is followed by ten years' war of attrition against Fascism ('every victory is the beginning'). Ada, the passionate young Communist of fourteen, at twenty-five years of age, and by the end of the war, has withdrawn from the political struggle, and is preparing to escape from 'the jungle of an industrial society' into private Socialism. Dave, the volunteer against Fascism in Spain, becomes the weary veteran of victory over Hitler but loses his faith in the process. The committed Comrades of 1936 become the soldiers of the Second World War—'men who . . . did not know what the war was about'. Monty's defeat is different. He goes not to Spain, but to Manchester, where he loses his political enthusiasm in business and the bourgeois comforts that it brings: 'There's nothing more to life than a house, some friends, and a family—take my word.' Finally Ronnie, the schoolboy Party worker just after the war, is plunged into despair in 1956 by the Soviet suppression of the Hungarian Freedom Fighters. This parade of defeat unfolds in the framework of family life. Harry grows senile, the creeping paralysis of his body accompanying that of his will. Ronnie and Ada grow away from Sarah into their own forms of compromise. Sarah, who is the mainstay of the Kahn family, remains the oracle whom they all acknowledge. If they cannot follow her counsel, it is only because her beliefs remain unaltered in a changing world. Like all oracles, she is a talker and not a listener. Hence, whatever the problems brought for her to solve, she can offer nothing more substantial than cups of tea and the promise of chicken soup with barley.

Roots

Chicken Soup with Barley is an urban, political chronicle spread over a period of twenty years, while *Roots* concentrates a picture of an isolated rural community into a few days in the life of one family. In fact the Bryants are hardly a family in Sarah's sense of the word. They are undemonstrative, almost impersonal towards one another, and are incapable of an exchange of ideas. Towards the world outside they are incurious to the point of superstition, in their own world conservative to the point of fatalism. Each reiterates the trivial circumstances of daily life—a private liturgy of commonplace. This being their substitute for communication, Beatie's message of enlightenment falls on deaf ears. Jim served in the last war, but when Beatie starts cross-questioning him in an attempt to needle him into life, he reacts with the obstinacy of the dead: . . . 'don't you come pushin' ideas across at us—we're all right as we are. You can come when you like an' welcome but don't bring no discussion of politics in the house wi' you 'cos that'll only cause trouble'. He is equating ideas with politics here, and is closing his mind to both, like the good ostrich he is.

The Bryants only tolerate Beatie because she is a Bryant, but her language is utterly foreign to them. It is Beatie's triumph that this language, which is essentially foreign to *her,* becomes her own at the end of the play. Her achievement is that she has mastered the art of communication at a level of which her family has never been aware. Ronnie has built the bridges for Beatie ('words are bridges'), but her family have never felt the need for bridges because they do not realize that there is anything to get across. Beatie's eventual fluency is a sign of hope for the Bryants, as is her instinctive condemnation of all that is cheap and shoddy in our society. 'The whole stinking commercial world insults us and we don't care a damn. Well Ronnie's right—it's our own bloody fault—we want the third-rate—we've got it!'

At this moment Beatie finds her cause. She has stopped trying to convert her family and begins to champion them. She submits to the law outlined by Harry: 'You can't change people—you can only give them some love and hope they'll take it.' *Chicken Soup with Barley* presents a succession of lost causes; *Roots* in its climax gives us a cause to fight for and win. For Beatie's discovery is not restricted to her family. Without adequate communication among its members society itself is at the mercy of commercial exploitation and phoney values. Lest we should dismiss *Roots* as a parochial play about a Norfolk family, Mr Wesker reminds us that the moral is universal (see p. 252).

Introduction

I'm Talking about Jerusalem

The last play in the trilogy opens in 1946, within three months of the beginning of Act Two of *Chicken Soup with Barley*. It is the story of the Simmonds' thirteen years in the wilderness. Ada and Dave emerge from the war painfully aware of the shoddiness of the values that their fight has helped to preserve. They have had enough of politics, of war, of the city, and of the factory. The wilderness of the Fens is for them full of the promise of creative labour, of health and strength, and of the spiritual nurture which only simplicity in a rural setting can bring. They see their experiment as a positive attempt to put socialism into practice. Sarah and Ronnie see it as a retreat from political and human commitment. Dave's New Jerusalem however has more powerful enemies than Ada's family. Libby Dobson points out that the William Morris ideal is illogical and dishonest. Worse, Dave finds that 'his ideals have got some pretty big leaks in places'. The episode of Colonel Dewhurst's lino costs him far more than his job. It shows him that Norfolk is not his spiritual home but a foreign country; his principles are compromised. But Ada proves as strong as her mother and will not let him give up. The real struggle now begins, and continues until their final retreat twelve years later. Dave finds his vision increasingly difficult to preserve. As the prophet of a way of life which becomes unreal and disappointing, he must continually lower his sights. England's land has proved neither green nor pleasant. Dave admits that the New Jerusalem is beyond his reach on earth. The Dark Satanic Mills of thirteen years ago now represent a reasonable way of life. The cottage is kept for holidays.

1965

A. H. M. BEST

MARK COHEN

NOTES

*The notes in this edition are intended
to serve the needs of overseas students
as well as those of English-born users*

Chicken Soup with Barley

3 *the East End of London:* the area east of the City, bounded on the
west by Bishopsgate, and stretching south to the river Thames
(see map on p. 216). It includes to the east and south, the districts of Whitechapel, Stepney, Bow and Stratford, and to the
north Shoreditch and Bethnal Green, and dates as an urban
development from the nineteenth century when it housed, gener-
ally in appalling conditions, London's poor and unemployed.
In the 1930's the inhabitants were principally Cockney, Irish and
Jewish. The area was ideal for Mosley's vigorous anti-Jewish
campaign (see Introduction p. 220).

a revolutionary song: examples from Collet's Record Shop, 70,
New Oxford St., London, W.1.

Nothing he knows!: a typical Jewish inversion, of which there are
many examples in the speech of Sarah's generation. The colloquial English retort would be: 'He doesn't know!'.

Upton Sinclair's book. . . . : Upton Sinclair, American author
of Socialist novels (1878-   ). *The Jungle* (1901) is a documentary
novel based on an investigation of the Chicago stockyards. As
well as being a best-seller, it led to the reform of some of the
worst horrors in the meat packing industry.

4 *Gardiner's Corner:* at the junction of Commercial Road and Whitechapel Road (see map on p. 216). Gardiner's is a clothier's shop
on the corner.

blackshirts: The first British Fascist party (see note on p. 242) was
formed in 1923, primarily as a counter-weapon to Communism,
but its chief, Miss Linton-Orman, did not adopt the uniform of
black shirts, worn by the German and Italian Fascist movement,
until several years later. By 1932, however, a new Fascist party,
the British Union of Fascists, led by Sir Oswald Mosley had taken
over the initiative, and its members wore black shirts from the
first.

(Touché): Sarah has scored a victory in the battle of wills between
herself and Harry. Harry has resisted her attempts to draw him
into conversation, but she has forced him to admit that he
knows more than he will say. This example sets the pattern for
their relationship throughout the play. *Touché* (Fr.), a fencing
term, indicates that a thrust has gone home after a series of
parries and counter-thrusts.

4 *nah!:* Yiddish exclamation: 'There you are!'

'Madrid today—London tomorrow': Madrid was fought over
savagely in the Spanish Civil War, then raging (see Introduction,

240

p. 222). The Communist Party saw the Civil War as a straight fight between the forces of good (the Republicans) and the Fascist evil (the Nationalists). The clash between Communists and Fascists in London's East End, described in this act of *Chicken Soup with Barley*, seemed a re-enactment of the same battle.

6 *strudel:* a light flaky pastry roll often filled with apple – an Austrian speciality.

demo: demonstration. A colloquial abbreviation.

like a Trojan I'm fit!: Jewish inversion, whose comic effect is increased by Harry's muddling two English expressions: 'fit as a fiddle' and 'strong as a Trojan'.

party members: Communists. For Prince there is scope enough for political activity in England, work within the trade unions and against Fascism. Dave sees the Civil War in Spain that had broken out in July 1936 as a far greater cause. This war now seems a complex one, but to Dave and the thousands of Communists and sympathisers who flocked to the front, the contest was simple. A legitimate democratic government was the victim of militarism, Fascism and eventually dictatorship.

7 *International Brigade:* In September 1936 the various Communist parties of European countries sponsored the formation of International Brigades. Thousands of volunteers to the Republican cause were thenceforward organized according to language groups (see note on p. 243).

the old cossack: a friendly allusion to Harry's Russian origin, with overtones of sarcasm: the Russian Cossacks are famed for their fighting spirit, but we know that Harry is unlikely to join the demonstration, despite his protesting 'Like a Trojan I'm fit!'

'All the nice girls love a sailor': Music-hall song from the first decade of the twentieth century. Monty's snatch of singing corresponds to the fourth line of the song:

> All the nice girls love a sailor,
> All the nice girls love a tar;
> All the nice girls love a sailor,
> For you know what sailors are!

Monty therefore sings as follows:

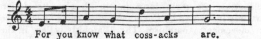

For you know what coss-acks are.

Aldgate: the main point of entry between the City and the East End (see map on p. 216).

Party loudspeaker vans: The Party is the Communist Party.

7 *Royal Mint Street . . . Commercial Road . . . Salmon Lane . . . Victoria Park:* (see map on p. 216).

8 *Mosley:* Sir Oswald Mosley (1896–   ), the wealthy son of a baronet, became a Member of Parliament on the Conservative side at the age of twenty-three, and a member of Ramsay Mac-

donald's Labour Government at thirty-two. He quarrelled with his party over the steady rise in unemployment, and threw up a brilliant parliamentary career to form his own party. In October 1932, he launched the British Union of Fascists. Its aim was to rid England of Communism and the Jews who, according to him, manipulated it, to rid the country of corruption and to give it firm centralized government (i.e. dictatorship). The party's foundation coincided with the appointment of Adolf Hitler, the Nazi leader (see note on p. 243) as Chancellor of Germany, but Benito Mussolini, the Italian Fascist leader, was a more decisive influence in Mosley's conversion.

Fascist meetings were invariably violent, but the so-called 'Battle of Cable Street' here described had worse after effects than usual. A week later a group of Fascist youths terrorized the Mile End Road (see map on p. 216), smashing the windows of Jewish shops and attacking Jews. The Battle of Cable Street was followed by the 'Mile End Road pogrom'.

8 *the Highway* (see map on p. 216).

they threw a seven-year old girl through a glass window: this happened in the Mile End Road pogrom (see Introduction p. 221), which in fact took place a week after the battle of Cable Street.

hammer and sickle: symbol of the Communist Party.

comrade: the usual form of address between Communists and Socialists.

the Underground: London's underground railway.

9 *Peter the Painter had a fight with Churchill:* A mysterious Baltic Anarchist (one who believes all government is evil) called Peter Straume was thought by the police to be connected with the notorious Houndsditch Murders of December 1910, in which three unarmed constables were killed. A few days after the murders the police raided an Anarchist hideout, 100 Sidney Street in the East End (see map on p. 216). Winston Churchill, as Home Secretary, was responsible for the police, and was present at 'The Battle of Sidney Street'. The house was burned to the ground, and the remains of a man and a woman found in the ashes. Peter the Painter was never caught, but he remained for Churchill a symbol of Bolshevik revolutionary ruthlessness. The Bolsheviks, the main force in the Russian Revolution, were certainly influenced by the other and far more violent revolutionary movement, Anarchism. The Anarchists believe in the abolition of organized government and the law. In a stateless society such as they advocate, social harmony is maintained voluntarily. Not surprisingly Communists and Anarchists proved uneasy bed-fellows once the revolution came in Russia.

After this incident the police were allowed to carry revolvers on dangerous assignments (see P. de Mendelssohn, *The Age of Churchill, 1874-1911*, p. 501).

per, per, per. . . .: East End Jewish exclamation of mockery.

dockers: dock workers in the Port of London had come out on

242

strike in protest against the Fascist meeting.

9 *the unions:* trade unions, i.e. organizations of workers formed to protect the interests of employees. Members of both the Labour Party and the Co-operative Party joined the Communists in barricading Cable Street against the Fascist marchers.

The Jewish People's Council: a socialist organization of Jews pledged to withstand Fascism. Its counter-march was ordered against the advice of the Jewish Board of Deputies (see below).

The Board of Deputies: founded in 1760, 'the premier body representing British Jews' needs, wishes and grievances to the Government'. (N. Bentwich: *The Jews in our Time,* p. 95). It is thus the voice of the Jewish 'Establishment' and the synagogues.

Hitler: Adolf Hitler (1889-1945), Nazi leader, and German Chancellor from 1933 until his death.

General Strike: On May 4, 1926, Britain's industrial life came to a standstill. All transport was suspended, factories closed, mines stopped, and almost four million men were on strike. The dispute arose in the mining industry, but the miners had eventually to return to work on unfavourable terms.

his aunts: Cissie and Esther; we meet Cissie in Act 1 Scene 2, and Esther in *I'm Talking about Jerusalem.*

11 *effing and blinding:* swearing.

'They shall not pass': 'No pasarán' was the slogan of the Republican armies in the Spanish Civil War when defending Madrid, and before them, 'Ils ne passeront pas' of the French troops in the Battle of Verdun, 1916. Here again (see note on p. 241) the anti-Fascists in the Battle of Cable Street identify themselves with the Spanish struggle. In fact, the barricades were effective and Mosley's marchers did not pass.

12 *The Edgar André . . . the Dombrovsky from Poland:* The first unit of the International Brigade (see above) to march to the Madrid front was largely made up of German volunteers, though it included a section of English machine-gunners. It was named after a German Communist leader, whom Hitler had just executed. It did not go to the front until November, 1936, i.e. a month after this act takes place. The second unit of the Brigade, the Commune de Paris, was composed of French and Belgians. It took its name from the Revolutionary Government which seized power in Paris at the end of the German siege of 1871. (Engels wrote of it as the classic example of the people's seizure of control) and also had an English contingent. The *Dabrowsky* (not Dombrovsky), the third unit of the first International Brigade, consisted of Polish miners.

Brass balls for breakfast: bullets.

calf-love: adolescent love. Ada is fourteen.

A midnight ramble . . . the back way!: Many foreigners joined the Republican forces by secretly crossing the mountains into Spain. Officially, the French police, as representatives of a neutral country, should have stopped them. Another vivid picture is given in W. H. Auden's *Spain* (1937):

> They clung like burrs to the long expresses that lurch
> Through the unjust lands, through the night . . .

12 *Sammy Avner* (actually Sidney Avener) *and Lorimer Birch:*
English volunteers, killed in December 1936 in a fierce battle at
Boadilla, twelve miles west of Madrid.

Felicia Brown(e): a Communist painter, the first English victim
in the Civil War. She was shot in Aragón in North Eastern
Spain in August.

Cornford: John Cornford, twenty-year-old post-graduate at Cam-
bridge, and the University's leading Communist, was the first
Englishman to go to the front itself. He was killed in the last
days of 1936 (once again Mr Wesker is anticipating) in the Sierra
Morena near Cordova in Southern Spain.

Ronnie Symes and Stevie Yates: both killed in the fierce fighting
for the capital in November 1936.

Casa de(l) Campo: one of the city's largest parks. In it was the
artillery that shelled Madrid. The rebels came across the park
to attack the city from the west.

Nat Cohen and Sam Masters: the first English volunteers in Spain.
They broke off their holiday to hurry to Barcelona, where they
organized a *centuria* (a group of about a hundred men) and
named it after *Tom Mann*, the English Communist and pioneer
of trade unionism at the end of the nineteenth century. Cohen
and Masters were Communists from the East End and were, like
Harry, garment workers.

2,762 British volunteers served in the Civil War (about five per
cent of the foreigners involved). Over half were wounded, and
500 (half of them Communists) were killed (N. Wood: *Communism and British Intellectuals*, p. 56).

16 *Toynbee Hall:* A community centre in Commercial Street (see
map), founded in memory of Arnold Toynbee (1852-83), an
economic historian and champion of social reform. He fought
hard for the cause of adult education and social work, both
perpetuated by Toynbee Hall.

Aspro: a brand of pain-killing drug, containing aspirin.

Sarah Nightingale: an allusion to Florence Nightingale (1820-
1910), pioneer of the nursing profession, whose task was to look
after the wounded British soldiers in the military hospital at
Scutari during the Crimean War (1854-1856).

18 *Hitler won't stop:* General Franco, the Nationalist leader in the
Spanish Civil War, and subsequently the country's dictator,
appealed to Hitler and the Nazi Party for help in July 1936.
Germany contributed money, troops, arms and aeroplanes. The
English Government strenuously preserved its uneasy neutrality.
One of Hitler's motives in helping was 'to distract the attention
of the Western powers to Spain, and so enable German rearma-
ment to continue unobserved'. His armaments were being built

up, of course, for the Second World War, three years later.

18 *bank holiday:* public holiday. Bank holidays were introduced in England in 1871 by Lord Avebury's Act in order to guarantee the working man some time off during the year. They take place on Boxing Day, Easter Monday, Whit Monday and on a Monday in August. On Easter, Whit and August bank holidays enormous crowds gather at seaside and other resorts. Monty's point is that the crowds in this instance had turned out as a matter of political conscience, and not in any idle or irresponsible way.

trade union organizer: an official employed by the union to build up membership and organize strike action etc. In the East End the number of small industries made organization difficult and the trade union movement was consequently far from strong.

19 *Monty takes a feather from a hat nearby and plants it among Hymie's bandages:* a humorous gesture. In this way Hymie is made to look like a Red Indian brave – which in a sense he is.

Mrs O'Laoghaire's vegetable barrow: O'Laoghaire is an Irish name (pron. O'Leary). In England, fruit and vegetables are often sold from barrows in the streets.

Russian Revolution: of 1917, in which the Bolsheviks overthrew Russia's Czarist government and founded the Communist state we now know as the USSR.

V. I. Lenin: (1870-1924), first Soviet leader.

20 *Capitalist bed-makers:* the Communist regards the Capitalist state and hence its products as rotten. The iron bed that gave way could hardly have provided better propaganda value, for *its* rottenness was patent.

social: a party for which the guests buy tickets in aid of a cause. In this case the social is to help a widow whose husband has been killed in an accident.

tram-line: tram-lines were rails sunk in the surface of the road along which the trams travelled. A bicyclist's wheels could jam in a tram-line, causing him to be thrown in the path of an oncoming tram or other vehicle. Trams no longer run in London.

21 *England arise:* the tune is as follows:

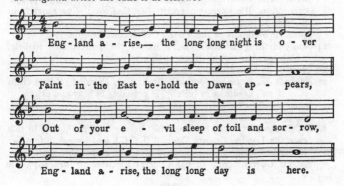

245

22 *As man is only human:* the tune is as follows:

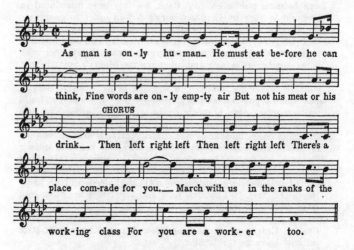

As man is on-ly hu-man_ He must eat be-fore he can think, Fine words are on-ly emp-ty air But not his meat or his drink_ Then left right left Then left right left There's a place com-rade for you._ March with us in the ranks of the work-ing class For you are a work-er too.

23 *Sir Philip Game:* The Commissioner of the Metropolitan (London's) police force. For the 'Battle of Cable Street' on Sunday, October 5 (not 4), he drafted 6,000 police constables and all his mounted men to the East End to forestall trouble. He intended to escort Mosley's marchers along their proposed route, and ensure his freedom of speech at the open-air meeting. When the march was in full swing, however, he banned it at the Home Secretary's instigation. The latter, Sir John Simon, had been warned by several Labour Party leaders of the likelihood of bloodshed if the demonstration took place. It nevertheless took a last minute telephone call from a Labour member on the spot to convince Simon. Before dismissing his Blackshirts, Şir Oswald Mosley said: 'The Government surrenders to Red violence and Jewish corruption. *We* never surrender' (see C. Cross: *The Fascists in Britain*, p. 161).

pioneers: members of the Young Communist League.

24 *penny-farthing whistle:* Harry mocks the policeman's whistle, which was the signal for the police to rally.

25 *There'll be blue murder:* There will be real trouble.

27 *Boobola . . . loolinka:* soothing diminutives (Yiddish) 'Little child . . . sleep'. Loolinka (a lullaby) is probably of Slavonic origin.

meine kindt: (Yiddish) my child.

Shuh! Shuh!: (corrupt form of 'shah'), Yiddish: hush!

28 L.C.C. block of flats: housing built by the local authority, in this case the London County Council (L.C.C.), and leased to families in need of cheap living quarters at a very reasonable rent.

Labour Government: In the General Election of July 1945, the government, including Liberals etc., numbered 412, the Conservative opposition 213.

28 Hackney: a district bordering the East End on the north.

The War! When everybody *made money:* In the Second World War, as in any other, racketeering flourished. Such foods as were obtainable were strictly rationed, as were clothes. There was thus a lively black market, and almost anything was saleable.

30 *May Day demo:* May 1 is the traditional day for Socialist rallies throughout the world. Note, however, that this act is dated June.

lousy: inefficient, poor. Ronnie comments on the postal service which has delayed Dave's letter number 215 so that it arrives at the same time as later letters, and after letters 216 and 217.

demobbed: demobilized. Men and women released from wartime service in the armed forces were said to have been demobbed.

31 *branch meetings:* meetings of the local Communist party.

Windy!: cowardly. A playful taunt.

I'll knock your block off: Playful. 'Block' (slang) means 'head'.

33 *Morgen . . . leite:* German proverb transmogrified into Yiddish, 'Tomorrow, not today, is what lazy people say'.

Labour majority in the House: nearly 200 (see note above).

Two of our own Party members: The two Communists returned to Parliament in 1945 were W. Gallacher (M.P. for West Fife in Scotland) and P. Piratin for the Mile End division of Stepney.

34 *Nationalization:* When the Labour Government came to power it was pledged to public ownership and control of the major industries and services. After four and a half years, and nine acts of Parliament, it had nationalized: the Bank of England, Civil Aviation, Coal, Cable and Wireless, Transport, Land Development, Electricity, Gas, Iron and Steel.

National health: The National Health Service was introduced on 5th July 1948. It entitles everyone in Great Britain to free medical, dental and hospital services. The citizen pays for this vast scheme of 'socialized medicine' through his National Insurance contributions (see note on p. 251). Certain additional fees have been imposed in later years.

blew raspberries: made rude sounds of disapproval.

the claptrap of a threepenny pamphlet: Ada, in her previous speech, is reacting violently against conventional left-wing notions of the natural dignity and idealism of the working-class. Here she refers to the propaganda circulated by socialist workers in order to win adherents. She despises this propaganda in the light of her and her husband's recent experiences.

bourgeois intellectual . . . Trotskyist . . . reactionary Social Democrat: disapproving labels attached by Communist Party members to those of their colleagues who deviate from the party line. Clearly in a State where the working class rules, both the middle class and the intellectual are suspect, a combination doubly so. A Trotskyist is a follower of Leo Trotsky (1879-1940), the Russian politician. He joined the Communist Party in 1917, the year of the Revolution, having been a prominent Social Democrat. He took a leading part in the Revolution and the early years of the Soviet state but fell foul of his leader, Stalin. He was more radical than the official Party line, for he believed in perpetual revolution. He was driven from power and exiled. In 1940 he was assassinated in Mexico, probably by a Stalinist agent.

The Social Democrats were middle of the road Socialists, and hence retrogressive to the mind of the true Marxist since they deny the need for Totalitarian rule. The British Labour Party is Social Democrat.

36 *up West to pictures:* to London's West End, where the expensive cinemas were.

37 *solo:* a card game for four players. See Act 3 Scene 2 (p. 57) and note on p. 251.

38 *Vie iss sie . . . mamma:* Yiddish: Where is she – my mother? . . . She is there – my mother?

39 The 'Egmont' Overture: Ludwig van Beethoven (1770-1827), the German composer, wrote in 1810 an overture and occasional music to accompany Johann von Goethe's (1749-1832) play *Egmont*. The play describes the revolt of the Netherlands against Spain.
cuppa: (slang) cup of tea.

What price partition . . . Power politics!: For years the Jews had claimed Palestine as their national home, and hoped that as soon as the Second World War was over, the survivors of Nazi tyranny would be allowed to emigrate there. Great Britain, however, which had administered the country since the end of the first war, disappointed them, for the Arab claim was also strong. In 1947, the problem was referred to the United Nations, and the country was partitioned between Arabs and Jews. When the independent state of Israel was set up in May 1948, five Arab powers immediately declared war upon it. The Arabs expected Russia to veto the UNO plan for partition as a move in the East-West cold war, but the Russians in fact backed the compromise.

40 *Jelly babies:* boiled sweets (candy), soft, shaped like babies.

41 *a cottage in the country:* Dave and Ada's life is the subject of *I'm Talking About Jerusalem*. At this point in *Chicken Soup with Barley* they have been in the cottage just over a year.
the Fens: fen country is flat and low-lying, and requires an elaborate system of drainage if it is to be of use agriculturally. It is characteristic of East Anglia, and of Norfolk in particular.
King's Lynn: a Norfolk market town, close by the Wash.
a Rabbi . . . to circumcise the baby: a rabbi, or Jewish priest, in this case performed the religious ceremony of circumcizing the new born boy. In fact the performer of the rite need not necessarily be a rabbi, but is called a mohel. The Jewish population of Great Britain is somewhat less than half a million, of whom 250,000 live in Greater London, and most of the others in large cities like Manchester, Leeds and Glasgow. Hence Ronnie's surprise at there being a priest in a market town.

42 *'Dillinger styles . . . for everywhere!':* Ronnie quotes sardonically. Commercial advertising is beginning to reach new heights after the Second World War, and Ronnie sees it as a debased form of language and a corrupting influence.

the big West End sales: the large shops periodically offer goods at reduced prices. Here it is suggested that these 'bargains' are not what they are made out to be.

sweat shops: domestic manufactories with particularly arduous and insecure working conditions. The sweat shop thrives in times of unemployment. The workers share a room for which they pay a rent themselves, and where they keep their equipment. Here they make up material (cotton for dresses, felt for hats, leather for gloves and shoes, etc.) and are paid by the piece for the finished article. Unless the work is done quickly and in quantity the reward is not adequate, and so the worker is 'sweated' by the wholesaler employer to achieve a minimum wage with no additional benefits whatever, and with no union protection. For a description of a sweat shop at the time when the system was rife (early twentieth century) see Jack London's *The People of the Abyss,* a classic eye-witness account of East End conditions.

43 *Board of Trade rate:* the Government department in charge of wages and prices fixes a *minimum* wage that workers in certain industries *must* receive. This would be lower than the price for which the Union was fighting.

Shop stewards: workers in the factory who are elected on the factory floor, and who call in their union when employment policy is at stake.

I read the Riot Act to them: I quietened them down, restored order. This expression is a survival from the days when, as the first step in bringing a public disturbance under control, the Riot Act of 1714 would be read out to the crowd ordering them to disperse. If they did not do so within an hour, they were guilty of a felony and liable to imprisonment. In any large and determined gathering the reading of the Act was clearly ineffectual.

sham: fraud, fake.

44 *strike meeting:* a meeting at which employees, with the advice of their union, decide whether to call a strike in protest against conditions, some action of their employers, or some other grievance. If the union does not back a strike, it is 'unofficial'.

45 *branch meeting:* see note on p. 247.

a political writer like Winston Churchill: (1874-1965), English statesman, historian, biographer and amateur painter, has in fact written only one novel, *Savrola* (1900), of which he claims to be heartily ashamed in *My Early Life* (1930). In that book he also reproduces correspondence with the American novelist, Winston Churchill (1871-1947) who published *Richard Carvel* in 1899 and sold over a million copies. As an aristocrat and a Conservative, Winston S. Churchill is hardly the political writer Ronnie would take as a model.

47 *rise:* an increase in pay.

48 *you're just drowning with heritage, mate!:* Ronnie comments jokingly that Harry is overburdened with the forces that have shaped his life: his Jewish ancestry and the Communist cause. For Ronnie's generation neither is a vital issue; eleven years and the war have passed since the opening of the play.

49 *You can't alter people, Ronnie. You can only give them some love and hope they'll take it:* This is the lesson that Ronnie learns for himself twelve years later by his love affair with Beatie Bryant. Beatie's story is the subject of *Roots*.

50 *Ravel's 'La Valse':* Maurice Ravel (1875-1937), French composer. His orchestral work *La Valse* (The Waltz) was written in 1920, but he is perhaps best remembered for his ballet score *Daphnis and Chloe* (1912), *Bolero* and *Introduction and Allegro*.

Blackfriars Bridge: a bridge over the Thames in London.

51 *National Insurance office:* Under the National Insurance Act, 1946, an overall scheme of social insurance was set up. Every adult worker has a card and weekly contributions in the form of a stamp are shared between employer and employee. The benefits cover sickness, unemployment, retirement, maternity etc. Since Harry was both sick and out of work, and her own employment is casual, Sarah is entitled to draw an allowance. She is only able to claim *National Assistance Board* help, on the other hand, if she can prove that her income is very low, and she is suffering real hardship.

52 *posh:* (slang) upper-class. Ronnie's accent is evidence of the post-war blurring of class distinction in England, which is being achieved by universal Secondary education and a more even spread of private wealth.

53 *ach a nebish* (Yiddish): silly, pitiable.

54 *Trotskyist* (see note on p. 247): There was undoubtedly acrimonious rivalry between the various Socialist groups and shades of Marxist faith fighting in the Spanish Civil War. For an account, see George Orwell's *Homage to Catalonia*.

Itzack Pheffer: one of the leading Soviet-Yiddish poets who fell victim to one of Stalin's purges (see below).

The great 'leader': Under the rule of Stalin (1879-1953) in the Soviet Union, political enemies were ruthlessly eliminated, critics of the regime disappeared for ever into prison, and racial minorities such as the Jews suffered persecution. In late 1948, Pheffer and other champions of Yiddish art, members of the Jewish Anti-Fascist Committee, were arrested and disappeared. Only when Stalin was dead did the world learn of their execution. The Committee had received Allied Jewish support during the war.

56 *Petticoat Lane:* the East End's most famous street market flourishes in the area around Middlesex Street (see map). Its highpoint is Sunday mornings.

phoney: (slang) false, fake.

56 *corn cures:* corns are painful callouses on the feet, caused by ill-fitting shoes.

Haricot beans: dried beans, also called Kidney beans (*Phaseolus vulgaris*).

57 *incontinence:* inability to control the bladder and/or bowels. A common affliction in the old.

solo: (see Act 2 Scene 1 p. 37). The game as it is played in this scene goes as follows:

	Clubs	Hearts	Diamonds	Spades
CISSIE:	K,4,3,2	3	K,2	A,K,J,6,4,2
SARAH:	A,Q,6	10,5,4	A,6,5,4	9,8,3
PRINCE:	J,10,8	K,7,J	J,10,9,8,7	Q,5
HYMIE:	9,7,5	A,Q,9,8,6,2	Q,3	10,7

> 1st Hand: CISSIE: 3 Hearts – 10 – K – A
> HYMIE: 3 Diamonds – 2 – 4 – J
> PRINCE: Q Spades – 10 – J – 9
> PRINCE: 5 Spades – 7 – 6 – 8
> SARAH: 5 Hearts – 7 – 6 – K Diamonds
> PRINCE: 7 Diamonds – Q – K Clubs – A
> SARAH: 3 Spades – J Clubs – 9 Clubs – 2 Spades
> [CISSIE shows Hand]

58 *Nu?:* (Yiddish) Exclamation capable of almost any meaning. Here! Well?

misère: the call in the card game of solo when the player claims he will not win a single trick. It is then the duty of his opponent to make him win one or more.

pass: i.e., no call at all.

lead: the player immediately to the right of the dealer of the cards plays first or *leads.*

65 *what happened in Hungary:* In the Revolution of 1956, many Hungarians rose against their Government in an attempt to liberalize the totalitarian regime. With the arrival in Budapest of Soviet tanks the uprising was suppressed, but some of the revolutionaries escaped to the West.

pop pop ... shmop!: Jewish form of mockery. The word to be debunked is repeated, and finally is given the 'shm' sound at the beginning, typical of Yiddish.

68 *Hendon:* A North-West London suburb to which many more prosperous Jews moved from the East End.

Blooms: Famous Jewish Kosher (see note on p. 261) restaurant in Whitechapel.

70 *You'll die ... if you don't care you'll die:* Ronnie sees this to be true three years later at the end of *I'm Talking about Jerusalem* (see Introduction p. 227).

Roots

This is a play about Norfolk people; it could be a play about any country people and the moral could certainly extend to the metropolis. But as it is about Norfolk people it is important that some attempt is made to find out how they talk. A very definite accent and intonation exists and personal experience suggests that this is not difficult to know. The following may be of great help:

When the word 'won't' is used, the 'w' is left out. It sounds the same but the 'w' is lost.

Double 'ee' is pronounced 'i' as in 'it' – so that 'been' becomes 'bin', 'seen' becomes 'sin', etc.

'Have' and 'had' become 'hev' and 'hed' as in 'head'.

'Ing' loses the 'g' so that it becomes 'in'.

'Bor' is a common handle and is a contraction of neighbour.

Instead of the word 'of' they say 'on', e.g. 'I've hed enough on it' or 'What do you think on it?'

Their 'yes' is used all the time and sounds like 'year' with a 'p' – 'yearp'.

'Blast' is also common usage and is pronounced 'blust', a short sharp sound as in 'gust'.

The cockney 'ain't' becomes 'ent' – also short and sharp.

The 't' in 'what' and 'that' is left out to give 'thaas' and 'whaas', e.g. 'Whaas matter then?'

Other idiosyncrasies are indicated in the play itself.

72 **Norfolk**: county in East Anglia, bordered on the north and east by the sea and on the south by the county of Suffolk. Its chief city is Norwich. The country is characterized by the fens (see note on p. 248), and is largely agricultural. The amenities and diversities of modern life have yet to come to the more remote parts of this county.

73 **tilly lamps**: paraffin lamps producing a harsh bright light. As the fuel is vapourized under pressure they burn with a hissing sound.

primus stoves: single-burner portable cooking stoves, operating on the same principle as tilly lamps.

74 *Armstrong*: Armstrong Siddeley, a make of motor car.

whist drive: whist is a card game for four players, a simple form of bridge. At a whist drive, a large number of people play in groups of four, and the personnel of each group is changed according to a rota system at the end of each game so that each partnership plays as many other pairs as possible. People pay to play at a whist drive and there are prizes. The object is usually to raise money for some local cause or charity.

76 *comics*: children's weeklies, containing strip cartoons and serial stories, e.g. *Dandy* and *Beano*.

riled: annoyed, aggravated.

77 *Manchester Guardian:* newspaper founded in 1821 as a weekly, becoming a daily in 1855. It upholds no particular political party, and is distinguished by its liberal and humanitarian viewpoint. Its feature articles are of a literary standard rare in journalism. Originally very much Manchester's newspaper, it now prints in London as well. Its name was changed to *The Guardian* on August 24, 1959.

rock 'n' rolling: form of dance popular at the time. It originated in the U.S. and was danced to *rock 'n' roll* music, as rendered for example by Bill Haley's *Comets.*

78 *barmy:* out of her mind.

allotment: a small plot of land. Pieces of land were parcelled up into small plots, a system which had a particular importance during the Second World War. Each plot was looked after by one family, who grew vegetables for their own consumption in order to lighten the load on the national resources. The system still persists where the land has not been taken over for some other use, such as building or large-scale farming.

unemployment benefit: see note on p. 250.

79 *the Storks:* the local public house, the 'pub'.

80 *the old mowld'll cling:* Beatie has suggested that digging the allotment must be heavy going in the autumn weather, when the damp and rain are on the increase. Jimmy contradicts her: It's not too bad just yet, but as the weather gets wetter the 'mowld' (mould, earth) will cling to his spade, making the work very arduous.

spuds: potatoes.

runners: runner beans, from a climbing, scarlet-flowered plant. They are eaten young, but if they are allowed to grow fully they produce the Haricot bean (see note on p. 251), which is dried in the pod before marketing.

a fair owle turn: 'a good run for your money'. Beatie comments that he has done well out of his allotment.

81 *that strike in London:* the 1958 bus workers' strike, when there were no buses on the streets, resulted in the total suspension of London's public road transport from May 5 to June 20. Many services were permanently curtailed as a result.

Territorials: part-time soldiers. It is in fact the regular troops who may be brought in to man essential services which have come to a standstill through strike action. Jimmy hasn't much sympathy with the strikers, who earn far more than his neighbours do.

the Hall: a good deal of rural England is privately owned. The landowner and his family live at 'the Hall', the Manor or the 'big house', where the administration of the estate also takes place. The estate usually comprises the owner's private grounds and farm, and farms let to tenant farmers. There may also be houses leased to tenants and 'tied' cottages (see note on p. 254). Only a small part of rural society still depends on 'the Hall' for jobs and housing. In *I'm Talking about Jerusalem* Colonel Dewhurst is the local landowner, and Dave Simmonds works for him.

81 *Territorials' Jubilee:* a commemorative celebration. Territorials send contingents from all over the country to the Jubilee.

82 *Chaucer:* (c. 1343-1400) English poet, reckoned to be one of the greatest poets England has produced. His influence has been felt at every stage of poetic development. He is best-known for *The Canterbury Tales,* but he wrote much else besides. Beatie takes him as a symbol of one aspect of English civilization which is worth defending.

the M.P. for this constituency: the Member of Parliament for one of the 630 areas into which the United Kingdom is divided for electoral purposes.

86 *squit:* nonsense, something not worth taking trouble to understand.

sand pits: pits made in the ground for the excavation of sand to be used in the building trade for concrete, mortar, etc.

87 *the club:* a simple form of hire purchase (see note on p. 255). A customer is enabled to buy an expensive item from either a shop or a travelling salesman by paying in regular weekly instalments. For instance, we discover later that Beatie's mother puts seven shillings and sixpence into the club a week, and thus pays for clothes. If the customer is a trusted one, she is allowed to bear off the article before it is fully hers, but if not she has to wait until she is 'paid up'. Many shops run 'Christmas clubs' on a similar principle. Susan is ashamed of having to buy on the 'never-never', or instalment plan.

council house: see note on p. 246.

89 *Poppy:* father.

tight: mean, close with money.

skint: make small savings. Mrs Bryant has to be very careful not to overspend her small housekeeping allowance.

90 *Labour Tote:* a lottery, run as a fund-collector by the local branch of the Labour Party. For the investment of a shilling, the prizes in this sweepstake were: first, £100; second, £75 (note Jenny's archaic inversion of the sum, incidentally).

Startson way: towards, in the neighbourhood of, Startson.

91 *compost heap:* a pile of vegetable and animal manure kept for fertilizing the soil. The use of compost is often supplanted by chemical fertilizers nowadays.

93 *Evening News:* one of the two London daily evening papers. The other is the *Evening Standard.*

95 tied cottage: a cottage tied to a job. In country districts the landowner will often provide accommodation free, or at a low rent, to his employee. This offsets the countryman's wage, which is low compared to an urban job. However, the right to the accommodation ceases if the employee gives up the job or is dismissed from it.

96 *vicarage:* the house in which the parish priest (Church of England) lives. Some vicarages are owned by the Church, others by local landowners. It is now common practice to amalgamate a series of small country parishes into one, particularly where an

increasing number of people leave the villages to find work in the towns. The sale referred to here is probably occasioned by an amalgamation of this kind.

97 *rum*: strange, unaccountable.

98 *a pick-up on the H.P.*: a pick-up is a portable electric turntable, which is attached to a wireless set. H.P. is the common abbreviation for hire purchase, where goods are bought on deposit, the remainder being paid in instalments with interest.

100 *Swan and Edgar's*: a large department store on the corner of London's Piccadilly and Regent Street, at Piccadilly Circus.

101 *in a jiffy*: very soon.

copper: a water tank encased in brick and fireclay with a grate beneath. The copper is filled by jugfuls of water from the cold tap and the fire lit whenever hot water is needed.

102 *skiffle*: a form of pop music, at its peak between 1956 and 1959. It arose in the coffee bars of London and the provincial towns, and its two best-known exponents were Tommy Steele and Lonnie Donegan. It is interesting in that it was the forerunner of the present fondness for folk music, and was sufficiently undemanding musically to be played and enjoyed by amateur groups, many of whom made their own instruments.

thrombosis: stoppage of a blood vessel by a clot.

gouache: here, simply water paint, in concentrated liquid or powder form. It can be used thickly as in oil painting, or diluted with water. Strictly, *gouache* is water paint thickened with gum.

103 *commission*: a percentage on sales which goes to the salesman.

'*Oh a dialogue I'll sing you ..!*: Beatie's fondness for the genuine traditional song is contrasted with her mother's unquestioning acceptance of commercial pop music. The tune is as follows:

104 . . . *it's nearly always me listening to you telling who's dead:* a withering comment on Mrs Bryant's inability to discuss anything other than local gossip.

105 *registers:* Ronnie was referring to levels of sensitivity. If you have no 'registers' for poetry it means you are incapable of ever appreciating it, you cannot register it, no matter how often its read to you. Some people have a failing of physical 'registers', such as colour blindness.

'*It's all going up in flames':* Ronnie's cry is that civilization is being corrupted and despoiled by the money-makers – no less.

106 'I'll wait for you in the heavens blue': the tune is as follows:

I'll wait for you in the hea-vens blue As my arms are wait-ing now___ Please come to me and I'll be true My love shall not turn sour___ I hun - ger, I hun - ger, I can - not wait lon - ger, My love— shall not— turn sour.___

109 *manager:* manager of the estate for which Mr Bryant works.

Union magazine: magazine sent to all its members by the National Union of Agricultural Workers.

112 *Let's hev grub and not so much o' the lip woman:* Let's have some food and not so much cheek, insolence.

I'll get my back on you my manny: I'll be revenged (get my own back) on you, my man.

115 '*Educated? No. She's a foreigner':* Beatie voices a classic English prejudice – that all foreigners are uneducated. Of course it is a prejudice held only by the *uneducated* English, and Beatie is only just beginning to realize how uneducated she is. It is becoming an equally common prejudice to measure education by examination results, as Beatie does in the same speech when she describes Ronnie as uneducated in that he failed his exams. Her final remark – 'They read and things' – is a curt dismissal of what goes to make an educated person; but Beatie will learn.

a club: a social club for young people, with facilities for games, dancing, sport and other activities. Many such clubs are run as missions by the churches or by charity, but local authorities are

115 increasingly making provision for youth clubs as part of their work in education. Much of the help in organizing activities is voluntary, and club members have a full part in running the club.

115 *furse:* first.

117 Mendelssohn's Fourth Symphony: The famous 'Italian' Symphony, composed while the composer and his family were in Rome in 1830-31. The slow movement is considered particularly fine. Felix Mendelssohn-Bartholdy (1809-1847), the German composer, was a particular favourite of Queen Victoria and her subjects. He was never held in quite such high esteem in his own country.

119 *You can't change people* .. : See Harry's speech in *Chicken Soup with Barley* on p. 49 – 'You can't alter people . . .' (see note on p. 250.)

120 Bizet's L'Arlésienne Suite: Georges Bizet (1838-1875), French composer, *L'Arlésienne Suite* is a concert arrangement of the incidental music he wrote to a successful play, *The Woman of Arles*, by Daudet, performed in both Paris and London during the 19th century.

121 *glass cherries:* 'glass' is written thus to show how Mrs Bryant pronounces the word 'glacé' – to rhyme with 'lass' (cf 'café' pronounced 'caff').

122 *article:* slang. The word used in this way is almost devoid of meaning, and shows that Frank is determined not to be impressed by Ronnie. In the early nineteenth century, this was high society slang, and implied a certain superciliousness.

124 *clan:* family. The word is used to describe a family which has strong loyalties and affections among its members. Frank's remark, 'A mighty clan I say', is in strong opposition to Beatie's 'What a bloody family!' A clan is of course suspicious of outsiders, and its members stick together in a crisis.

126 *casual labour:* a job which depends entirely on the availability of work. The work is paid for by the piece, and there is none of the guarantee of a weekly wage.

127 *children:* yet Beatie's remark 'Presents for the kid', of Act 1 suggests that Jimmy and Jenny have only the one child.
State Registered Nurse: a fully qualified hospital nurse entitled to put the initials SRN after her name.
pack up: stop, cease.

128 *Who do you think'll win today? Well, Norwich won't:* a reference to the local football team, Norwich City.
head: head of the clan.

130 *You brewed up yit?:* Have you made the tea yet?

136 *The apple don't fall far from the tree:* Proverb, meaning: Offspring are not as unlike their parents as they may like to think. A clannish remark, and like all proverbs no more than half the truth.

139 *living in mystic communion with nature:* see Introduction, p. 220.

I'm Talking about Jerusalem

145 Beethoven's Ninth Symphony: Ludwig van Beethoven (1770-1827), in his final symphony, known as the 'Choral', introduces a choir and soloists into the last movement. The burden of the words to this movement, from the German poet Schiller's *Ode to Joy*, is: All men shall be brothers. This paean may be interpreted as Beethoven's vision of a new Jerusalem. Hence it is an apt, if ultimately ironic, opening to the play.

shlapping: (Yiddish) dragging.

146 *the army is marching on its stomach:* Ronnie perverts the old saying, attributed to Napoleon: 'An army marches on its stomach', i.e. an army cannot march to victory unless it is properly fed.

147 *We just put a Labour Party in power:* see note on p. 246.

National Health: see note on p. 247.

millenium: golden age. Originally a period of a thousand years. In the *Revelation of St John the Divine*, XX, Christ's Second Coming is to last that period.

schmulz herring: herring pickled in brine. Here it typifies a scanty diet.

Wandering Jews: The legend springs from the story of a Jew who refused to allow Christ to rest at his door when bearing the Cross to Calvary. He was therefore condemned to wander for ever.

148 *like Miriam:* Ronnie is actually referring to the meeting between Moses and Sipporah (Exodus, II, 16). Miriam was the wife of Moses' brother Aaron.

Autumn Journal by Louis Macneice (1907-1964): Ronnie quotes two extracts from the poem. These quotations commemorate a moment of life-changing decision.

river of the dead: the Styx, which in Greek mythology the dead soul crossed into Hades, ferried by Charon.

Lethe: another of the rivers of Hades. The dead drank its waters, which made them forget all that had gone before.

149 *the Rubicon:* a river in the Appenine mountains. It formed the boundary between Rome and Gaul and by crossing it and thus overstepping the boundaries of his own Province, Julius Caesar committed himself to war and changed the course of history.

150 *primus stove:* see note on p. 252.

calor gas: gas stored under pressure in cylinders, marketed and distributed by the Calor Gas Co. Ltd. It is used for gas appliances where there is no mains supply.

152 *shambles:* mess, state of untidiness.

153 *Communist. . . . That's a dirty word, ain't it?:* by this date, Russia was a potential enemy and Communist was indeed a term of abuse in the Western World.

Civvy Street: Soldier's slang for civilian life.

a ship in the night: from the phrase 'Ships that pass in the night' in H. W. Longfellow's poem *Tales of a Wayside Inn*. The point is that the plans discussed by Dave and Libby Dobson during the war were only a passing phase.

154 *an ivory tower:* an expression meaning a place or way of life removed from the harsher realities.

155 *chippy:* a rough sort of carpenter. Dave's ambition is to do the finer work of furniture making.

China: cockney rhyming slang; china plate = mate. Cf. loaf of bread = head, as in 'Use your loaf'; plate of meat = feet, as in 'Don't shuffle your plates'.

160 *get our bearings:* expression from the use of a compass to determine one's position; meaning to get accustomed to a new place.

fencing: making boundary fences or pens for animals.

soft water: water ideal for washing, since soap lathers easily in it. Hard water contains chemical salts.

164 *black and blue:* to swear black and blue means to insist emphatically.

Beethoven ... based on a Hungarian folk song: Sarah may have been right. The classical composers often used folk songs as a basis for their music, e.g. Dvorak (1841-1904) in his *Symphony from the New World* (symphony in E minor, op. 95).

165 a soft and melodic Yiddish folk song: the tune is as follows:

Roughly translated, the words mean:

Blow, blow you winds of evil. Now is your time. Winter will last a long time yet. Summer is still far off. If a light flickers, extinguish it with rage. Tear the frames from the windows. This *Winter Song* was written by Abraham Reisin (1876-1953), the Polish-Yiddish poet. It had much of the universality of the folk-songs it derives from, but the words also imply revolution. The song became a workers' hymn at the turn of the century, but the pessimistic refrain, *Winter will last a long time yet . . '* was amended to *the winter will not last much longer, spring will soon appear.* Victory seemed nearer.

166 YHA: Youth Hostels Association. Dave is planning to make some extra money by letting space for Youth Hostellers who want to stay overnight.

'Linden Lea': a song in the English folk tradition, with words by William Barnes (1800-86), the Dorset regional poet. It has been set to music by Ralph Vaughan Williams (1872-1958). It is published by Boosey & Hawkes Ltd.

167 *A business consultant:* a deliberately vague description of a type of job that has only arisen in England since the Second World War. Business consultancy ranges from fitting a new office with furniture (probably taking a commission on sale from the manufacturer) to advising the management of a company on the employment of high-grade personnel.

170 Libby Dobson . . . lóoks as though he wants to be a fisherman and can only be one on holidays: a comment on the urban fashion of wearing the clothes of manual workers when not in the office. The popularity of jeans for leisure wear is an example. Libby is probably wearing a thick high-necked sweater, stout flannel or corduroy trousers, and ankle-length rubber boots.

hale and hearty: healthy and energetic. By his interjection of 'bloody' Libby shows that he despises such people.

171 *nettled:* irritated, anoyed.

Simmonds: the use of the surname is faintly contemptuous, and shows Dave that Libby means to keep his distance.

I'll even dance round the may-pole: the old rural custom of dancing round the may-pole no longer takes place except as a self-conscious rustic revival. Libby's remark is an indication that he sees little purpose in Dave's life in the country.

172 *the Salvation Army:* a reference to Ronnie's latest marriage plans: he'll marry a prostitute to 'save' her. The Salvation Army was founded by William Booth in 1865 to bring the Gospel to the poor and sinful. The Army waged campaigns against drunkenness and prostitution in the latter half of the 19th century.

173 *the beautiful, rustic estate:* the country way of life.

you're bristling: you're beginning to fight back.

174 *Jerusalem:* an ideal world (see Introduction p. 239).

175 *William Morris:* (1834-1896), poet, painter, craftsman and socialist. In his book *News from Nowhere* (1891) he describes a Utopian socialist England in which everyone has the satisfaction of being a craftsman and money and ugliness have disappeared.

Robert Owen: (1771-1858), Welsh socialist. As owner of several cotton mills, he brought in schemes for his workers' welfare and the education of the children who worked part-time in the factories. At his New Lanark Mills, and in America, he pioneered community living and the collective ownership of factories. Although his ideas were greatly in advance of the first half of the nineteenth century, he became a much respected authority on social policies and education and his factories were much visited.

174 *no strings:* no further conditions or restrictions.

175 *benevolent dictatorship:* absolute rule in the interests of the people. Catherine the Great of Russia and Frederick the Great of Prussia are taken as examples of this kind of despotism.

177 taking maybe something to chew from the table: as his first wife used to do.

179 *pilfering:* petty stealing.

181 an olive branch: the traditional symbol of armistice, deriving from the return of the dove to Noah's Ark with an olive leaf, to symbolize the end of God's anger (Genesis VIII, 11). Ada and Dave's conflict is over (see 'the battle dies in silence').
horse: sawing frame.

182 *curf:* here, the sawing away of a layer of wood equal to the thickness of the saw-blade. The craftsman saws down the join between two pieces of wood which are clamped together in a vice.
smasher: splendid person.

183 *You taking the mickey out of me?:* are you teasing me? making fun of me?

184 *cocker:* (slang) chum, mate.

185 *philistine:* insensitive to good or beautiful things.

187 *Words are bridges:* see *Roots*, Act 1, p. 78.
During the war, when you were overseas: see *Chicken Soup with Barley*, Act 2 Scene 1.

191 *For peace and quiet . . :* Esther sarcastically quotes a typical boarding-house advertisement.

192 *I'm keeping in training:* a market-stall keeper needs a powerful voice to compete with the other salesmen and the market noise.

193 *William Morris:* see note on p. 260.
A Yiddisha fellow?: Esther shows her Jewishness – Morris is a common first name among English-speaking Jews.
Beatie Bryant: Beatie's story is the subject of *Roots*.

194 *bricks:* splendid, reliable people.

195 *nuts to yers all:* an affectionate dismissal of the others – 'You can all take care of yourselves from now on' (Yers = you).
you can lay down deposit on two machines and pay off over three or five years: this can be done under a Hire Purchase agreement (see note on p. 255).
school dinners: midday meals available to all children at State schools for a nominal sum. The meals service is subsidised out of rates as part of the education service.

196 *grasshopper mind:* a mind which jumps erratically from one idea to the next.

197 *kosher:* prepared according to the very strict Jewish dietary laws. The orthodox Jew is never allowed to eat pork.

198 '*muzzeltov*': Hebrew – good luck!

199 *selling flags at a football match:* flags giving the colours and supporting slogans of the two teams. Members of the crowd would buy one or the other to show which side they supported.

261

199 *Aylesbury:* a market town in Buckinghamshire, north of London.
   Flower and Dean Street: (see map on p. 216) was the home of
   Harry, Cissie and Esther's parents. Harry ran back to the
   'prison' only too readily, even in the thick of 'The Battle of
   Cable Street' (See *Chicken Soup with Barley*, Act 1, Scene 2).

200 *jerry houses:* jerry-built means inadequately built, with thin walls
   that let in the damp, unseasoned woodwork, and plaster that too
   easily flakes away from the walls.
   Straight Jane and no nonsense: Esther's personal market slogan.
   Straight = honest.
   forfeits his deposit: if a candidate in a parliamentary election
   polls less than ten per cent of the total votes for the constituency,
   he loses the one hundred pounds he deposited when putting his
   name forward.

202 *Mr Gaitskell:* Hugh Gaitskell (1906-1963), the leader of the Labour
   Party and hence of the Parliamentary Opposition from 1955
   until his premature death. In the election of October 8, 1959,
   the Conservative Party won 365 seats, Labour 258, Liberal 6,
   and Communists none (compare the results with July 5, 1945, the
   election referred to in *Chicken Soup with Barley*, Act 2 – see note
   on p. 246).
   Transport House: In Smith Square, Westminster: headquarters
   of the Labour Party.
   loo-ves: loves, after the pop singer's fashion!
   Come O my love: old American folk song.

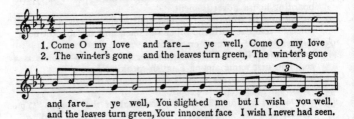

1. Come O my love and fare— ye well, Come O my love
2. The win-ter's gone and the leaves turn green, The win-ter's gone

and fare— ye well, You slight-ed me but I wish you well.
and the leaves turn green, Your innocent face I wish I never had seen.

203 *There ain't a lady livin' in the land:* Ronnie pervert's Albert
   Chevalier's music-hall song, *My Old Dutch*, as follows:

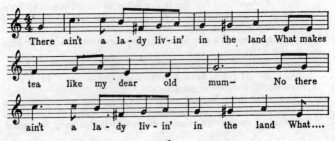

There ain't a la-dy liv-in' in the land What makes

tea like my dear old mum— No there

ain't a la-dy liv-in' in the land What....

262

203 *old dutch:* wife (slang). Comic comparison with a Dutch clock.
204 *You know what my father once said to me? 'You can't change people . . .'* See *Chicken Soup with Barley*, Act 2, Scene 2; also Beatie's story in *Roots*.
   shrapnel: flying fragments of bomb and shell.
   a Zanny Hora: popular Israeli round dance of Slavonic origin.
205 *millenium:* see note on p. 258.
   Maxim Gorky: (1868-1936) Russian novelist. *Mother* dates from 1907 and is very much a propaganda book for Socialism.
   Howard Spring: (1889-1965), English novelist, whose most famous novel is *Fame is the Spur* (1940).
   Gustave Flaubert: (1821-1880), French novelist. *Madame Bovary* is one of the world's most celebrated novels. It is a story of adultery in a French provincial town.
206 *the silver lining:* from the expression, Every cloud has a silver lining.
207 Al Jolson: (1886-1950) American entertainer, most famous for his renderings of pseudo-Negro (coon) songs, which he performed with a blackened face and whitened lips in 'minstrel' style, accompanied by exaggerated histrionic gestures. He reached the peak of his popularity during the 1930's with his songs *Sonny Boy* and *April Showers*, published in the U.K. by Chappell.
   We've got sixpence: Ronnie sings *I've got Sixpence* as follows:

208 *put us on pedestals:* set us up as an ideal.
   out went six million Jews in little puffs of smoke: In the Nazis' Final Solution of the Jewish Question, approximately that number of Jews, German, Hungarian, Polish, Czech, etc., were murdered in the concentration camps of which Auschwitz was perhaps the most notorious. The death camps were equipped with gas chambers and crematoria, and when Auschwitz was working at full capacity in the summer of 1944, it could dispose of 9,000 corpses in a single day.
   . . . sang the Red Flag . . : on coming to power, the Labour

Party sang the British Socialist Party's traditional hymn, but continued to pour money into the production of nuclear weapons. Since the 'enemy' against whom such defence was considered necessary was the leading socialist country, the U.S.S.R., the irony of the situation is obvious.

208 *Remember what you said about carrying bits and pieces of each other?:* see *I'm Talking about Jerusalem,* Act 3, Scene 2, p. 204.

209 *There aren't many flies on me:* I know what I'm doing.

210 *maybe you can't build on your own:* see Sarah's comment, 'What's socialism without human beings?' in *I'm Talking about Jerusalem* Act 1, p. 155.

 . . . somewhere . . . I fail as a human being. Like my father . . : see *Chicken Soup with Barley,* Act 2, Scene 2 (end) p. 49.